# Baptism by Fire

ALSO BY MARK K. UPDEGROVE

*Second Acts: Presidential Lives and Legacies
After the White House*

WITHDRAWN

# BAPTISM
## *by* FIRE

Eight Presidents Who Took Office
in Times of Crisis

MARK K. UPDEGROVE

THOMAS DUNNE BOOKS
St. Martin's Press  New York

THOMAS DUNNE BOOKS.
An imprint of St. Martin's Press.

www.thomasdunnebooks.com
www.stmartins.com

Library of Congress Cataloging-in-Publication Data

Updegrove, Mark K.
  Baptism by fire : eight presidents who took office in times of crisis / Mark K. Updegrove.—1st ed.
     p.  cm.
  Includes bibliographical references and index.
  ISBN-13: 978-0-312-38803-4
  ISBN-10: 0-312-38803-9
  1. Presidents—United States—History.  2. Crisis management in government—United States—History.  3. Political leadership—United States—History.  4. Presidents—United States—Biography.  I. Title.
  E176.1.U688 2009
  973.09'9—dc22

                    2008033055

First Edition: January 2009

10  9  8  7  6  5  4  3  2  1

To my parents after fifty years of marriage

And to their grandchildren,
Chelsea, Jake, Elizabeth, Meredith, and James,
and our Charlie and Tallie

# Contents

# Contents

# ACKNOWLEDGMENTS

I have been very lucky. A number of people have taken an interest in this book and have provided me with guidance and support in seeing it through. To them, I owe my sincere gratitude.

This is the second book on which I've teamed up with my editor, Rob Kirkpatrick, of St. Martin's Press, whose wise literary direction has once again enhanced the work. It was further aided by Robert Cloud and Lorrie McCann, also at St. Martin's.

Additionally, I vetted the book's concept and the content with many who encouraged me to go forward or helped put me on the right road, while others were generous in giving me insight into the men I discuss in these pages. They include Gerald Baliles and George Gilliam, both of the Miller Center, one of the nation's foremost places of research and study on the presidency; Don Carleton; David Hume Kennerly; my agent, Ed Knappman; Tim Naftali; Dave Overton; Cathy Saypol, who spurred on my literary efforts from the beginning; Hugh Sidey; Richard Norton Smith; Theodore Sorensen; Harrison Tyler; and Peter Varley. Gerald Ford, George H. W. Bush, and Brent Scowcroft also graciously provided valuable perspective germane to this project in interviews I had conducted with them for my previous book, *Second Acts: Presidential Lives and Legacies After the White House.*

I am indebted to others, too: my in-laws, Peter Cundill, and Roger and Kay Wiewel; Steve Huestis; Jim Popkin; Lee Rosenbaum; Nick Segal; Sarah Simpson; Hal Stein; Ray Walter; and Josef Zankowicz. Thanks, as always, to my devoted family: Susie, Glenn, Elizabeth, Meredith, and James Crafford; Marjorie Kaskey; Jeff and Loretta Kaskey; Cindy Kaskey; Mike and Andria Kaskey; Herbert Krombach; Jim and Nancy Krombach; Randall, Chelsea, and Jake Updegrove; and Stuart and Christine Updegrove. My parents, Jake and Naomi, worked four jobs between them in order to give their children every advantage, and encouraged us to pursue our passions. Their support on this project was no exception.

While I was writing this book, my immediate family of three happily became a family of four with the addition of Tallie Reed Updegrove, born on August 8, 2006, who came into our lives in December 2007 with the consent of the American and Guatemalan governments. Tallie's first literary work is preserved here—"Cvc nbb BbVBNBb"—saved from one of the many times she sat on my knee and tapped on my keyboard, a welcome brown-eyed distraction as I tried to set about my work. The duties of writing meant time taken from my beloved son, Charlie, who often (though not always) resisted all the instincts of a seven-year-old and minded my recurrent requests for quiet. I hope to make it up to him. Most of all, I am indebted to my wife of fifteen years, Evie, whose love, support, counsel, and faith in me I value beyond measure—and can never adequately acknowledge.

MKU
*Isle of Palms, South Carolina*

# Baptism by Fire

# INTRODUCTION

It was the hottest summer in thirty-seven years, or so said many of Philadelphia's elders who could remember the stifling humidity of midcentury as they struggled with the heat of 1787. At eighty-one, Benjamin Franklin, Pennsylvania's president and one of its oldest residents, was one of the few among the city's forty-two thousand souls who could recall those earlier years. In his time he had borne witness to the evolution of thirteen English colonies into the United States of America, a country unique in its character, which he in many ways personified. Eleven summers before, in 1776, Franklin had been among the fifty-six men who had convened in Pennsylvania's State House as battles with English troops were waged throughout the colonies, to formalize a Declaration of Independence from King George's empire. Now he would return to the State House with fifty-four delegates from twelve states of the union—Rhode Island abstained—who braved soaring temperatures along the Delaware to keep the country united by framing the outlines of a binding federal government.

The sun, if not the heat, was on Dr. Franklin's mind when, in

mid-September, he queued up with his fellow delegates to sign the Constitution of the United States, forged after four months of discussion, debate, and accord. On the back of the chair occupied by the convention's
president, George Washington, a half sun was etched, painted in a spectacular gold. Franklin turned the attention of his colleagues to the carving, musing that artists frequently found it difficult to differentiate a
sunrise from a sunset. "I have often in the course of this session, and the
vicissitudes of my hopes and fears as to its issue, looked at that behind the
President without being able to tell whether it was rising or setting,"
he told them. "But now at length I have the happiness to know that it is a
rising and not a setting sun."[1]

Yes, it *was* rising. Truly morning in America. But there was no certainty
as to what the day would bring. Much of its fate would fall to the man who
had occupied the sun-adorned chair during the convention's proceedings.

The Constitution allowed for the office of president of the United
States but said very little about what the role entailed. Washington,
elected unanimously to the post a year and a half later, would have to
figure much of it out for himself—and set the precedent for those who
would succeed him—as the states that composed the newly formed but
tenuous union, of different economic makeup and disparate agendas,
took their first wobbly steps toward nationhood. Given the intrinsic political differences throughout the country, many flatly believed the Constitution would fail to lead to a binding federal government. There were other
crises brewing, too: the massive debt accrued during the revolution, which
had the potential to undermine the economy, and hostilities among foreign powers—in particular, Britain, which was in no mood to see its former colonies succeed as an independent nation. No surprise then that
Washington's inaugural speech in the spring of 1789 was more "a fervent
supplication to that Almighty Being" during the "present crisis" than an
address to the young republic's free population of two million four hundred thousand citizens. His faith in God was one of the few things he
could be sure of as he led the country forward.

Every generation, it seems, has a tendency to glorify the past, to look
back and marvel at their earlier innocence. In the last half century alone

we have lamented the end of American innocence around the cold war, John F. Kennedy's assassination, Vietnam, Watergate, the Iran hostage crisis, Iran-contra, Monica Lewinsky, 9/11, and, more recently, the war in Iraq, our fading status abroad, and the global economic crisis, imagining the simpler times that preceded them. All were occasions to decry the state of the union.

In fact, Washington's times illustrate that America has never been either simple or innocent. As Arthur M. Schlesinger Jr. reminded us in *The Cycles of American History,* "We carelessly apply the phrase 'end of innocence' to one or another stage of American history. This is an amiable flourish when not a pernicious delusion. . . . No nation founded on invasion, conquest and slaughter was innocent. No people who systematically enslaved black men and killed red men were innocent. No state established by revolution and thereafter rent by civil war was innocent."[2] America can never lose something she never had.

Myopia in our collective consciousness is nothing new. The important thing is that we not only remember that crises have often played out in our history—brought about by our vulnerabilities, ambitions, and flaws—but also that we ultimately overcome them. Our system of government and the principles on which it was founded, laid out with such forethought in Philadelphia in 1787, coupled with the spirit of the American people, ultimately prevail. And we go on.

No institution has been more instrumental in shaping our country and guiding us through the crossroads we have faced than the presidency. It is, as Hugh Sidey wrote, "a symbol of the nation's ideals and administrator of American life."[3] This book examines eight chapters in America's history when the threat of constitutional morass, the dissolution of our union, economic collapse, nuclear holocaust, or ebbing faith in our government hovered over the nation as a new president took office, and the leadership he put forth in response.

The stories focus on men who took the reins of presidential authority as storm clouds gathered or a hard rain fell, not those who took office during a more placid time only to face turmoil later in their tenure: Washington, the first president of a fragile and fledgling nation; Thomas

Jefferson, the first president as the government emerged into a two-party system; John Tyler, the first vice president to assume the presidency upon the death of an incumbent; Abraham Lincoln as civil war loomed; Franklin D. Roosevelt during the depths of the Great Depression; Harry S. Truman at the close of World War II and the dawn of the cold war; John F. Kennedy at the cold war's height; and Gerald R. Ford, in the wake of Watergate, as the first person to become president through the Twenty-second Amendment, unelected by the national electorate.

All of these presidents faced unique crises at the outset of their administrations that offered no precedent. Though all except Washington may have drawn strength in knowing the challenges of those who went before them, they had nothing on which to base their leadership except their own faith, instincts, and best judgment. While each man had his own flaws, some pronounced and explored here, the best among them tapped into what Lincoln may have described as "the better angels of [their] nature" to face the central trials of their administrations. For the most part, the country had the good fortune of having in its highest office a man who complemented the moment by rising to the occasion.

In contemplating historical hypotheticals—

What if John Adams—a patriot to be sure but headstrong, irascible, and often polarizing—had been the first president?

Or Lincoln's presidential rival, Stephen Douglas, unopposed to the extension of slavery in new states as America expanded west, had beat him in 1860?

Or Franklin Roosevelt's second vice president, Henry Wallace, the most liberal member of Roosevelt's cabinet and a Russian sympathizer, had remained on the ticket to take over for the deceased Roosevelt as the cold war began?

Or what if Richard Nixon's original vice president, Spiro Agnew, who resigned in 1973 amid allegations that he had accepted kickbacks as governor of Maryland, had ascended to the presidency after Nixon's resignation in 1974?

—we can appreciate the importance of having in place the right man at the right time. In almost all cases, by examining the tests they faced and the leadership they offered, we can get a glimpse of their greatness, or at very least, their goodness.

How were those qualities manifest? And why did they make a difference, particularly in the crucial, formative days and months after these men assumed the presidency?

Words can ease the soul just as knowledge sustains the mind. During trying times, a leader can summon them to inspire faith and quell fear by pointing to intention. It is fitting then to begin by drawing on words spoken by each man upon taking office, which serve to frame the crisis he confronted while portending the attributes that would most define him as president.

Washington's address was more a benediction of sorts, appropriate for America's commencement as the Constitution was put into practice. He believed ardently that the "invisible hand" of God had much to do with the country's rise and would continue to act in its favor. But as important as God's blessings may have been in its founding, it is impossible to imagine America's successful beginning without Washington himself.

In his address he noted his anxiety at being drafted into the role of president but yielded to the wishes of the electorate as he was "summoned by my country, whose voice I can never hear but with veneration and love." Washington always answered its call, without pause or thoughts of personal gain, as the commander in chief of the Continental army in the revolutionary fight against the British, as the presiding officer at the Constitutional Convention, finally as president of the union.

We can summon immortal words from many presidents, but we struggle to recall enduring words written or spoken by Washington. With him, it's more about image: the whitewashed "I cannot tell a lie" myths first spun by Parson Weems, or his strong, stolid countenance protruding from Mount Rushmore or staring back from Gilbert Stuart canvases, exuding a piety that seems altogether out of place in today's age. Those renderings were meant to inspire awe, much as Washington did in his own times. Revered for his honor, a virtue seldom invoked today outside military circles, Washington had a peerless standing that was based less on his words—he was challenged as a writer and public speaker—than his deeds.

As president he remained above partisan fray and popular opinion, always acting in what he saw as the best interest of the country. His cabinet contained a mix of Federalists and Anti-Federalists (or Republicans), whose major disagreement was how much power should be given to the national government and how much reserved for the states. While Washington was inclined toward the Federalist camp, he ruled with an even hand. Rarely did he reveal his own views until policy decisions were required, fearful that a split of the body politic into opposing political parties would break the union. As war raged between the British and French in the wake of the French Revolution, he resisted the pro-British sentiments of his secretary of treasury, Alexander Hamilton, and the French leanings of Jefferson, his secretary of state, insisting the United States remain neutral until it had gained strength and stability. Achieving the latter meant avoiding a war with the British, which seemed inevitable given the lingering antagonisms between the two countries in the wake the American Revolution.

To that end, Washington supported a treaty negotiated with the British by Supreme Court chief justice John Jay, despite the disastrous reception it got from the public, which saw it largely as caving in to its former enemy. Finally, after two successful four-year terms in office, Washington refused to run for reelection, setting a precedent for his successors by willingly relinquishing power, a decidedly American tradition now ensured by the Twenty-second Amendment. Given his unequaled stature and the ambiguities of the presidential office, he could have been the nation's first king; he chose instead to be a public servant, a steward.

Though he was not immune to criticism and could be thin-skinned when it was directed at him, it was Washington's integrity more than anything else that set the standard for American leadership and gave the young republic the confidence of its ideals. His decisions were led by what he considered to be in the best interest of the country, as was the case with Jay's Treaty. Moreover, his steady presence and restraint kept the country united despite the fissures that threatened to divide it. Without Washington, Jefferson's words in the Declaration of Independence might be nothing more than philosophical flourishes, and American democracy a mere abstraction.

But Jefferson's vision gave Washington an ideological foundation on which to sustain a revolution. As president of the union he helped found, Jefferson would rely on his ideals to help crystallize the country's destiny. Still, there was no guarantee that the country would remain united as the election that eventually rode Jefferson into office—the election of 1800— vociferously played out.

Despite Washington's worries of "riot and insurrection" as a consequence of partisan politics, by the dawn of the nineteenth century the government was divided into two distinct political parties: the Federalists with their pro–central government stance, and the Anti-Federalists, who wanted to give individuals and state governments more sovereign powers to determine their own direction. Washington's fears were well-founded. Never in world history had a nation seen one "party" peacefully yield power to another. In Europe, shifts in power often resulted in a monarch being put to a violent death or in bloodshed in the streets. Given the heated passions around the election of 1800, the first time in the young nation's history that candidates from opposing parties vied for the presidency, there was no reason to believe that those fears would not be realized. Both candidates—John Adams, the incumbent Federalist president, and Jefferson, the Republican candidate—were eviscerated in a campaign as ugly as any since. Jefferson was derided by Federalist newspaper editors as "the Jacobin anti-Christ" who would tear down the nation that Washington had built, a view subscribed to by many in the party.[4] Nevertheless, the Republicans carried the election. Yet even then, the results were uncertain. Due to a quirk in the Electoral College, Jefferson's running mate, Aaron Burr, received the same number of electoral votes as Jefferson. When the unprincipled, opportunistic Burr refused to give way to Jefferson, the contest's outcome was tossed into the House of Representatives to decide—and the country braced for conflict. In the course of a week, thirty-five votes produced only deadlock. On the thirty-sixth, Jefferson won a narrow victory.

Jefferson called the election "the Revolution of 1800," though crisis had been averted when no blood spilled in its waging, signifying that the country and its ideological underpinnings were strong enough to sustain opposing viewpoints—no matter how fervently held. But it fell to Jefferson to bring the country together under his Republican leadership.

His inaugural remarks set the right tone. "Every difference of opinion is not a difference of principle," he reminded the electorate. "We have been called by different brethren of the same principle. We are all Republicans, we are all Federalists. . . . Let us then with courage and confidence, pursue our own federal and republican principles, our attachment to the union and representative government."

The most enigmatic of the Founding Fathers, Jefferson would enact a Republican agenda but would show his own Federalist side in the most momentous act of his presidency, as he subordinated his instincts to resist broadening the powers of his office when opportunity for the country to realize its destiny serendipitously arose. A Virginia country squire, Jefferson believed, as others did, that America's future lay in its expansion westward; its teeming ambition could be realized only in its inexorable growth across the continent. Manifest destiny it would later be called. That conviction, along with a Renaissance man's boundless curiosity, led to his sending Meriwether Lewis and William Clark and a permanent team of thirty-one men to discover the uncharted territory and bounty that awaited west of the Mississippi in 1804. But a year earlier, he had ensured the country's western expansion, testing constitutional limits by ordering the acquisition of more than eight hundred thousand square miles that stretched from the Mississippi River to the Rocky Mountains from France's Napoleon Bonaparte for a fire-sale price of $15 million. The Louisiana Purchase doubled the size of the United States overnight, becoming Jefferson's singular presidential triumph. In making the purchase, Jefferson strengthened the presidency, likely an unintentional consequence for the anti-Federalist. But had he stuck to his Republican guns, America's future might have been far different.

While penning the Declaration of Independence a quarter of a century before his presidency, Jefferson came up with a plan to abolish slavery over time by taking the children of those in bondage and teaching them trades, before recolonizing them and granting them lives as "free and independent people." The idea, quickly rejected by Southern delegates, never made it into the declaration. Had abolition been pressed, there would have been no document at all, for no union would have been viable. Jefferson and many of his contemporaries knew that slavery was a great wrong, but they knew also that it would have to be attended to by future generations.

The slavery issue would continue to seethe well after Jefferson passed on to the ages in 1826, fifty years to the day after the immortal date appearing on the Declaration of Independence. But in 1840, as America set about electing—or perhaps reelecting—its president, the country cared less about issues than image. The Whig Party, organized around national policies, offered General William Henry Harrison as its presidential candidate to square off against the Democratic incumbent, Martin Van Buren. The Whigs cast the general as the hero of the 1811 battle of Tippecanoe, a precursor to the battle of 1812, employing the catchy campaign phrase, "Tippecanoe and Tyler too." "Tyler" was John Tyler, a compromise candidate to be Harrison's running mate. An old-style Virginia patrician, Tyler was a former Democrat who, along with other states' rights Southerners in his party, forged a tenuous alliance with the Whigs aimed at driving Van Buren—and Jacksonian Democracy—out of the presidency. The Whigs' campaign, light on substance, heavy on populist packaging, won the favor of the American electorate, sending "Tippecanoe" to the White House . . . and eventually Tyler, too.

A month after taking the vice presidential oath, Tyler was awakened at sunrise at his Williamsburg home by a messenger from Washington who informed him that Harrison had died of pneumonia. Tyler would become the first man to ascend to the presidency with the death of an incumbent. But would Tyler be the *acting* president or would he take on the position outright? At best the Constitution was vague on the matter. And what was Tyler's obligation to honor the ideology and policies of his deceased predecessor?

Within hours of learning of Harrison's death, Tyler was on his way to Washington. Shortly upon his arrival, resisting his own inherent stubbornness and yielding to the advice of members of the cabinet, he took the oath of office; Tyler had believed that since the Constitution provided for the ascendance of the vice president to the presidency with the death of the incumbent, reciting the oath was a redundant exercise. But taking the oath was a clear indication that he had *become* president, not merely a presidential surrogate. The only significant aspect of his inaugural address—not spoken but issued in writing three days later—was that he offered one at all, reinforcing the impression the he was, as he referred to himself several times during its course, "President" or "Chief Magistrate."[5]

Dubbed "His Accidency" by detractors who continued to doubt his authority, Tyler made it clear that he would be his own man. He rejected the nationalist policy of Harrison and the Whigs, racking up his most significant achievement with the annexation of Texas, thus giving a boost to the states' rights cause—and the westward expansion of slavery. When the Whigs took revenge by staging a presidential impeachment trial, Tyler narrowly staved off disaster. His strong will in forming his own administration strengthened the presidency, setting a precedent for vice presidents who found the presidency thrust on them. But his stubbornness, which he didn't keep in check for long, alienated the Whig Party that had ridden him into office, diminishing his influence, further divided the country on slavery and put him on the wrong side of history.

The slavery question—and the nation's most grave crisis—would eventually fall squarely in the hands of Abraham Lincoln. He took office in 1861 as seven Southern states had seceded from the union in response to his election. Lincoln's resolve to preserve the union was plain. "*You* have no oath registered in heaven to destroy the union," he told his "dissatisfied countrymen," the would-be secessionists, upon his first inauguration. "While *I* have the most solemn one to 'preserve, protect, and defend it." But ostensibly, his determination to keep the union intact was a response to the symptom of secession, not the disease of slavery. In order not to alienate the border states, whose support would be pivotal if civil war broke out, and despite a lifetime opposition to slavery, he declared in the same address; "I have no purpose, directly or indirectly, to interfere with the institution of slavery. I believe I have no lawful right to do so, and I have no inclination to do so."

But of course, the war, which raged soon after Lincoln took office, *was* about slavery. The Emancipation Proclamation, handed down by Lincoln in 1863 as Union troops began to turn the tide on the Confederate army after heavy losses, made that clear. Lincoln's strong will in preserving the union was manifest in the win-at-all-costs strategy that led to a staggering loss of life and a trail of scorched earth throughout the South. But while condemning the sins of slavery and secession, he was careful not to cast out the sinner. In his second inaugural address, in 1865, as the war drew to a close after the brutal toll it had taken for four years—far longer than anyone had anticipated—Lincoln responded empathetically to the plight of his now vanquished countrymen in the Southern states: "With malice toward none," he stated, "with charity for all, with firmness in the right as God gives us to see the right, let us strive on to finish the work we are in, to bind up the nation's wounds, to care for him who shall have borne the battle and for his widow and his orphan, to do all which may achieve and cherish a just and lasting peace among ourselves and with all nations." His compassion, like that of the father welcoming his prodigal son home, ensured that the country would continue anew—and reinforced an American ideal.

In the latter part of the nineteenth century and into the twentieth, America had moved along and risen in the world at the brisk pace of its own boundless ambition, fueled by its belief in itself and the rewards of its labor. Economic opportunity, as it always had been, was at the heart of the promise of American liberty. However, three score and a dozen years after Lincoln's first inaugural address, as one hundred thousand witnessed the inauguration of Franklin Delano Roosevelt on a cold, dreary March day in 1933, the country once again found itself in crisis, this time around the economic ravages of the Great Depression. The Depression had continued unabated for three and a half years while Herbert Hoover, who believed that remedies lay in the private sector, passively presided over the country.

The results had been devastating: twelve million—almost a quarter of the labor force—were unemployed; nearly all the country's banks, more than ten thousand, had failed; thousands of farms across the Great Plains foreclosed as their topsoil was swept up by Dust Bowl winds.[6]

Roosevelt's unbridled buoyancy in the face of despair and suffering was audacious. "This great Nation will endure as it has endured, will revive and will prosper," his voice rang out after taking the presidential oath, like coins jingling in a pocket. "So, first of all, let me assert my firm belief that the only thing we have to fear is fear itself—nameless, unreasoning, unjustified terror which paralyzes needed efforts to convert retreat into advance."

Roosevelt never retreated, just as his faith in the resilience of the country never waned. Using all the tools at his disposal, he put in place the policies of the New Deal, which included sweeping measures that spilled over every segment of the population, heightening the role of federal government in American life. Though the Depression would not see its nadir until several years after FDR took office, the president's optimism and confidence in the American government and people bred hope during the worst of times. That same quality would help sustain the country as he mobilized the population to embark on its second world war after the Japanese bombed Pearl Harbor in December 1941.

Roosevelt died on April 12, 1945, as the war wound down, leaving Harry Truman, just two months into his tenure as vice president, to deal with its end and muddled aftermath. Though Truman took the presidential oath just hours after Roosevelt was pronounced dead, he offered no inaugural remarks to the American people. But his comment to the press the following day spoke volumes: "Boys, if you pray, pray for me now." He added that upon hearing the news that he would become president, "I felt like the moon, the stars, and all the planets had fallen on me."[7]

Had he known then what he would soon discover, he might have felt as if a few other celestial bodies had struck him as well. Japanese troops had all but been defeated, but the country seemed unlikely to surrender given the premium it placed on honor. Though Truman had known a little about the nuclear program the United States was developing through the Special Committee to Investigate the National Defense Program, which he had chaired, the White House hadn't briefed him on the extent of the Manhattan Project, which put at the military's disposal a weapon whose awesome power might compel the Japanese leadership to accept their fate. Nor was Truman aware of the extent of the tensions that were developing between the United States and the Soviet Union, its ally in the war effort. In early 1945, two months before his death, Roosevelt met with British prime minister Winston Churchill and Soviet premier Joseph Stalin at Yalta in the Crimea to draw up plans for postwar Europe. A clearly ailing FDR acquiesced to Stalin's demand to control Poland's borders, secure land in the Far East, and levy heavy reparations on defeated Germany. Stalin's aggressive posture portended a cold war between the United States and the Soviet Union as the two countries jockeyed for geopolitical advantage for much of the latter half of the twentieth century.

Soon into his presidency, Truman gave the order for American planes to drop atomic bombs on Hiroshima and Nagasaki, forcing a Japanese surrender, while tensions between the United States and the Soviets began building over the spoils in Europe. "Sherman was wrong," Truman said at the time. "*Peace* is hell."[8] It fell to Truman to keep the peace while standing up to the Soviets in Berlin, Turkey, and Greece; rebuilding wartorn Europe and Japan; and dealing with labor strikes and discrimination against African Americans at home. But in 1950, in not wavering when Communist North Korea, with the backing of China, invaded South Korea, he led the United States into a drawn-out war resulting in a virtual stalemate and his own diminished popularity. However, though not appreciated at the time, Truman's formidable character and common sense enhanced America's moral standing and fortified its position in the world at one of the most crowded hours in American history.

By 1961, as John F. Kennedy took office, tensions between the two superpowers had escalated, as the threat of a nuclear war loomed behind America's halcyon façade. U.S. foreign policy, as in Truman's day, was defined by its measured effect against Soviet domination. Stalin died in

1953, succeeded by Nikita Khrushchev—truculent, aggressive, and willing and able to exploit weakness. Kennedy, callow in the minds of many—including Khrushchev—confronted the issue of Communist aggression head-on. "Let every nation know," he said, "whether it wishes us well or ill, that we shall pay any price, bear any burden, meet any hardship, support any friend, oppose any foe, in order to assure the survival and the success of liberty." To the Soviets he made the direct plea "that both sides begin anew a quest for peace, before the dark powers of destruction unleashed by science engulf humanity in planned or accidental self-destruction." To his "fellow Americans" he made his famous entreaty to enlist in the cause of freedom: "Ask not what your country can do for you—ask what you can do for your country."

While contending with the simmering civil rights movement at home, Kennedy spent the better part of his 1,036-day presidency consumed by the threat of communism abroad. He began his regime inauspiciously with a botched attempt to overthrow Cuban dictator Fidel Castro in the Bay of Pigs invasion in April 1961. Later in the year, struggling to gain ground in the cold war, he sent additional military advisers to Vietnam to help fend off Communist troops from the north, and he boldly jump-started America's feeble efforts to compete with the Russians in the space race. But the central crisis of Kennedy's presidency—and perhaps of the cold war—would come in October of the following year as Khrushchev, emboldened by Kennedy's failure at the Bay of Pigs, sent Russian ships carrying nuclear warheads to Cuba in an attempt to establish a Soviet nuclear presence just ninety miles off the coast of Florida. After carefully considering his options, Kennedy resisted his military chiefs' call for direct engagement and instead ordered a naval blockade around Cuba. The move prevented the Soviet ships from gaining entry to the island while buying time in the hope that cooler heads would prevail. Kennedy's composure during the crisis, and his determination to set his own course, kept the cold war from becoming hot.

In the first lines of his 1956 Pulitzer Prize–winning book *Profiles in Courage,* Kennedy used Ernest Hemingway's phrase "grace under pressure" to define courage. Detractors described Kennedy as "all profile, no courage." Certainly image played into the telegenic Kennedy's appeal. That in itself can be a virtue. Washington was a master of the heroic pose; Roosevelt's outward jauntiness inspired public trust. Still, Kennedy showed a grace in the midst of the Cuban missile crisis that went far beyond superficial and reflected real guts, to use Hemingway's word.

Had it not been for a few hundred votes in Illinois and Texas, where voting irregularities were widely reported, the election of 1960 would have gone not to Kennedy but to the incumbent vice president, Republican Richard Nixon, himself an unflinching cold warrior. Nixon considered contesting the election but accepted defeat rather than throw the country off balance in the eye of the Soviets. After narrowly losing a 1962 election for California's governorship, Nixon ran for president again in 1968 in another close election, this time winning. Having finally taken the ultimate political prize, Nixon savored power, thwarting the path of political enemies—perceived and otherwise. A bungled break-in at the headquarters of the Democratic Party in Washington's Watergate office complex led to the slow unraveling of Nixon's presidency as the administration was mired in scandals revealing its corruption.

A beleaguered Nixon resigned the presidency on August 9, 1974. Never before had a president resigned the office. Nine months earlier, Nixon had reluctantly appointed House Minority Leader Gerald Ford to the office of vice president, the first under the provisions of the Twenty-fifth Amendment. Not elected by the American people, Ford succeeded Nixon as president as the country's trust in its government and the presidency ebbed.

Uncomplicated and down-to-earth, Ford proved an antidote to the enigmatic, imperious Nixon. After taking the presidential oath, Ford gave the nation what he called "a little straight talk among friends." "Our long national nightmare is over. Our Constitution works. We are a nation of laws and not men. Here the people rule." Americans responded to the refreshing openness of the Ford administration, but Ford's brief honeymoon wouldn't last. A month later, in an effort to bind up the country's deep divisions and move on to more pressing matters, he pardoned Nixon of any wrongdoing in Watergate. Ford claimed it was "the right thing to do." But was it? The "people" didn't think so. Overnight his lofty approval ratings plummeted. While contending with the ensuing controversy, Ford grappled with rampant inflation, the last gasps of the failed war in Vietnam, and an unflattering image as a dim-witted, albeit good-natured, clod. Nonetheless, the county was moving on as the dark cloud of Watergate began to dissipate over time.

Though it certainly cost him the 1976 presidential election to Democrat Jimmy Carter, the American public eventually came to accept the pardon of Nixon as Ford had intended it, and began to appreciate the politically selfless measures he took to heal the country. Ford's inherent decency ultimately helped restore America's faith in its government.

Even before television and the Internet, history was drawn by sound bites. Clare Boothe Luce, playwright and wife of *Time* magazine mogul Henry Luce, often challenged political leaders by telling them that history would remember them in a single line. She cited Lincoln as an example: "He freed the slaves," she would say, then demand, "What will be your sentence?" (Kennedy got so tired of hearing the question he grew exasperated in her company. She flattered Nixon by suggesting that his line would be, "He went to China," but that was before the full revelations of Watergate.)[9] History is neither so succinct nor so regimented. But underlying the deeds and policies that will underscore the legacies of our presidents is the character that inspired them. It should be just as memorable. Washington's integrity and sense of duty; Jefferson's egalitarian ideals; Tyler's stubbornness; Lincoln's resolve and compassion; Roosevelt's buoyancy and activism; Truman's courage of conviction; Kennedy's composure; Ford's decency.

Jefferson once pithily described the office of the presidency as a "splendid misery." One suspects the misery lies in the constant strain of power, the splendor in what one can do with it. Forty-two men have surveyed the job firsthand, and a forty-third now takes the stage. (There have now been forty-three men who have been president, though Grover Cleveland, who was elected to two non-consecutive terms, was both our twenty-second and twenty-fourth president.) Barack Obama will be the forty-third man to hold the presidency, but will be our forty-fourth president. As he takes office, the country is once again at a crossroads. America's involvement in Iraq has been met with doubt and scorn at home and abroad even as the threat of global terrorism remains and the country's moral authority is in doubt along with the policies of George W. Bush. And the possibility of sustained recession—or even depression—looms despite government bailout schemes. Faith in our financial institutions has receded, and the nation's economic leadership has diminished with the rise of free market economies throughout the world—China, Russia, and elsewhere—which bubble up with possibility.

In October 2008, in the wake of the global financial crisis, an ABC News/*Washington Post* poll revealed that 90 percent of Americans think the country is on the "wrong track," an all-time low in the twenty-five years the poll has been taken. Similar polls are just as gloomy, with results that reflect thirty- or forty-year lows.[10] Furthermore, a CNN/ Opinion Research poll released on July 4, 2008, showed that only 29 percent of Americans believe that the country's Founding Fathers would approve of the state of the nation today, down from 54 percent in 2001.[11] While it is too early to tell whether Bush's vindication will, in some measure, come with history's verdict, the quagmire of drawn-out wars in Iraq and Afghanistan; the continued threat of terrorism at home and abroad; a faltering economy blighted by deregulation and plagued by colossal debt;  the nation's diminished stature overseas and its increasingly ambiguous leadership politically and economically; and the consequent demoralization of the American people are burdens Obama must take in hand.

What can Barack Obama do or say in his first days in office to rally the nation, to unite us, and to boost our self-assurance? What steps can he take to dispel our fears of economic calamity and to restore our standing in the world—and our own faith in our role within it? And what lessons can he draw from those who went before him as he faces his own unprecedented crises?

Writing these narratives, I was often reminded of a passage written by Robert F. Kennedy in the introduction of a memorial edition of his martyred brother's *Profiles in Courage*: "This book is not just the stories of the past but a book of hope and confidence in the future. What happens to the country, to the world, depends on what we do with what others have left us." If past is prologue, these stories too should instill hope and confidence in our future.

Like Washington, Jefferson, Lincoln, Franklin Roosevelt, and perhaps Kennedy, had he not been cut down in his prime, President Obama can be a transformational leader; someone whose vision and character take us in a new direction; someone who uses a time of crisis to inspire us to reach beyond ourselves. Or, like Truman and Ford, he can be a president whose leadership is less inspirational but whose moral courage helps us to weather the storm and emerge stronger, more resilient. One thing is certain: As America faces another crossroad in its turbulent history, we are invested in the hope that Barack Obama is the best of us. And, there are reminders in these stories of who we can be at our best.

# I

# GEORGE WASHINGTON

## *The First*

The moment was bound to be awkward. As the delegates at Philadelphia's State House debated the role and responsibilities of president of the United States for the Constitution they were creating, several questions arose: Should the country's chief magistrate be one man or a council consisting of several, perhaps from different regions of the union? They had, after all, broken away from a monarchical government in which one man reigned supreme. What if the president was imprudent in his ambitions or died before his term? Wouldn't a plural executive allow for moderation and render moot the question of succession? And what about remuneration? Should the chief executive—or executives—be salaried, or by the very nature of money, would it lead to greed and corruption?[1]

"The first man put at the helm will be a good one," Benjamin Franklin, the oldest delegate, told his fellow delegates. "Nobody knows what sort will come afterwards." He had scribbled his thoughts on the subject on paper, and, being of thin voice, had them read to the delegation by his fellow Pennsylvanian James Wilson. Franklin was inclined toward a plural executive and believed that no compensation should be offered.

19

"There are two passions which have a powerful influence on the affairs of men," he had reasoned. "These are ambition and avarice, the love of power and the love of money."[2]

The matter required delicacy. The entire room knew that the first man to assume the role as head of the government in any form was the very man who was presiding over the convention: George Washington. James Madison, who sat with Washington at a table for the Virginia delegation, would later write to his friend Thomas Jefferson, in far-off Paris serving as America's minister to France, that the moment was "peculiarly embarrassing."[3] Washington himself, he of renowned dignity and glacial reserve, simply let the moment pass.

After deliberations, the state delegations voted seven to three for a single president, with Delaware, Maryland, and New York opposed. "Gen. W., ay," wrote Madison in his notes, signifying that if the Constitution were ratified, General Washington alone would be the nation's first president.

Several months earlier, when Jefferson had read the names of the men who would compose the constitutional delegation—among them Madison, Alexander Hamilton, George Mason, Gouverneur Morris, Roger Sherman, Elbridge Gerry, and Charles Pinckney—he proclaimed them "an assembly of demigods." But neither Jefferson nor any of the other delegates had any doubts that George Washington—by his sheer stature and indispensability—stood above all others. Washington, after all, had served as commander in chief of the Continental army in the war against the British for six long years, which, at times, seemed mere folly. His natural facility as a leader and his bold military strategy drove the revolutionary troops to victory despite the dreadful hardships they faced. Well before there was a United States of America, General Washington had been referred to as the Father of the Country, a sobriquet that first appeared in 1776.[4] After the fighting was over, when the Articles of Confederation proved flawed in guiding the federal government, it was Washington's support of a Constitution for the new republic that, more than anything, served as a catalyst for the convention—and inevitably it was Washington who oversaw it.

Seventeen months after the Constitutional Convention disbanded, in February 1789, the Electoral College confirmed what the members of the delegation—and perhaps the entire nation—already knew. By unanimous vote, Washington was elected to be the nation's first president.

Washington at the helm as the country's first chief executive may have given almost universal comfort to Americans, but not to the fifty-seven-year-old Washington, who ostensibly wanted nothing more than to live out his years as a gentleman farmer at his beloved Mount Vernon. "I fear I must bid adieu to happiness," he confided to his former aide-de-camp, Colonel David Humphreys, shortly before taking up the office, "for I see nothing but clouds and darkness before me; and I call God to witness that the day which shall carry me again into public life will be a more distressing one than any I have ever yet known."[5] But the duty-bound Washington had always seen his way through the hardships his country served up due to his unyielding belief in the "glorious cause" of America and the magnificence of its future.[6]

Still, the "clouds and darkness" Washington saw in the task ahead were not an illusion. The mammoth debt accrued during the revolution threatened to cripple the American economy, and antagonisms with the British had not vanished with the war's end. Those troubles and others would require the attention of a skilled and steady hand, one who could handle the enormous burdens of the job. The crowned heads of Europe would look with keen interest upon the experiment America was conducting. Like the American people, they knew that the success or failure of the new republic and its untested, academic Constitution—indeed, the audacious notion of egalitarian liberty itself—rested largely on the president's shoulders. It was up to him more than any other to keep the country united despite the differences—regional, economic, and ideological—that threatened to tear at the country's newly sewn and fragile seams and divide its citizenry. What's more, each step he made in a march toward a stable government would set the standard for those who succeeded him. No one knew this more than Washington. "I walk on untrodden ground," he observed soon into his first term. "There is scarcely any part of my conduct which may not hereafter be drawn into precedent."[7] However, as he wrote to Madison, he "devoutly wished" that "these precedents be fixed on true principles."[8]

That Washington would establish the principles on which the presidency would rest was America's good fortune. Above all else, integrity was seared into his character. As Jefferson put it in a letter to Dr. Walter Jones well after Washington's death, Washington's "integrity was most pure. His justice was the most inflexible I have ever known, no motives of interest or consanguinity, of friendship or hatred, being able to bias his decision."[9] Tench Tilghman, one of Washington's lieutenants during the revolution, called him "the most honestest of men that I believe ever adorned human nature."[10] The grade school tale of a young Washington chopping down the cherry tree and fessing up to the act is an allegory capturing the essence of his greatest strength as a leader; the nation needed a president who could be trusted not to exploit the ambiguities of the powers granted to him in the Constitution and to do what was best for the country.

But there was more than integrity to Washington's legend, which Americans embraced as a point of pride to rally around. There also were his feats of bravery. In a skirmish that marked the beginning of the French and Indian War when Washington was a twenty-three-year-old aide-de-camp, he averted death when four bullets penetrated his coat, while two horses were shot from underneath him before his retreat. (Later Washington logged a report detailing the foray. After reviewing it in London, King George II was rumored to have speculated that the entire incident came from the active imagination of a glory-seeking young man.[11]) Those battlefield heroics and others—Washington was that rare man who was oblivious to the peril of warfare—gave him the air of invincibility, adding to his myth.

Then there was his physical prowess. Washington personified the image of a strong leader. He was considered the best horseman in his home state—the equivalent in Virginia aristocracy to being a football hero at Notre Dame—giving him an advantage on the battlefield, where he was fearless, or on a leisurely country fox hunt, which he relished.[12] His strength was such that he could crack nuts between his outsized fingers, and David Humphreys heard the general boast that he never came across a man who could throw a stone farther than he could.[13] In almost every case, Washington literally stood above all others, ramrod straight. In a day when most of his contemporaries were between five and six feet tall, Washington, at six two and just over two hundred pounds, was an imposing presence, albeit one seemingly constructed of spare parts. His nose was big and broad, his complexion deeply pockmarked, and his lips thin. Decaying teeth meant dentures, ill fitting and painful in his case, made up of the teeth of horses and donkeys and, it is believed, human slaves.[14] His hips were heavy, while his chest was sunken owing to a childhood pulmonary illness. Marquis de Lafayette, the young French general who fought under Washington during the revolution, claimed Washington's hands were the biggest he had ever seen.[15] Still, the assemblage resulted in physical grandeur. As Lafayette put it, "General Washington seemed to arrest fortune with one glance."[16]

Many of his countrymen had the opportunity to capture a glance of their soon-to-be president as he journeyed to New York to be inaugurated into his new role. After borrowing $50 for expenses, currency being in short supply, Washington set out on the fortnight's journey from Mount Vernon in a coach-and-four, accompanied by two aides. (Martha Washington, who shared her husband's despair over reentering public life, would join him in New York after he was settled.) Venturing through six of the country's thirteen states, mostly along the Old Post Road, he was received like a conquering hero with an unprecedented series of receptions en route. Wreaths were bestowed upon his brow, feasts prepared, and toasts and speeches made in his honor. Veterans who fought alongside him in the revolutionary cause came out to reminisce about their struggles and ultimate triumph, and to wish him well in his new battle.[17]

It was the kind of outpouring that might have been accorded an emperor in ancient Rome. But Washington was not—and refused to be— Caesar. Rather, he emulated Cincinnatus, the Roman general who humbly went back to his farm after leading his country to military victory when it was under siege by barbarians. These were celebrations of hope and gestures of good faith; Washington could be trusted to lead an *American* government, a decided departure from the European imperialism that had characterized Western regimes to that point in history.

On April 30, 1789, at the corner of Wall and Broad streets in lower Manhattan, Washington was sworn into office on the colonnaded balcony of Federal Hall, which would temporarily house Congress. He was escorted to the dais by the man who would become his vice president, John Adams of Massachusetts, who had secured the position by receiving the second-greatest number of electoral votes—thirty-four to Washington's sixty-nine. The presidential oath was administered by Robert Livingston, chancellor of New York. Washington, purposely dressed in a plain brown broadcloth Hartford suit and white silk stockings with a dress sword at his side, recited as designated in the Constitution, his right hand on a Bible, left hand on his heart, then, unscripted, kissed the Bible. "It is done," Livingston said before shouting to the masses gathered to witness the inauguration, "Long live George Washington, President of the United States!" as church bells pealed.[18]

The ceremony was followed by Washington's address in which "virtue was personified," in the words of one observer, then a service at St. Paul's Chapel of Trinity Church and, by early evening, a display of fireworks and illuminations. When it was all over, braving a crowd of thirty thousand or more, the greatest the city had ever witnessed, preventing his transport by carriage, Washington walked downtown to the quarters at 39 Broadway that would serve as his home and office for seven months before Philadelphia became the nation's capital. The first president's tenure, and the fruition of the Constitution, had begun promisingly. But the daunting challenges of the office remained.[19]

It was by no means a certainty that Washington would rise to exalted heights. He was born in Tidewater, Virginia, on February 22, 1732, to the well-to-do tobacco planter Augustine Washington and his Mary Ball Washington. Augustine died when George was eleven. The young Washington honed his leadership skills early on, acting as a surrogate father to

his younger siblings, three brothers and two sisters, under the reproach-
ful gaze of his mother. Washington would forever remain self-conscious
about his lack of formal education—seven or eight years of private tutor-
ing at best. He was "not a scholar to be certain," claimed John Adams,
an observation that may have arisen out of petty jealousy. "That he was
too illiterate, unread, unlearned for his station and reputation is equally
past dispute."[20]

In 1752, at age nineteen, Washington embarked on a career in the
military, joining the militia as major after his mother forbade him to
enlist in the Royal Navy as he had hoped. The ambitious and able Washington rose steadily through the ranks to become commander in chief of
Virginia Militia just three years later. In 1759, he resigned his commission and stepped back into civilian life upon his marriage to Martha
Dandridge Custis. Mrs. Custis, the wealthiest woman in Virginia by the
estimation of many, brought assets that included six thousand acres of
Virginia farmland and 150 slaves to work it, adding to the five thousand
acres and 49 slaves he already owned, some of which was inherited from
his older half-brother Lawrence. Washington happily adopted the life of
a wealthy farmer, overseeing the harvest of tobacco, corn, and wheat
crops. Agriculture became his lifelong passion, albeit an unrequited love
at least financially and one that would be interrupted for years at a time
when the duty of his country called.

The first call came in 1774. Like many Virginians, Washington had
become increasingly resentful of the burdensome economic policies of
the British and was selected to represent Virginia as a delegate in the first
Continental Congress in Philadelphia. He was chosen again the following year, beginning his term in May 1775, a month after the death of
eight colonial minutemen at the hands of British troops in Lexington,
Massachusetts, led to a call for revolution. When the Congress proposed
a Continental army to go up against the British, Washington was elected
unanimously to the post of commander in chief. In a letter to his wife
sent after he received his commission, he wrote, "Far from seeking this
appointment, I have used every endeavour in my power to avoid it, not
only from my unwillingness to part with you and the Family, but from a

consciousness of its being a trust too great for my Capacity . . . it has been a kind of destiny that has thrown me upon this service."[21] Perhaps his reluctance was sincere, but the old military uniform he wore to congressional sessions may well have suggested otherwise to his fellow delegates.[22]

That Washington did much with very little as commander in chief is a vast understatement. His army—small in number and even smaller with frequent desertions, short on training and supplies and often morale—was ill suited to go up against the British. Although he made early tactical mistakes and lost more battles than he won, he chalked up significant victories, among them defeating a battalion of British troops in a surprise attack after crossing the icy Delaware River on Christmas night in 1776, a win that buoyed spirits throughout the colonies. But the war would drag on for five more years, ending in 1781 with a victory over the British general Charles Cornwallis at Yorktown, Virginia. Unable to bring himself to surrender his sword to Washington, Cornwallis delegated the task to his second in command.[23]

The key to success had less to do with military victories, however, than simply keeping the army united. As long as they remained together, wearing down British patience and resolve, the flame of the revolution flickered.[24] Without it, the Declaration of Independence would have been nothing but a bold decree and lofty ideals on parchment. Washington's leadership, tenacity, and devotion to the cause kept the army intact and sustained the revolution over six bleak years. As one historian put it, Washington's "moral fortitude surmounted problems of misery and want seldom equaled in military history."[25] He would face similar challenges—and offer the same overriding virtues—as president.

The Treaty of Paris between England and the United States, effectively ending the war, would come later, in 1783. Then, his duty done, Washington resigned his commission. Shocked at the notion of Washington relinquishing power at a time when it could be seized immutably, King George III was rumored to have said, "If he does that, he will be the greatest man in the world."[26]

Despite Washington's ostensible disinclination to serve in "a trust" he deemed "too great for [his] capacity," destiny would not stop calling him after he laid down his sword and returned to his fields at Mount Vernon.

That Washington would be the first president was all but certain even before his election; the power he would wield in the role, however, was not. Here again, Washington's towering stature was paramount in shaping the government. The Constitution's outline of duties around the office of the presidency was vague at best—the delegates seemed content simply to hand the office over to Washington to determine for himself what it meant—but no more so than on the subject of a president's cabinet. It stated simply that the president—a "He," of course—"may require the opinion, in writing, of the principal officer in each of the executive departments, upon any subject relating to the duties of their respective offices." What the departments were and whether the officers reported to the president was a matter of interpretation. What was less ambiguous was that the officers, like Supreme Court justices, were to be appointed by the president and approved by the Senate.

But the matter of the Senate's ability to exercise a veto dismissal was not clear—a central question in determining whether the president would be a watered-down figurehead whose cabinet officers would be subject to the Senate's political whims. Aided by his friend and frequent adviser Madison, Washington engineered a narrow victory when the Congress voted on whether the Senate would be entitled to veto dismissals. The vote in the Senate was decided by Vice President Adams's tie-breaking ballot. Had it not been for Washington's prestige, the power of the presidency would likely have been greatly diminished.[27]

The men who would compose Washington's cabinet were among the greatest political minds in America, revolutionary all-stars who had all put their stamps on the republic at its conception: Thomas Jefferson, secretary of state; Alexander Hamilton, secretary of the treasury; Henry Knox, secretary of war; Edmund Randolph, attorney general. In addition to boasting impressive credentials, the selections, like Washington and Adams, struck a desirable geographic balance between North and

South, which held the population roughly evenly. The cabinet represented the three most populous states. Jefferson and Randolph hailed
from Washington's native Virginia; Hamilton was from New York; and
Knox, like Adams, was from Massachusetts. Though Knox and Hamilton had served under Washington in the Continental army, cronyism
and nepotism were absent in Washington's selections. Conscious of the
scrutiny his nominees might receive, he reflected, "No step will pass unnoticed that can be improved into a supposed impartiality for friends or
relatives."[28]

In addition to creating a cabinet, Washington would have to set a
tone, a style by which the institution of the presidency would reflect the
country's core principles. The balance Washington strived for was to
"maintain the dignity of Office, without subjecting himself to the impu-
tation of superciliousness."[29] But while the United States had broken
away from monarchical England, it did not—and perhaps could
not—make a clean break from the intrinsic pomp and pageantry associated with nobility. Maybe it was force of habit.

One of the hallmarks of American democracy is openness. (Indeed,
one of the reasons the European ruling class thought America would fail
was that they believed democracy to be little more than mob rule.) One
of Washington's challenges was to create a classless executive office in
which the people were recognized. Initially, he maintained an open-door
policy—citizens could drop by and have their concerns addressed by the
man in charge. This well-intentioned experiment was short-lived. "From
the time I had done breakfast and thence till dinner and afterwards toward bedtime," he wrote, "I could not get relieved from the ceremony of
one visit before I had to attend to another."[30]

Just three days into his term, a more practical solution was announced
in the *Federal Gazette of the United States*. "We are informed that the President has assigned every Tuesday and Friday between the hours of two
and three for receiving visits," it read, "that visits of compliment on other
days and particularly Sunday, will not be agreeable to him. It seems to
be a prevailing opinion that so much of the President's time will be engaged by various and important business imposed on him by the Consti-

tution that he will find himself constrained to omit returning visits, or accepting invitations to entertainment."[31]

A public backlash over the president's relative inaccessibility ensued, after which Washington solicited the opinions of Adams, Hamilton, and James Madison on how often he should receive the public. Three opportunities for the citizenry to interact with the Washingtons were proffered. On Tuesday afternoons, on the dot of three, Washington held levees, receptions not unlike those held in the salons of the aristocrats of Europe. Suitably attired men with an invitation or a letter of introduction in hand were admitted and invited to greet the president not with an egalitarian handshake but with a bow. As the biographer Richard Norton Smith put it, "Washington did a convincing imitation of himself." He stood formally dressed in black velvet, one hand on his dress sword and the other on his feathered cockade hat, greeting as many attendees as fifteen minutes would allow, before the door would close. Presently he would circulate through the room making small talk. Inside the hour, the gatherings would end with another round of bows at four.[32] The affairs were strictly stag; woman who met similar criteria (as well as men) could enjoy tea with the president and Mrs. Washington on Friday evenings. Formal dinners for invited guests were held on Thursdays. Though the frozen formality of the levees seems now to contradict American sensibilities, they set the precedent of the executive residence as "the People's House," a tradition that stands.

There were other apparent contradictions. Washington was transported through the city in a canary-yellow carriage drawn by six white horses and ornamented by gilded cupids and Washington's coat of arms. The flamboyant chariot, though, had less to do with Washington's grandiosity than perhaps his tacit complicity in showing European observers that the American presidency was not to be trifled with.[33] But through his comportment, Washington himself did that. "There is not a king in Europe," noted Benjamin Rush, Philadelphia physician and Founding Father, "that would not look like a *valet de chambre* by his side."[34]

When congressmen grappled with what the official title of the president should be, it led to some highfalutin suggestions: His Elective

Majesty, His Highness, the President of the United States and Protector of the Rights of Same, and His Mightiness. Temperance prevailed after James Madison advised that those designations would "diminish the true dignity of the first magistrate himself." The modest, self-explanatory title President of the United States would do.[35]

Congress also weighed in on Washington's salary. Those constitutional delegates, including Franklin, concerned about presidential avarice needn't have worried about Washington. As in his days as commander in chief, Washington renounced "every pecuniary compensation," which he made clear in his inaugural address, stating, "I must decline, as inapplicable to myself, any share in the personal emoluments which may be indispensably included in a permanent provision for the executive department." He would accept only expenses incurred as part of his official duties. Ignoring Washington's magnanimity, Congress apportioned an annual salary of $25,000.

It was a good thing. Washington hadn't had much financial success as a farmer, and though his and his wife's landholdings made him one of the richest men in the country, he was more often than not short of ready cash. His yearly salary would be much needed to provide for the hefty expenditures he would incur as president, including his rent at 39 Broadway, in addition to the costs of his opulent carriage, at least a dozen horses, slaves, and scores of social events where he and Martha spared no expense to ensure the pleasure of their guests.[36] Those expenses and others meant not a penny of his earnings would end up in his anemic bank account.

Despite Washington's fear that an ideological chasm would imperil the nation's shaky union, Alexander Hamilton and Thomas Jefferson, the dominant forces in his cabinet, would define opposing principles, portending rifts in the administration and eventually, when Washington was no longer at the government's helm to hold opposing parties at bay, result in a dual-party government.

Hamilton, an up-from-the-bootstraps wealthy New York City lawyer, was a devout Federalist, in favor of a strong, active federal government that would cater to urban interests. Jefferson, the Virginia country squire and plantation owner, was "not a friend to a very energetic government."[37] He envisioned instead an agrarian America and a decentralized government in which the individual states controlled their own fates. American democracy, in his mind, centered around the rights of individuals. Jefferson believed Hamilton to be "not only a monarchist, but for a monarchy bottomed on corruption."[38] His conflicts with Hamilton were not restricted to their different visions for the country they had helped found. There was a natural antipathy between them, a clash of background and regional sensibilities. Jefferson had been born into the gentry in Virginia, where he inherited his father's thousand-acre estate at age fourteen: Hamilton came into the world in the West Indies, the bastard child of a down-on-her-luck French mother and a ne'er-do-well Scottish father, moving to New York at fifteen to be educated at King's College (later Columbia College), where he displayed prodigious scholarship. Jefferson's aristocratic Southern background, like Washington's, did not allow for unseemly displays of naked ambition, although he was just as eager as Hamilton to determine the direction of the new government.

Both men were calculating and possessed among the finest minds of their generation. And both would vie for Washington's ear in the crucial early decisions of his presidency around the nation's economic foundation. In all important matters of state, Washington sought out the opinions of his advisers, usually presented in written form, without revealing his own mind until it had been made up. "I am anxious, always, to compare the opinions of those in whom I confide with one another," Washington said, "and these again with my own, that I may extract all the good I can." The secretary of a British diplomat wrote that Washington "possesses the two great requisites of a statesman, the faculty of concealing his own sentiments and of discovering those of other men." John Adams recognized those requisites as Washington's "gift of silence," a quality he himself did not share. Though Washington's reserve was innate, it also served a purpose: Conscious that political passions threatened to split the country, he kept his voice still so as not to add to them. But though he considered all the views of those close to him—and none were closer at the outset of the administration than Hamilton and Jefferson—Washington's final policy decisions were his alone, framed in his own language.[39]

Much to Washington's dismay, personal enmity would eventually develop between Hamilton and Jefferson. But in one of the first key fiscal policies of the administration, Jefferson helped Hamilton broker a deal that would pave the way toward economic stability—and gave Hamilton early advantage in a rivalry to shape the administration, which Hamilton would ultimately win outright.

The national debt, accrued during the Revolutionary War, was the dominant crisis Washington faced as he took office. The young republic owed enormous sums of money to European countries, primarily France and the Netherlands, with no cash reserves to pay it off. The sheer immensity of the debt threatened to break the American economy, the vitality of which was pivotal to the country's future. Inherent in the American ideal, after all, was the prospect of financial gain—doing better through hard work and ingenuity, and reaping pecuniary rewards. The first found its revolutionary fervor in the taxes imposed by the British to protect trade monopolies. English tea that sank to the bottom of Boston Harbor was tossed there by angry colonists protesting what they saw as economic tyranny—even as they enjoyed the highest standard of living in the world. The "shot heard 'round the world" at Lexington and Concord, inciting the Revolutionary War, was sounded as much in the name of economic independence as individual liberty, and in many ways the two were intertwined.

At Washington's behest, Hamilton quickly set to work devising plans to resolve the crisis. Washington claimed no expertise on economic matters and seemed content to let his former aide-de-camp play a sort of prime ministerial role in the administration—much to the chagrin of the other cabinet officials, particularly Jefferson. All of Hamilton's schemes provoked controversy on some level, but such was Washington's popularity that Hamilton's proposals—with the president's approval—became policy without major opposition. Excise taxes on local goods were an immediate tonic but not one that was swallowed easily by Congress and the public. A number of the items Hamilton recommended taxing were the same as those the British had taxed before the war, arousing the ire of colonists. But Washington supported the measures knowing they would give a much-needed boost to the federal budget.

Hamilton also suggested offering creditors of the government bonds at the same value as old, depreciated continental bonds. This proved difficult for the original holders of the bonds to stomach; the majority of them were soldiers and Southern farmers who had sold the bonds at a fraction of their worth for much needed cash. The beneficiaries were those who bought them, mostly wealthy speculators—stockjobbers— concentrated in the North.[40] Hamilton was accused of catering to the interests of the wealthy mercantile class at the expense of the original holders, who had contributed much to the war effort. As a component of the plan, he advocated the federal assumption of all state war debt, another move that alienated Southerners. Most of the Southern states, including Virginia, had already paid down the bulk of their debt, making the plan advantageous to the Northern states. The latter two issues were touchy enough among Southerners to give rise to talk of secession, and Hamilton's plan ran into a major obstacle when Southern congressmen led by James Madison balked.

Here Jefferson made himself useful to Hamilton, hosting a dinner for Hamilton and Madison at which he oversaw a compromise: Madison would lead dissenting congressmen in supporting the federal assumption of debt in return for Hamilton's sway in moving the U.S. capital to a permanent place on the banks of the Potomac River, which bordered Virginia and Maryland, just upriver from Washington's Mount Vernon and, not incidentally, farther away from Hamilton's New York power base. The agreement entailed moving the capital temporarily to Philadelphia in a southward journey that would take it to its new and final home in ten years' time. Though Jefferson, like Madison, was opposed to the federal government's incurring the debt, he "saw the necessity of yielding for this time . . . for the sake of the union, and to save us from the greatest of calamities."[41]

Though Jefferson would soon come to regret facilitating Hamilton's plan, giving rise to what he saw as his pernicious influence, the move eventually served Jefferson and Madison. Hamilton was able to consolidate the wealthy creditor class behind the federal government, giving it a vested interest in the government's future. As for Jefferson and Madison, in the words of the historian Joseph Ellis, "They would not abandon the government but capture it. The new capital would become an extension of Virginia, or at least the Virginia vision of what the American Revolution meant and the American republic was therefore meant to be. Jefferson would oversee and orchestrate this campaign and provide its rhetorical foundation. Madison would actually lead the troops and do the necessary political infighting."[42] But that would come in time.

Hamilton's next proposal, the creation of a national bank to be situated in Philadelphia for a period of twenty years, also touched a nerve along ideological and sectional lines. Well before Hamilton became secretary of the treasury, he was intrigued with the notion of a national bank as the cornerstone of America's economy, a concept he borrowed from European models. The proposed bank would have the power to issue a uniform currency, safely hold government funds, extend credit to the public and private sectors, and with a market capital of $10 million, would be more than five times bigger than all the nation's existing banks combined.[43] It was to be a joint venture with the private enterprise; 80 percent of the bank's stock would be funded privately while all of its board would be nongovernment officials.

Once again Hamilton ran into stiff opposition from Jefferson and Madison, who worried that the bank's location in Philadelphia would jeopardize the move of the capital to the Maryland-Virginia border and rejected it on constitutional grounds. Nowhere in the Constitution, they maintained, was it written that the government had the authority to create a national bank. In his fifteen-thousand-word response, a memo to Washington, Hamilton countered that not all the government's powers were outlined in the Constitution; some, he argued, were implied in its clause permitting Congress to "make all the laws which shall be necessary and proper." Though reserved in expressing his opinions, Washington revealed his tacit but increasingly evident Federalist bent, ruling in favor of Hamilton and broadening the federal government's role in American life. "His wishes flowed from his policy," wrote his biographer Richard Brookhiser.[44]

Years earlier, during the war, Washington had given a clue to his belief in a robust central government working in tandem with the state governments when he likened the American system of government to the inner workings of a clock that would cease to function if the smaller wheels were maintained at the expense of the larger ones.[45] Still, Washington's policy was less about rigid ideology and political considerations than about protecting and upholding the Constitution that bound the union together. "While others formed ranks around party standards or economic systems or European alliances," writes Richard Norton Smith, "Washington planted his banner where he had always stood, upon a Constitution whose delicate balance was threatened by the ancient enemies of republics, domestic factionalism and foreign influence."[46]

A sweep of Washington's quill quelled any fears that the capital would remain in the North. In 1790 he signed an act of Congress that would bring the Federal City to the Potomac's banks by the new century and put the project under Washington's direct authority. Through a number of negotiations with nineteen of the area's landowners, Washington and a board of commissioners secured six square miles that would make up the new city.[47] Raw, humid and swampy, the habitat was more suited to mosquitoes than government bureaucrats. Not a single school or church could be found in the area, and pasturing cows roamed the field that would become the mall.[48] Abigail Adams called it "the dirtyest Hole I ever saw."[49]

As with setting precedents, the president recognized the importance of splendor in the edifices that would permanently house the nation's government; if the capital were to rival those in Europe, it must be steeped in majesty reflecting the country's character. A student of architectural design who had designed his home at Mount Vernon himself, Washington took keen interest in the project—in particular, the mansion that would become the President's House—and began to make his mark.

Given the dearth of architectural talent in the country, Washington accepted the solicitation of Pierre Charles L'Enfant as the project's chief designer in 1791. L'Enfant had come to America in 1777 as one of a number of French troops who fought in the revolution, and had gone on to design New York's Federal Hall in the style of the senate in Rome.[50] His vision for the Federal City rivaled the splendor of Europe, characterized by wide boulevards and architectural grandeur, including a "palace" as the President's House that would have been five times larger than today's White House. Though Washington supported both L'Enfant and his palace plan, neither would last. L'Enfant, an arrogant prima donna in the eyes of the city's planning commission, was fired by Washington a year later, while his plans for the President's House were scrapped due to a shortage of labor and building materials.[51]

Jefferson proposed an open design contest for a new architectural plan for the President's House, with a first prize of $500. An ardent student of architecture himself, Jefferson had his own view of what the capital city and the President's House should look like, which contrasted with the more majestic view of Washington. Jefferson favored a modest city of small brick buildings and, under a pseudonym, entered his own design for the President's House, a Palladian-style Villa Rotonda. But it and seven other entries were rejected in favor of the plan of the architect James Hoban, an Irish immigrant whose plans for a stately stone mansion were said to be modeled on Dublin's Leinster House, and who had caught Washington's attention years earlier for his work in Charleston, South Carolina. Though Washington subscribed to Hoban's plan for the house, he added his own touches, including intricate carvings and other design flourishes along with an entreaty to enlarge the structure by 20 percent, which would make it the country's largest house until late into the next century.[52] Jefferson sneered at the final design, which, like the growing federal government, was both larger and more imperial than to his liking.

In the autumn of 1792, amid speeches and ceremony, the house's cornerstone was laid in the spot L'Enfant had earlier designated. Though Washington declined to attend, he would continue keen oversight of the project from Philadelphia and would visit to measure its progress on his intermittent travels back to Mount Vernon for presidential respites.

Washington's travels as president went far beyond the road from the capital to Mount Vernon. Even though the weekly levees gave the people a chance to visit the president, he believed that he, as the head of the federal government, should also go to see the people. In his first term, as Hamilton and Jefferson battled in New York awaiting his yea or nay, he journeyed by coach to every state that made up the union, inspiring from town to town the kinds of stately welcomes he had received when he trekked from Mount Vernon to New York City for his inauguration. In 1790, he toured the New England states, where a question of protocol arose when the Massachusetts governor John Hancock refused to call on the visiting president in Boston, expecting rather that the president should call on him as governor of the state. Washington declined, knowing that it could be construed as a precedent that the federal government was subordinate to the state governments. Hancock eventually backed down, establishing the fact that the president outranked the governors of any state. The following year, Washington toured the Southern states, logging nearly two thousand miles in his travels.[53]

One of the few things Hamilton and Jefferson could agree on, along with nearly everyone else, was that Washington should remain as president for a second term. Only Washington himself had reservations. Even two years into his first term he felt the warm tug of his beloved Virginia plantation drawing him home to a quiet life on the Potomac far from the burden of public office, and had planned to step down after the term was over. But being the one unifying figure in the country, the one who transcended partisanship, he allowed himself to be drafted by his country once again. The election of 1792, a forgone conclusion, really, resulted in Washington's victory by another unanimous vote and Adams again as his number two. With tensions mounting among political factions at home, and between the United States and powers abroad, Washington's next four years would hardly be quiet.

Like the president whose sense of duty she shared, Martha Washington resisted the longing to be at home at Mount Vernon, accepting four more years as first lady, a role she found tiresome. "I am still determined to be cheerful and happy in whatever situation I may be," she wrote to a friend. "For I have also learned from experience that the greater part of our happiness or misery depends on our dispositions, and not upon our circumstances."[54] She made the best of hers.

A year older than the president and more than a foot shorter, Martha Washington was, in her husband's words, "a quiet wife, a quiet soul."[55] The daughter of a wealthy planter, she grew up at her family's plantation outside Williamsburg, Virginia. At eighteen, she married Colonel Daniel Custis and soon produced four children, two of whom died just past infancy. In 1757, Custis also died, leaving her a widow at twenty-six with their two surviving children, Jack and Patsy. Two years later, she married another colonel, the dashing Washington, who took her children into his life as his own.

Though thought by historians not to be the true love of Washington's life, Martha Washington was a good social match for her husband, and the two were bonded by their affection toward one another. Throughout Washington's career, she had been a wholly supportive wife. When he took command of the Continental army and was headquartered throughout New England and the Mid-Atlantic, she would travel—often weeks at a time—to be with him without complaint of the wretched conditions. She not only kept house for Washington but also mended clothes and knitted socks for the troops, and nursed the wounded and sick. Though it clearly wasn't the life she wanted, she proved just as stoic as first lady.

The excise taxes Hamilton had put into place continued to be a sore spot for a number of Americans who believed the system favored the Eastern establishment. Among them were a band of farmers and distillers in four counties in western Pennsylvania who were particularly worked up over the hefty tax on whiskey, a product common to the hardscrabble area. In the summer of 1794, anger led to uprising as the mob drove troops guarding excise agents—who had been terrorized—to surrender. The insurgency unnerved Washington, who viewed it as a direct threat to the federal government and was concerned that the fervor would swell beyond the region.[56] In August, he ordered a militia of thirteen thousand—far more than the number he had commanded during the Revolutionary War—to set out to the area, west of Pittsburgh, under the command of the Virginia governor Henry "Light-Horse Harry" Lee, father of Robert E. Lee. In a patent show of executive force, Washington himself joined the troops, riding in full military regalia with Hamilton, his former revolutionary sidekick. In a sense the pair was returning to their glory days.

The insurgents quickly backed down, and the Whiskey Rebellion was quashed with barely a whimper. The overwhelming military force was as much a statement as a means to quell the uprising. In a Proclamation of Militia Service, Washington justified incursion "when it is manifest that violence would continue to be exercised upon every attempt to enforce the laws; when, therefore Government is set at defiance, the contest being whether a small proportion of the United States shall dictate to the whole union, and, at the expense of those who desire peace, indulge a desperate ambition."

Just as Hamilton and Jefferson were divided on domestic policy, so they differed in foreign allegiances. As France and England, along with their allies, resumed a century-old war to become the world's dominant power, Hamilton advocated support of England, while Jefferson sided with America's ally in the American Revolution, France. Hamilton's choice was largely a function of economics; a better relationship with England would help propel the American economy, opening up trade opportunities that would benefit the mercantile class largely concentrated in the port cities of the Northeast. Jefferson, on the other hand, embraced France on ideological grounds; he saw the French Revolution as an extension of the American Revolution, despite the river of blood flowing from the guillotines that betrayed American ideals.[57] England, to his mind, was an anachronism, "the dead hand of the past."[58]

Washington was against allying with either England or France. A political pragmatist, he believed that the country should avoid foreign entanglements altogether as it began its ascent in the world. America simply wasn't ready; it needed time. He stated as much to France in 1793, in what would become the nation's first decisive foreign policy position, a

Proclamation of Neutrality unequivocally asserting that America would abstain from involvement: "The duty and interest of the United States require that they should with sincerity and good faith adopt and pursue a conduct friendly and impartial toward the belligerent Powers."

Washington wrote of his decision: "Every true friend to this country must see and feel that the policy of it is not to embroil ourselves with any nation whatsoever, but to avoid their disputes and politics; and if they will harass one another, to avail ourselves to the neutral conduct we have adopted." He counseled patience, presciently envisioning a time a generation forward when the country, bigger and stronger, would be able to hold its own against any truculent nation. "Twenty years' peace, with such an increase of population and resources as we have a right to expect; added to our remote situation from the jarring powers, will in all probability enable us in a just cause to bid defiance to any power on earth."[59] (A victory against England in the War of 1812, nineteen years later, would prove as much.)

But averting war with England—directly or indirectly—wouldn't be that easy. Though the Treaty of Paris had been signed by England and America in 1783, effectively ending the War for Independence, tensions between the two countries escalated over time due in large part to the fact that British troops still occupied Northwestern U.S. territories, in violation of the treaty, and that British naval ships routinely seized American merchant vessels, forcing the captured crew to enlist in the English military and fight in its war with France. What's more, the ill will got in the way of a more advantageous trade relationship between the two countries that would help boost the American economy.

Keeping sabers from continuing to rattle would require a treaty with England, which would be negotiated a year later through John Jay, whom Washington had made the country's first Supreme Court chief justice in the first months of his presidency. In April of 1794, Jay departed for London at Washington's behest, sailing across the Atlantic in the hopes of hammering out a binding agreement between the two nations that would ease the threat of war. Washington had instructed Jay to negotiate an agreement that would have the English withdrawing troops from the

Western territories, a particularly important concession since, well before manifest destiny, Washington saw America's future as a world power inextricably linked to its governance of land across the North American continent.[60] Additionally, he asked Jay to secure a deal that would open up lucrative trade markets in the British West Indies, and compensate ship owners for vessels captured by the British navy and slave owners for slaves abducted by British troops in the war. Finally, Jay was not to accept anything that would "denigrate our treaties and engagements with France."[61]

Those in the Jefferson camp—the Anti-Federalists and later the Democratic-Republicans and finally the Republicans—were wary of Jay, an unabashed Federalist whom they considered an anglophile and a monarchist, and who, along with Madison and Hamilton, had written a number of the essays comprising *The Federalist Papers*. Their suspicions were further aroused when word got back to America that Jay had kissed the hand of the queen when he was presented at court.[62] After finalizing negotiations on November 19, Jay returned to Philadelphia with an agreement in hand that would prove far more objectionable to Republicans and other supporters of the French than a buss on the hand of an English monarch.

Yes, the United States would maintain its neutrality, but on decidedly English terms. In effect, the agreement Jay struck would sever the alliance America had formed with France during the Revolutionary War, which had bolstered America's flagging efforts by securing much-needed French military support.[63] Despite Jay's diplomatic efforts, few of the provisions Washington had stipulated made it off the bargaining table and into the treaty's twenty-eight articles. What he got was an English commitment to repatriate troops from the Western territories by 1796 and to negotiate a settlement to American shipping merchants who had lost vessels to the English navy. Additionally, he secured an agreement to allow American trading vessels into the British West Indies, albeit with restrictions on the size of the ships and their ultimate destinations.[64] In return, he granted the extension of "most-favored nation" status to England an offer not reciprocated; the British would retain the right to levy tariffs on American exports. Furthermore, the treaty placed a statute of limitations on the capture of American sailors forced from the merchant vessels seized by the English navy and obliged payment of American debt amassed during the revolution.

The fruits of the negotiation, formally called the Treaty of Amity, Commerce and Navigation, between His Britannic Majesty and the United States of America, by their President, would be known infamously among the American people as Jay's Treaty. "It must speak for itself," Jay told Washington of the deal. "To do more was not possible."[65] He was probably right, and Washington, though ambivalent about the treaty, knew it. The British had the upper hand in the negotiations, knowing well that America was disinclined to join with a number of smaller European countries prepared to take up arms to defend their neutrality.[66] "My opinion respecting the treaty," Washington wrote to Jefferson, "is the same now as it was: namely, not favorable to it." But, he added, it was better "than to suffer matters to remain as they are, unsettled."[67] A flawed treaty, in other words, was better than none at all.[68] But if the treaty spoke for itself, as Jay suggested it must, its words would be an abomination to the majority of Americans, its substance seen as an unmitigated sellout to British interests.

In June, Washington called Congress back to Philadelphia, where they engaged in heated debate over the treaty, the most pressing foreign policy question since the nation's founding. With the exception of its constraints on trade in the West Indies, it was passed by the Senate—barely. By twenty votes to ten, with pro-British senators outweighing their pro-French counterparts on party lines, the two-thirds needed for passage was secured with not a vote to spare.[69] (Vermont and Kentucky had entered the union in 1791 and 1792, respectively, increasing the number of senators to thirty.)

Though Washington had wisely attempted to keep the details of the treaty from the American people, word leaked out before the Senate's vote. The reaction was unlike anything else Washington would see in his public life, and he was completely unprepared for it. Angry mobs stormed the executive residence in Philadelphia "from day to day," as Adams recalled, "buzzing, demanding war against England, cursing

Washington, and crying success to the French patriots and virtuous Republicans."[70] The "Father of his Country" was now mocked as the "Stepfather of his Country" and called a "dictator"; eloquent toasts previously made in his honor in taverns across the nation on any given night were replaced by a far simpler one: "Damned George Washington!"[71] Newspapers that had extended a hands-off policy toward the redoubtable president now took at him with fury. The assault was almost too much for Washington, who complained bitterly to Jefferson that the "exaggerated and indecent terms" hurled at him during the onslaught "could scarcely be applied to a Nero; a notorious defaulter; even to a common pickpocket."[72] Neither did the senators who supported the treaty escape wrath. Senator Humphrey Marshall of Kentucky was, in the words of one writer, "burned in effigy, vilified in print, and stoned in Frankfort," Kentucky's capital, where the state legislature proposed a constitutional amendment allowing for his recall.[73] But it was Jay himself who incurred the full thrust of the public's scorn. "Damned and double damned" in every part of the country, he was burned in effigy throughout the summer.[74]

Popular opinion, however, had not been a deciding factor in Washington's support of the treaty. "I have weighed with attention every argument which has been brought into view. But the Constitution is the guide which I will never abandon," he wrote at the time. The Constitution allowed the president and Senate to enact foreign policy "without passion and with the best means of information available." For Washington, supporting the treaty in the face of a hostile public was a matter of "conscience."[75] Here again, Washington's integrity set the tone for American leadership.

Jay's Treaty widened the gulf between the Federalists and Republicans, ensuring the inevitability of a two-party system, which not even Washington could forestall. While that consequence surely troubled Washington, as did the maelstrom of controversy that came his way—"No man should aspire to the presidency unless he has a thick skin and a light heart," he was to say later—he would not live to see the policy vindicated by historians.[76] The consensus would generally be that the treaty was the nation's only hope of sidestepping a war it could not afford to fight, and that the administration made the right move by aligning its future with England, which would prove a better economic complement for the United States.[77]

By 1796, tired and, at sixty-four, well past his prime, Washington was more than ready to pack it in and return to Mount Vernon to tend to his farm. It was time. His original cabinet had resigned their posts: Jefferson, in 1793, to Monticello in a huff over continuing to be on the losing end of his feuds with Hamilton; Hamilton, in 1795, off to a lucrative law practice in New York; Knox and Randolph left late in Washington's second term. Of Washington's original staff, only Adams remained, by Adams's own estimation Washington's "heir apparent."[78]

In May, Washington resurrected long dormant notes Madison had prepared for him as thoughts for a valedictory address when Washington had first contemplated retirement near the end of his first term. Using them as a guide, and with considerable input from Hamilton and John Jay, Washington fashioned what would for all practical purposes be his parting words to the nation, which would not be uttered by Washington but would rather appear in newspapers in September, first in Philadelphia's *American Daily Advertiser,* then across the country. The themes he sounded were a summary of the ideological framework on which he had based his presidency and that characterized the key policies of his administration.

The obvious message was one of unity. As in the days when he led the Continental army, unity was the key ingredient in the country's viability. "The unity of government which constitutes you one people is also now dear to you," Washington's words read. "It is justly so, for it is a main pillar in the edifice of your real independence. The support of your tranquility at home, your peace abroad; of your safety; of your prosperity; of that very liberty which you so highly prize."

Aware of the regional differences that threatened the union, Washington reminded his "friends and fellow citizens" that "every portion of our country finds the most commanding motives for carefully guarding and preserving the union of the whole." In essence, he was saying that whole of the union was greater than the sum of its parts. To that end, he warned of "baneful effects" of the split of the government into political "parties in the state." While he conceded that in a democracy political parties "are useful checks upon the administration of government and serve to keep alive the spirit of liberty," he added it was "a spirit not to be encouraged." This, of course, was a battle Washington would not win. Conversely, his withdrawal from the political scene would ensure that political differences in the government, already manifest in his administration but kept in check by his unifying presence, would soon mean an open two-party system. But that would be another's crisis.

"Observe good faith and justice towards all nations; cultivate peace and harmony with all," he advised on foreign affairs, but he further warned to "steer clear of permanent alliances with any portion of the foreign world." Rather, he counseled, as was the case with Jay's Treaty, "temporary alliances for extraordinary emergencies." Parenthetically he stated, "I hold the maxim no less applicable to public than to private affairs, that honesty is the best policy," an old saw that perhaps best captured the core of Washington's moral code.

Several months after Washington had disseminated his address, John Adams was elected to succeed Washington, capturing seventy-one electoral votes in the nation's third election. Thomas Jefferson, who finished second in the balloting with sixty-eight votes, would be Adams's vice president.

On March 4, 1797, Washington donned one of his finest formal black velvet dress suits on what would be his last day as president and cemented another American tradition: the seamless transfer of power to successive presidential administrations. Within the House Chamber of Congress Hall before a standing-room-only crowd of federal government officials, he watched as his successor, his vice president, took the presidential oath of office. Adams, feeling swept up in the drama of the occasion as if in a play, would later tell Abigail that it was "the most affecting and overpowering scene I ever acted in."[79] As invigorating as it may have been for Adams, Washington was relieved to give up the starring role—even if the audience and the nation at large looked upon his departure from the stage with great unease.

On the week-long journey from Philadelphia back home to Mount Vernon, the ex-president and ex–first lady stopped by the place that would become the nation's capital. There they visited the President's House, still under construction. Building materials and debris were strewn about the site amid worker's shanties, and the structure lacked a roof, under which Washington would never live. But, as if an apt metaphor, the foundation, built for the ages under Washington's careful guidance, was in place for those who would go after him.

Washington made his final exit on the eve of the eighteenth century. On December 14, 1799, ailing from a throat infection he had caught two days earlier while inspecting Mount Vernon's fields in inclement weather, he lay in his bed, gravely ill. Just before midnight, he placed his fingers on his wrist to take his own weakening pulse after whispering, "'Tis well." As those words were his last, he may well have been referring to the country he loved and had forged and sustained. The fledgling United States of America and the fruition of the principles on which it was founded were realized largely out of the bedrock of his character; his legacy would resound throughout the nation, its borders ever pressing west as he had envisioned, well after he drew his final breath. Though a crisis over sectionalism was brewing around the election of 1800—despite his call for unity—and many more crises would follow, 'twould be well indeed.


Revolutionaries are inherently impassioned. It is unflagging zeal that sustains causes often fought against overwhelming odds. But despite the ardor of country that upheld Washington as he led revolutionary forces to victory, making him the essential Founding Father, it was his restraint that made him great as a president. While broadening the authority of the federal government, he never exploited his stature or the ambiguity of his position to wield power to the detriment of the republic, nor did he do anything that would compromise the dignity or integrity of the office. Furthermore, he kept his political opinions in check until policy decisions were required so as not to add to the political divisions that threatened to split the country.

He also kept the nation out of war, rejecting the passionate pleas of Jefferson and Hamilton to support France and England, respectively, and allowing the country to find its way through its tenuous infancy. In fact, dispassion marked Washington's most vital foreign policy decision. He would probably not have prevailed in the revolution if not for the French, who provided money, weapons, and troop support. Yet, by mobilizing John Jay to negotiate with the British and endorsing the resultant treaty, he did not allow a sentimental attachment with his former ally—or a lasting grudge against the British—to get in the way of making the right call for the future of the country.

Most important, he didn't lust for power. Imagine Lenin, Mao, or Castro—revolutionaries all—willingly ceding power and giving it back to the masses (or at least to a voting constituency of white male property owners) to decide who would succeed him. Washington was the one man in American history who was bigger than the government itself; the hero of the revolution could have been the emperor of the state he, more than any other, helped found. Instead, he ensured that government would remain in the hands of the people. In doing so, he set his most important precedent, leaving office after two terms in office and exemplifying a fundamental democratic ideal. (Another seminal revolutionary, Nelson Mandela, would follow Washington's lead, holding on to office as South Africa's first democratically elected president for only five years before relinquishing power.)

Henry Lee famously eulogized Washington as being "first in war, first in peace, first in the hearts of his countrymen." The men in the following chapters made the presidency stronger, bolstering it during times of trial and uncertainty. But Washington *made* the presidency. Everyone who comes after him is subject to his standard. He was the first.

# II

# THOMAS JEFFERSON

## *"We are all Republicans,*
## *we are all Federalists"*

On March 4, 1801, under a clear night sky lit by a crescent moon, the 4:00 A.M. stagecoach departed from the newly named Washington, District of Columbia, bound for Baltimore, Maryland. Among the passengers was John Adams, the second president of the United States, who had risen before dawn on his last night in the White House to make the long trek home to Quincy, Massachusetts, where his wife, Abigail, awaited his return. Somewhere along the day's route, at noon, Adams's status would change to former president. Back in Washington, at the Capitol Building, still under construction, Thomas Jefferson, Adams's vice president and former friend and protégé, who had defeated him in the national election the previous fall, would take the oath of office to become the nation's third chief executive.

For Adams, leaving the capital before dawn rather than bear witness to his successor's inauguration may have been a practical matter. He anticipated a long, unpleasant journey "five hundred and fifty to six hundred miles to ride through the mud"—and may have been eager to get on with it.[1] Or maybe it was a lack of protocol. Since no man had ever lost the presidency before, no precedent had been set. Besides, there was no evidence that he had been invited to Jefferson's inaugural ceremonies in the first place. Though George Washington had stayed on in Philadelphia, then the capital, to see Adams inaugurated four years earlier, Washington had willingly relinquished office and surely would have won a third term if he had chosen to run. But bitterness almost certainly played a part in Adams's early departure. He was "obstinate, opinionated, vain, ill-tempered, impatient, and lacking in sound judgment" in the uncharitable judgment of one historian; the ascendance of Jefferson to the presidency likely got the best of Adams—and brought out the worst.[2] Even Adams's supporters were put off by his hasty retreat.

With Adams's departure from the White House went the Federalist Party's reign of the presidency, which nominally began with Adams's four-year tenure but spanned George Washington's eight years in office during which the first president claimed no political party but subscribed largely to the Federalists' evolving views. Jefferson's entrance marked the beginning of Republicans' control of the government's executive branch. A lack of graciousness surrounding Jefferson's inauguration and the change of ruling parties extended well beyond Adams. The *Columbian Centinel,* a Federalist newspaper in Boston, wrote an obituary rather than extend a note of congratulations to the new president:

YESTERDAY EXPIRED
Deeply regretted by MILLIONS of grateful Americans
And by *all* GOOD MEN
THE FEDERAL ADMINISTRATION
Of the
GOVERNMENT of the *United States*
Animated by
a WASHINGTON, an ADAMS—a HAMILTON, KNOX,
STODDERT AND DEXTER
Aet. 12 years.[3]

The election marked a crossroads for America—and the potential for crisis. Throughout his eight-year presidency, Washington had expressed grave concern that opposing political parties would be the ruin of the republic, devoting much of his farewell address to warning of their "baneful effects." A two-party system, he maintained,

> *kindles the animosity of one part against another, foments occasionally riot and insurrection. . . . There is an opinion that parties in the free countries are useful checks upon the administration of the government and serve to keep alive the spirit of liberty. This within certain limits is probably true. . . . But in those of the popular character, in governments purely elective, it is a spirit not to be encouraged. From their natural tendency, it is certain there will always be enough of that spirit for every salutary purpose. And there being constant danger of excess, the effort ought to be by force of public opinion, to mitigate and assuage it. A fire not to be quenched, it demands a uniform vigilance to prevent its bursting into a flame, lest, instead of warming, it should consume.*

Others across the states agreed with Washington's judgment. Washington himself had given the country stability as it teetered along, unifying it through his steady presence and giving greater strength to the Constitution that bound it together. But with the "Father of His Country" dead and gone, and no other unifying figure to replace him—and the prospering nation's diverse economic and political interests growing—a party split was all but inevitable. "[Washington] got off just as the bubble was bursting," observed Jefferson when Washington left office in 1797, "leaving others to hold the bag."[4] Maybe. But Washington's exit alone would have precipitated a burst bubble.

Was Washington's concern over a two-party system ill founded? *Was the U.S. government and the ideological foundation on which it was built strong enough to sustain two parties, factions that could mean a house divided?* If so, it would mark the first time in world history that a peaceful transfer in a republic would occur from one "party" to another.[5] But even then, what did Republican rule mean for America, and how would it differ from the Federalist visions held by Washington and Adams?

There was a time, of course, when Adams and Jefferson had come together as brothers in arms in the cause for America. A quarter of a century earlier, the two were among the nation's Founding Fathers who convened in Philadelphia to form the Continental Congress. Adams, the flinty elder, took the thirty-three-year-old Jefferson, eight years his junior, under his wing. They were both part of a five-member team, including Benjamin Franklin, Roger Sherman, and Robert Livingston, that was given the responsibility of drafting the document that would serve as the breakaway republic's Declaration of Independence from Britain. A skilled and proven scribe, Jefferson was charged by Adams with writing the decree due to the former's "peculiar felicity of expression."[6]

He labored at the task in his small house on Market Street for two and a half weeks in June of 1776. Each morning he set to work after a cold footbath—a lifelong practice—writing without notes on a portable writing desk he had designed and made himself, taking occasional breaks to play his violin.[7] His work was augmented by Adams and Franklin, who offered amendments to the declaration. Adams's chief duty was to sell the document to his sundry peers in Congress, a job Adams considered the more pressing duty. When it was approved by the assembly, Adams had managed to preserve most of its substance, a triumph given the widely divergent views of the delegates. Of its original 1,800 words, only 460 were scratched, though the edited version notably excluded Jefferson's sweeping denunciation of slavery.[8]

Of the two men, only Adams felt that they were involved in something seminal, believing, as he expressed to his wife, that he was "present at the creation." Jefferson thought more significant deeds toward independence were taking place at the state level, and he spent his time in Philadelphia concerned that he was missing the real action happening in his home state of Virginia—while fretting that the integrity of his declaration had been compromised in the editing process. Perhaps sullen, or the result of his natural diffidence, Jefferson said little during the sessions. "During the whole time I sat with him in Congress," recalled

Both of the parties chose running mates that gave their ticket geographic balance. Charles Pinckney of South Carolina was chosen by the Federalists as Adams's running mate, while the Republicans paired Jefferson with Aaron Burr, whose hold on his home state of New York, where he had the support of the Tammany Hall political machine, would prove decisive in the election's outcome. With tensions between the two parties mounting, the election was perhaps the most indecorous display of democracy in the nation's history. In the fashion of the times, the candidates themselves did not participate directly in the proceedings, ostensibly beyond the ugliness of campaign wrangling. Adams and Jefferson watched from the sidelines as they were both brutally savaged by their opposing parties in discourse that played out across the country in newspapers, pamphlets, and word-of-mouth rumor. Even by later standards, the election was the most scurrilous in American history.

Adams was depicted as a monarchist, more British than American. One rumor had it that he planned to marry off one of his sons to one of the daughters of King George III, thus creating an American dynasty that would return the nation to the bosom of its mother country.[16] His mental state was questioned and decried as "quite mad," as he was lampooned as being decrepit and toothless.[17] Perhaps just as insulting, much of the criticism came from a dissenting wing of his own party led by Alexander Hamilton.

Jefferson fared even worse, particularly since the Alien and Sedition Acts didn't water down the slurs of rivals as it did for President Adams. Jefferson's early support of the French Revolution, the bloody excesses of which would eventually alienate him, opened the door to opponents to depict him as a radical. His dangerous ideas would mean, in the words of the *Connecticut Courant*, "Civil War," contending further that "murder, robbery, rape, adultery and incest will be openly taught and practiced, the air will be rent with the cries of the distressed, the soil will be soaked with blood, and the nation black with crimes."[18]

Even more damning, he was eviscerated as the devil incarnate, an atheist whose godlessness would rear its ugly two-horned head in domestic policy. According to one rumor circulating in puritanical New England, family Bibles would become illicit in a Jefferson administration.[19] The *New England Palladium* speculated, "Our churches will be prostrated."[20] Jefferson unwittingly played into this demagoguery by proclaiming, as he did years later in his *Notes on the State of Virginia,* "It does me no injury for my neighbor to say there are twenty gods or no gods. It neither picks my pockets nor breaks my legs." But while unfounded, the party line resonated. Martha Washington, the first president's widow, remarked to a visiting member of the clergy that she found Jefferson to be "one of the most detestable of mankind."[21]

Neither candidate was spared personal slander: Adams was an alleged adulterer who preyed on young maidens; Jefferson was said to have cavorted with slave women (a rumor that gained credence in 1998 when a DNA test proved the bastard child of a young slave mistress, Sally Hemings, was linked to the Jefferson family bloodline, though not necessarily to Jefferson himself).

When the election results were tallied in November, Jefferson and Burr each got seventy-three electoral votes. Adams and Pinckney came up shy with sixty-five and sixty-four, respectively. The Republicans had taken the presidency. But a burning question arose: Which Republican? Jefferson and Burr each received the same number of electoral ballots. A glitch in the system (which would be rectified with the Constitution's Twelfth Amendment four years later) meant there was no designation between president and vice president in the balloting process. And while there had been an understanding in the party that Jefferson was the presidential candidate and Burr his running mate, partisan members of the Electoral College in New York refused to yield their votes to Jefferson. Instead of demurring, the unscrupulous and opportunistic Burr allowed the predicament to unfold in the hopes that somehow he, not Jefferson, would gain the White House.

Three months later the matter was taken up in the House of Representatives, where the Federalist-controlled body would determine who would take the nation's helm. The threat of violence hovered over the country as Congress deliberated, and wary Republicans feared their rivals would use the situation to rob Jefferson of the presidency. In Penn-sylvania, Republican governor Thomas McKean warned that he would call out the state's twenty thousand militia if the Federalists ruled in favor of Burr. In Virginia, several prominent Republicans, fearing the worst from the Federalists, called for drafting a new constitution to redraw the lines of the federal government, while in the North there were threats of secession at the prospect of a Jefferson presidency.[22]

For a week in mid-February, the House held a series of votes to final-ize the election's outcome. Thirty-five ballots resulted only in stalemate, but on the thirty-sixth, the presidency went to Jefferson. In an odd twist of fate, it was Jefferson's adversary, Alexander Hamilton, who engineered his victory, ultimately holding sway over his Federalists colleagues at the expense of his fellow New Yorker, Burr. While the prospect of a Jefferson presidency was undoubtedly abhorrent to Hamilton, Burr's immorality was even more objectionable. "[Burr's] private character is not defended by his most partial friends," Hamilton maintained, concluding that he was "the most unfit man" to be president.[23] Thomas Jefferson, it seemed, was the lesser of evils.

Just under eight hours after John Adams's predawn departure from Washington, Thomas Jefferson emerged from Conrad and McCunn's, one of the city's finest homes newly turned into a boardinghouse, a mere two hundred steps from the unfinished Capitol, where he would be sworn in at noon. Dressed simply in "plain cloth," by one account, and forgoing transport by carriage, the president-elect advanced on the Capitol by foot, a parade of militia from the District of Columbia and nearby Alex-andria, Virginia, marching before him, and a small group including Republican congressmen and two members of Adams's cabinet trailing him.[24] The "small parade," simple and unpretentious in contrast to the more lavish inaugural displays of Washington and Adams, reflected the incoming Republican administration's intrinsic promise of modesty and prudence.[25]

If Jefferson needed a reminder that Federalism did not fade away with Adams, now en route to Massachusetts, he needed only to look into the eyes of the man administering his presidential oath. John Marshall, newly tapped by Adams as chief justice of the Supreme Court—one of forty-two "midnight judges" he appointed in the waning days of his presidency to ensure ongoing political influence—stood firmly in the Federalist camp. Marshall had been an indispensable aide to President Adams, just as he would become a maddening nuisance to President Jefferson. But that would come in time. On this day, Jefferson would extend an olive branch to those in the Federalist Party and emphasize that ideological fissures in the American political spectrum did not mean an end to civil discourse or to the advancement of "common effort for the common good."

In his soft voice, barely audible to any of the dignitaries beyond the first several rows of seating in the Capitol's Senate chamber, Jefferson acknowledged the "animation of discussions and of exertions" that characterized the election but exhorted his "fellow-citizens" to "unite with one heart and one mind." His message, crafted as skillfully as his immortal declaration, further defined the American ideal. "But every difference of opinion," he said, "is not a difference of principle."

> *We have called by different names brethren of the same principle. We are all Republicans, we are all Federalists. If there be any among us who would wish to dissolve this Union or to change its republican form, let them stand undisturbed as monuments of the safety with which error of opinion may be tolerated where reason is left free to combat it. I know, indeed, that some honest men fear that a republican government cannot be strong, that this government is not strong enough; but would the honest patriot, in the full tide of successful experiment, abandon a government which has so far kept us free and firm on the theoretic and visionary fear that this government, the world's best hope, may by possibility want energy to preserve itself? I trust not. . . . Let us, then, with courage and confidence pursue our own federal and republican principles, our attachment to union and representative government.*

In calling all Americans "Republicans" and "Federalists," Jefferson reminded his countrymen that, however divided in their politics, they were united in their support of a nation that divided its power between the federal and state governments—a departure from the monarchical regime from which it had broken away. Furthermore, he suggested that American liberty required being able to have a difference of opinion without fear of reprisal or disunity. That virtue contributed toward making the United States government "the strongest on earth."[26]

Afterward, Jefferson walked back to Conrad and McCunn's, where he later enjoyed dinner with two dozen or more fellow residents of the house, assuming his regular place at the foot of the table, and retired to his room early.[27]

That the "Revolution of 1800" ended with the defeated Federalists yielding power to their opponents orderly and peacefully—no shots fired, no swords drawn—was a sign that the nation, now fourteen years into its Constitution, had entered into stable adolescence. The American experiment was working. Perhaps Washington was wrong; maybe there *was* room for two parties and divergent political opinion—no matter how impassioned—without giving rise to the threat of "riot and insurrection." "I subscribe to . . . the true principles of the Revolution of 1800," wrote Jefferson later of the election. "[N]ot affected indeed by the sword, as that, but by the rational and peaceable instrument of reform, the suffrage of the people."[28] But beyond Jefferson's conciliatory inaugural remarks, what would the change in party rule—Jeffersonian Republicanism—mean for the "rising nation"?

Jefferson remained at Conrad and McCunn's for more than a fortnight, in no hurry to move into the White House, which he deemed "big enough for two emperors, one pope, and the grand lama in the bargain," and which stood vacant upon his arrival.[29] It was evident from the beginning that he was not going to be a leader in the Washington mold—the daunting archetype for the presidency—in style or substance. But there were similarities in background.

Both Washington and Jefferson were born into the aristocratic families in Virginia—"my country," as Jefferson called it—and were strongly connected to the land. Jefferson came into the world at his family's plantation, Shadwell, in the foothills of the Blue Ridge Mountains near Charlottesville, on April 13, 1743. Thomas was the first of the ten children of Peter and Jane Rudolph Jefferson; his well-to-do father was a tobacco planter and surveyor, and his mother, a descendant of one of Virginia's oldest and most distinguished families. He inherited the family home and its five hundred fertile acres in his fourteenth year, after his father's death, the same year he enrolled in a boarding school twelve miles from the family home. There he voraciously read the classics, acquiring a lifelong love of books. Two years later, he attended college at William and Mary in Williamsburg, where he studied law, graduating in 1762. After a five-year law apprenticeship, he passed the Virginia bar in 1767 and went into private practice while managing the affairs of the family's landholdings.

As with Washington, Jefferson married "up" to a well-to-do widow also named Martha. A beautiful twenty-three-year-old five years his junior, Martha Wayles Skelton became Jefferson's wife on the first day of 1772, shortly after the death of her four-year-old son. Their life together at the newly constructed Monticello, a one-bedroom brick house that would evolve into Jefferson's architectural marvel over time, was clouded by death. The Jeffersons produced six children: five daughters and a son. Only two daughters survived into adulthood, and only one, Martha, outlived her father. On what would become the worst day of his life, his wife died of complications surrounding the birth of their youngest child in September 1782, leaving him a widower at thirty-nine. He did not remarry.

Finally, like Washington, Jefferson was obliged to leave the bucolic life on the Virginia plantation he loved for prolonged periods to serve the republic he helped create. After serving in the Virginia House of Burgesses, where he was elected in 1769, writing the declaration as a member of the Continental Congress in 1776, and taking on two single-year terms as Virginia's governor from 1779 to 1781, he had had enough, writing, "I have taken my final leave of everything of that nature, have retired to my farm, my family and books from which nothing will ever more separate me."[30] But though he had already left his eternal mark through the declaration, the nation was not done with Jefferson.

In leaders, style can say as much about one's values and ideals as substance can. Jefferson's distinct Republican manner marked a further shift from the European imperialism that characterized world powers at the time, reflecting his vision of American government marked by egalitarianism. As his inaugural signaled, much of the pomp of the Washington and Adams years was done away with; Jefferson introduced a style that reflected the Republican modesty and classlessness he envisioned for the nation's government.

His administration had an informal air about it. The president, who at six two stood awkwardly over most of his peers, often padded around the White House in threadbare slippers, his once sandy, now graying hair worn freely, not constrained in a queue in the fashion of the times. A British diplomat noted with some disdain his "utter slovenliness and indifference to appearances, and in a state of negligence actually studied."[31] Jefferson dispensed with protocol, insisting that all his guests were equal, occasionally putting off visiting foreigners who expected the red carpet treatment. A minor diplomatic gale was touched off when Jefferson refused to escort the wife a British diplomat to dinner.[32]

A deemphasis on ceremony meant an end to the levee, the stilted, formal receptions for members of the public favored by Jefferson's predecessors, replaced by small dinners for a select few over French cuisine; guests were expected to serve themselves and allowed to sit where they pleased, buffet-style.[33] On those occasions when Jefferson greeted the public, it would be with a handshake, not a bow as had been the custom for Washington and Adams.[34] One of the opportunities the people had to see the president might be a chance spotting on his daily afternoon horseback rides seven miles or so through the Washington countryside, though even then passersby would likely not know who he was. The president usually rode alone on his favorite horse, Wildair, and showed none of the trappings of the nation's highest office. On at least one occasion, a

constituent failed to recognize him, greeting him as a stranger, whereupon
the man began a verbal assault on the president. As the two conversed,
Jefferson, maintaining his anonymity for the moment, politely suggested
that it might not be fair to render such harsh judgment on a man he had
never met.[35]

The new president's leadership approach was, in the words of the
historian Joseph Ellis, "a more indirect expression of authority and [he]
attempted to create a consensual context within which all decisions had
at least the appearance of being voluntary. His chief duty was to render
the federal government over which he was to assume control unobtrusive
and politically impotent."[36] Oratory was not his strong suit, as witnesses
at his inaugural address may have attested. He seldom spoke before
crowds. In fact, his two inaugural addresses are thought to be the only
speeches he made during his entire presidency. He was far more adept at
and inclined toward the written word. Citing its unacceptable similarity
to the ceremony the British monarchy used to open parliament, in violation of Republican principles, Jefferson refused to give his State of
the Union address to Congress. Instead, he submitted his in writing,
though this move may have had just as much to do with his dislike of
public speaking.[37] Much of his workday was spent at his writing desk in
contemplative solitude. Rising at dawn, he worked alone in the early
morning hours. Later in the morning he met with cabinet officials and
congressmen, and, after a horseback ride and an afternoon respite, had
an early supper and spent much of the evening back at his desk for more
writing before retiring to bed by ten.[38]

Jefferson used his pen to address one of the most stinging accusations
against him in the campaign, that of his alleged atheism. On the first day
of 1802, he crafted a letter to the Baptist Association of Danbury, Connecticut, in which he presented himself as a friend to religion while re-
minding the recipients of the Constitution's promise of the separation of
church and state:

> *Believing with you that religion is a matter which lies solely between man and*
> *his God, that he owes account to none other for his faith or his worship . . . I*

*contemplate with sovereign reverence the act of the whole American people*
*which declared that their legislature should "make no law respecting an es-*
*tablishment of religion, or prohibiting the free exercise thereof," thus building a*
*wall of separation between Church and State. Adhering to this expression of the*
*supreme will of the nation in behalf of the rights of conscience, I shall see with*
*sincere satisfaction the progress of those sentiments which tend to restore to*
*man all his natural rights, convinced he has no natural rights in opposition to*
*his social duties.*[39]

If opponents still wished to accuse Jefferson of being Godless, they could do so with impunity. Jefferson had indirectly repudiated Adams's Alien and Sedition Act in his inaugural speech by espousing free speech as an intrinsically American virtue; now he put his money where his mouth was.

Just as the Federalists had lost the White House in 1801, so they lost their hold on Congress. The new assembly, the nation's sixth, was as eager for reform as the new president and worked in tandem with him toward a distinctly Republican agenda. Budgets were nipped and tucked, including marked spending reductions in the military, which cut the national deficit by a third. Jefferson's agenda also included the repeal of many of the excise taxes Alexander Hamilton had put in place during the Washington administration, among them the tax on whiskey that had spurred the Whiskey Rebellion in western Pennsylvania. The cuts proved as popular as the original taxes were unfavorable, boosting Jefferson's esteem among the American public.

His popularity grew with his stand against pirates off Africa's Barbary Coast who had long tormented American trade ships. To keep the buccaneers at bay, American seamen held to the practice of paying them off. But when the pirates off the coast of Tripoli increased the amount of the bribes, the United States refused, leading the pirates to declare war. Jefferson sent naval vessels to the region, where they engaged in a military standoff, inaugurating America's new fighting force, the Marine Corps. Though the pirates and their payoff demands remained in place after the smoke cleared, Jefferson's bold stand against them was recognized abroad and became a point of pride at home.

While the executive and legislative branches worked harmoniously in Republican unison, the judicial branch, headed by Chief Justice John Marshall, was a decidedly Federalist check on the balance of power. That became evident in the Court's landmark case *Marbury v. Madison*, settled in 1803. James Madison, the secretary of state, was a friend and protégé of Jefferson's, and a fellow Virginian and Republican. William Marbury was one of the forty-two Federalist "midnight judges" Adams had appointed as his presidency neared its end under the Judiciary Act of 1789, through which Adams had gotten the judges approved through a lame-duck Federalist Congress. However, Marbury's commission as a Washington County justice of the peace was not delivered during Adams's term—and Madison, who along with Jefferson was intent on repealing the act, was not about to grant it during Jefferson's term. Marbury took the case to the high court where Marshall, another midnight judge, presided over it with great interest and, it turned out, deftness.

Though the chief justice could have ruled in favor of Marbury, forcing the administration to grant the commission, he knew the order could be disregarded by Madison, and, with the court having no power to enforce its rulings, the precedent would weaken the Court. Instead he poked the Jefferson administration in the eye, opining that Madison *should* have granted the commission but ruling that the section in the Judiciary Act allowing for the federal court system was unconstitutional as it exceeded the Court's authority under Article III of the Constitution. In doing so, he asserted the Court's authority as the arbiter of the Constitution, putting the judicial branch of government on an equal footing with the executive and legislative branches in the triumvirate of federal power. "It is emphatically the province and duty of the judicial department to say what the law is," wrote Marshall in his opinion. "Those who apply the rule to particular cases, must of necessity expound and interpret that rule."[40] Marbury did not get his judgeship: Marshall, with one shrewd decision, appreciably enhanced the power of his.

Much has been made of Jefferson's paradoxical nature. Recent biographers have deconstructed his contradictions, endeavoring to shed light on the enigma of his character. The champion of the common man was a decided aristocrat who was anything but common. Prudent and frugal as a civil servant, insisting that the federal budget never bleed red ink, he let his personal finances run amok. His $25,000 presidential salary was invariably exceeded by his personal expenses, which included a $10,855 bill for the European wines that flowed freely during his two terms. Even as financial hardship threatened bankruptcy, in his retirement he renovated and expanded his beloved architectural masterpiece, Monticello, resulting in part in his inability to will the estate to his heirs. A deist (like Washington) and champion of religious freedom who made reference to God in either of his inaugural speeches—invoking "that infinite power which rules the destinies of the universe" in his first—he approached organized religion warily—and often antagonistically. Perhaps most striking, the man who professed that "all men are created equal" and had proposed the abolition of slavery in the original draft of the declaration in 1776, was himself a master of several hundred slaves, freeing only five upon his death, a function largely of the debt he left. And, though he condemned interracial mixing as abhorrent, his alleged relationship with his slave Sally Hemings still remains in question. No surprise then that ideological compromise would mark Jefferson's greatest deed as president.

The Louisiana Purchase has its rightful place as one of the great bargains in American history, right up there with the purchase of Manhattan by the Dutch from an Indian tribe for $24 worth of beads and mirrors, and the New York Yankees' acquisition of Babe Ruth from the Boston Red Sox for $125,000 in cash and the promise of a $300,000 loan to fund the Sox owner's Broadway production of *No, No, Nanette*.[41] As with those episodes of good fortune, there was more than a little serendipity in Jefferson's procurement of the Louisiana territory from France. But the matter of dealing with France over the territory, which comprised land far beyond the eponymous state, began less auspiciously than suspiciously and became the central leadership test for Jefferson in his White House years.

As America expanded westward, the Mississippi River and the port of New Orleans near the river's mouth became increasingly important as a means of shipping goods east, allowing the circumvention of the Appalachian Mountain range, which stood in the way of transport by land. When Jefferson began his presidency, the Mississippi and the vast Louisiana territory were owned by Spain, which had taken control from France in 1762, and access to the Mississippi for commercial purposes had been secured through the Pinckney Treaty of 1795. Spain's "pacific dispositions, her feeble state," in Jefferson's words, made this an agreeable arrangement. After a coup d'état elevated Napoleon into French rule as military dictator, he had designs on taking back the territory and reestablishing France's presence in North America—just a small part of a larger ambition of world domination. Spain, which had poured money into the territory without return, benignly ceded control of the territory to Napoleon in 1802. Prior to the transfer of authority to France, a Spanish court blocked American access to New Orleans's port warehouses, an act that put at risk the $1 million worth of American produce that annually moved through the port.[42]

"This little event, of France's possessing herself of Louisiana," wrote a distressed Jefferson to an unofficial emissary for Napoleon, Pierre Samuel du Pont, in April of 1802, "is the embryo of a tornado which will burst on the countries of both sides of the Atlantic and involve in its effects their highest destinies." In Jefferson's view America's destiny was, in essence, manifest destiny, a term that would be coined during James Monroe's presidency but a concept that was very much alive during Jefferson's. Like Washington before him and Monroe after, Jefferson believed that America's future was in the country's westward push, from the banks of the Mississippi across the continent to the shores of the Pacific. At present, France stood in the way.

But also like Washington, Jefferson appreciated the importance of averting a war that might throw the young nation off-kilter. As the Federalist Party and factions in the Western territories called stridently for war, Jefferson and Madison attempted in vain to resolve the matter diplomatically, including overtures to Britain to join together economically against the French. By the new year, concerned that Federalist opposition might lead to secession, Jefferson took another tack: He would attempt to buy New Orleans from France.

Unwilling to leave the fate of the negotiation solely in the hands of his minister to France, James Livingston, who was already in talks with Napoleon, he called on James Monroe to lend his services in the mission. In soliciting Monroe to take on the assignment, Jefferson displayed all the subtlety of Napoleon's ambition. "All eyes, all hopes, are now fixed on you," he wrote his fellow Virginian, who would become the nation's fifth president in fourteen years' time. "And were you to decline, the chagrin would be universal and would shake under your feet the high ground on which you stand with the public . . . for on the event of this mission depends the future destinies of this republic."[43]

No pressure, of course.

Monroe did not disappoint the president, setting sail for France soon after Jefferson's entreaty with his approval to buy New Orleans, and all or parts of Florida if it was also on the table, with a budget of up to $10 million (though Congress approved only $2 million.)[44] By the time Monroe arrived in Paris on April 12, Livingston had already made headway in his talks with Napoleon—and a far larger opportunity presented itself.

Napoleon's aim of staking a claim on the North American continent had faded as his luck had turned. The French army's foray to put down an uprising of slaves and free blacks in Saint Domingue, current-day Haiti and the Dominican Republic, where Napoleon had hoped to corner the sugar market, had turned disastrous as an outbreak of yellow fever took down troops. Strategically, France would need the island as a fortress to defend its interests in North America. In addition, France's on-again-off-again war with Britain was about to resume. Badly in need of cash, the French dictator was keen to divest himself of his North American assets beyond just the sale of New Orleans. "They ask for only one town of Louisiana," he said, "but I already consider the colony as entirely lost."[45] The whole Louisiana territory—it would eventually become

Louisiana, Arkansas, Oklahoma, Missouri, Kansas, Iowa, Nebraska, nearly all of South Dakota, and parts of Minnesota, North Dakota, Colorado, Wyoming, Montana New Mexico, and Texas—was on the table, and, in real estate terms, Napoleon was a motivated seller.

Wide-eyed at the proposition at hand, unable to communicate the terms of the new deal to Jefferson without a lag in the negotiations of a month or more, and worried about a potential change of heart from the mercurial Napoleon, Monroe and Livingston made a bold decision.[46] Ignoring the limits of presidential and congressional authority, they spent most of April carving out a treaty with their French counterparts. For $15 million, the United States acquired 828,000 square miles west of the Mississippi, effectively increasing the nation's size by half. Once confirmation of the fruits of the negotiation hit Washington, following rumors that had preceded it across the Atlantic, official word went out to the country on July 4, a date inextricably associated with Jefferson's broad vision for the country.[47]

But what of Jefferson's political principles? Where was it written in the Constitution that the president had the authority to make such a purchase? Wasn't he a strict constructionist? There was nothing expressly constitutional about presidents buying land from foreign powers independent of the Senate. And what about the effects on the federal budget? Fifteen million dollars would have the treasury drowning in red ink, hardly the prudent policy of a man who wanted to reduce the size of government and keep the budget in the black, or at least balanced. Furthermore, implicit in the buy was an increase in the power of the executive branch and of the presidency itself, a wholly anti-Republican concept.

Jefferson acknowledged that he was outside the bounds of constitutionality, believing the action would require a constitutional amendment. "The Executive in seizing the fugitive occurrence," he maintained, "have done an act beyond the Constitution." Secretary of the Treasury Albert Gallatin and Madison, the Constitution's author, disagreed and tried to persuade the president otherwise. In the end, though, the question became moot. Fearful that Napoleon might renege on the deal if there was a lengthy delay, Jefferson put aside constitutional fears in favor of political expediency, rationalizing that "the good sense of our country will correct the evil of [broad constitutional] construction when it shall produce ill effects."[48] As for the matter of money, he reasoned that this was "the case of a guardian, investing the money of his ward in purchasing an important adjacent territory; and saying to him when of age, I did this for your good."[49] Furthermore, he believed that the acquisition would keep the country safe. "[G]iving us the sole domination of the Mississippi," he wrote, "excludes those bickerings with foreign powers, which we know of a certainty would have put us at war with France immediately: and it secures to us the course of a peaceable nation."[50]

Not surprisingly, the acquisition met with resistance among Federalists due to its political implications: The incorporation of the Southern and Western territory as states in the union would tilt the electoral balance farther away from federalism, which drew its strength from the industrial Northeast. Even some of Jefferson's fellow Republicans expressed worry that greater diversity in regional concerns would lead to political fragmentation. Jefferson would have none of it. The West was America's future, worth putting his political principles temporarily on ice, worth the uncertainty of America's changing political dynamic. "Whether we remain in one confederacy or form into Atlantic and Mississippi confederacies, I believe is not important to the happiness of either part," he wrote in 1804. "Those of the western confederacy will be as much our children and descendants as those of the eastern, and I feel myself as much identified with that country, in future time, as with this."[51] On October 20, the Senate deferred to Jefferson's vision, ratifying the treaty that allowed for the purchase twenty-four votes to seven.

A month later, at a ceremony in New Orleans, the transfer of the land was recognized as an American flag was raised in place of France's; a similar rite took place in March in Saint Louis. On the latter occasion the American government was represented by Meriwether Lewis, who would soon lead a team of men in blazing a trail from the Mississippi across the continent in search of the bounty and opportunity the new land held for the country.

Just over a year earlier, in January 1803, before negotiations for the territory had begun, and as France's hold on it threatened American interests, Jefferson called on Congress to appropriate $2,500 to send a volunteer regiment across the continent on an exploratory mission. (In fact, he had proposed such an expedition as early as 1792, while serving as Washington's secretary of state.) As the party would be trespassing through much of their journey—France and Spain owning the bulk of the territory—the expedition was positioned as a commercial and scientific endeavor.[52] True enough, its impetus was in part to find a navigable waterway from the Pacific to the Atlantic (which clearly never materialized), rouse American efforts in the profitable fur trade at present dominated by Britain, and record and bring back some of the scientific fruits of the vast, uncharted land. But its principal basis was first and foremost a political one: to assert America's domain.[53]

Lewis, who hailed from outside Charlottesville, Virginia, was a family friend of Jefferson's. An army officer who had risen to the rank of captain on the Ohio and Tennessee frontier, Lewis resigned his commission in 1801 to serve as Jefferson's private secretary in the White House, drawing his $500, later $600, annual salary directly from Jefferson's pocket. His "knowledge of the Western country, of the army and all its interests & relations," in Jefferson's words, as well as the passion he shared with Jefferson for botany and natural history, made him the ideal candidate to lead the expedition.[54] He chose as his coleader William Clark, also a Virginian, who had put in time on the frontier as an army officer, fighting in the Indian Wars.

The party of forty began their journey in the winter of 1803–04 in Saint Louis, divided on the Mississippi between a fifty-five-foot keelboat equipped with twenty-two oars and two seven-man canoes.[55] They were aided en route by a French Canadian trapper and his pregnant Indian wife, Sacagawea, who proved invaluable as guides; their journey lasted twenty-eight months, bringing them to the Pacific Ocean, where they arrived near Astoria, Oregon, and back to Saint Louis by September 1806. Along the way they battled inhospitable terrain; unfriendly Indians; grizzly bears, rattlesnakes, and other menacing wildlife; venereal disease (soldiers being soldiers); and one case of appendicitis, which accounted for the lone death in the entire party. The journey was carefully chronicled by the party in journals containing nearly a million words and accompanied by detailed drawings, stoking the American imagination and enhancing the country's growing identity.[56] Jefferson was captivated by the expedition, personally examining the specimens yielded by the explorers and showcasing them at the White House, which he turned into a natural history museum of sorts.

By almost any measure, Jefferson's first term had been a resounding success. Four years after the ugly "revolution of 1800," Jefferson was re-elected by what might have been called "the Rout of 1804." With New York's George Clinton replacing Burr as his running mate, the Republican ticket bested the Federalists, led by Charles Pinckney, 162 electoral votes to 14.

Jefferson's second term did not prove nearly as rewarding.

The aptly named Burr, though rendered politically impotent by the administration as vice president during Jefferson's first term, continued to barb at Jefferson in his second. Fleeing out west after killing Alexander Hamilton in a duel off the banks of the Hudson River, Burr, ever ambitious, attempted in vain to lead a revolution of the Western states in the hopes of crowning himself emperor. Jefferson, who had once written "a little rebellion now and then is a good thing," was not amused. After Burr was captured and brought to Richmond, Virginia, for a trial presided over by Chief Justice Marshall, Jefferson let it be known that he believed Burr to be guilty of treason, a momentary lapse in the civil liberties that Jefferson championed.[57] Marshall, no less a thorn in Jefferson's side, obtained a not guilty verdict by narrowly defining the parameters of treason to a malleable jury.

Toward the end of Jefferson's presidency, in 1806, tensions from the Napoleonic Wars had Britain and France ignoring American neutrality. American ships in the Atlantic were routinely harassed—including an attack on the frigate USS *Chesapeake*—and members of the crew often were impressed under the pretext that they were British deserters, which in many cases rang true. Determined not to draw the country into war, Jefferson responded with economic sanctions, ceasing all foreign trade with Europe, reasoning that its dependence on American agricultural products would bring the truculent nations to their knees. Instead, it had the same effect on the American economy. Imports plunged from $108 million a year to $22 million, eroding Jefferson's popularity among the public and in Congress.[58] In the last months of his term, Congress overturned the embargo, which, by Jefferson's own estimation, had cost three times more than a war.[59]

Depleted by his second term, Jefferson upheld Washington's two-term precedent, strengthening it for his successors, and stepped aside in favor of Madison, his chosen heir. Madison went on to keep the White House in Republican hands, handily beating the Federalist opponent in the election of 1808, once again Charles Pinckney, 122 electoral votes to 47. Just two days before yielding power to his successor, Jefferson wrote to his old friend Pierre Samuel du Pont, "Never did a prisoner, released from his chains, feel such relief as I shall on shaking off the shackles of power. Nature intended me for the tranquil pursuits of science, by rendering them my supreme delight. But the enormities of the times in which I have lived, have forced me to take part in resisting them, and to commit myself on the boisterous ocean of political passions."

The fact that the ocean of political passions that churned in 1800 never boiled over was a testament to the American political system that Jefferson helped craft in 1776 and continued to shape through the end of the eighteenth century and throughout his presidency at the dawn of the nineteenth century.

He returned to his cherished Monticello, where he toiled in the "tranquil pursuits" he had put on hold and founded the University of Virginia in nearby Charlottesville in 1819, one of his proudest accomplishments.[60] Unwilling—or unable—to curb his lavish lifestyle, Jefferson fell into insurmountable debt, which he tried in vain to pay off by selling some of his precious books to the government, volumes that became the nucleus of the Library of Congress, and hatching an ill-conceived plan around a lottery with Monticello as its prize.

The epilogues for those who played central roles during Jefferson's White House years range from triumphant to tragic. Madison, after two successful terms in office, was followed into the White House by James Monroe, who would himself serve two terms, maintaining the Virginia Republicans' hold on the White House and ensuring that Jefferson would remain influential as a mentor and elder. John Marshall made certain that federalism would continue to flicker, consistently ruling in favor of federal law over that of the states, long outlasting the Republicans' twenty-four-year run on the presidency with a formidable reign over the Supreme Court that spanned thirty-four years. Aaron Burr, though escaping charges of treason, fled the United States for Europe, leaving wrathful countrymen and anxious creditors in his wake, and later returned to New York virtually unnoticed in 1812. He spent his remaining years uneventfully in a moderately successful law practice before dying in 1836, his days as a power-hungry rogue long forgotten. Meriwether Lewis, appointed by Jefferson as governor of the Louisiana territory in 1807 as a reward after his grand expedition, failed in the role. A year later, journeying back to Washington to answer for the mishaps of his administration, he died of gunshot wounds, thought to be self-inflicted, at an inn outside Nashville.

The most heartening postscript is the reunion, embodied in letters to and from Quincy and Monticello, between Adams and Jefferson. In some respects, Adams and Jefferson were the Lennon and McCartney of their day; they were better together than apart, and the fruits of their partnership were bigger than both of them. Also like John and Paul, though estranged and embittered by their breakup, they took pride in their seminal, immortal collaboration and a formative friendship meant that sentiment would ultimately trump residual bad blood after passions had subsided. For Adams and Jefferson that moment of reconciliation would wait four years after Jefferson followed Adams into private life, when Adams penned his old friend a letter in 1813 suggesting that "You and I ought not to die before We have explained ourselves to each other."[61] An exchange of gracious letters followed in which the two carefully laid out—for each other and for history—their own versions of the meaning of the revolution of 1776, all the while watching the nation they had helped forge in the hands of the next generation. In that sense, the revolution of

1800, which pitted their opposing views against each other for the nation's highest office, continued well after the contest was decided and ended in an affable whimper.

As if by divine providence, the two withered revolutionaries died on the same day—July 4, 1826—as America celebrated its fiftieth year of independence. Though Jefferson had died just hours before, Adams's last words, "Jefferson still survives," would, at least figuratively, ring true.

Jefferson's epitaph, self-written with strict instructions not to change a word, reflects just three achievements: "Author of The Declaration of American Independence and Statute of Virginia For Religious Freedom, and Father of The University of Virginia." Notably absent are his two terms as president.


What to make of Jefferson? He began his presidency intent on limiting the size of government and ended up irrevocably expanding it. Though he rejected the imperial presidencies of Washington and Adams, with one grand signature on parchment he doubled the size of the country, bypassing his own principles—constitutional and otherwise—along the way. At the same time, his style and substance enhanced the country's identity, giving the world an increasingly American version of democracy, while further shaping the nation's destiny.

Agreeing with most other historians that his was a "powerful and important" presidency, Daniel Boorstin added, "It was not the presidency he had promised. One of the things about Jefferson is that he loves theory, so that every incident will call forth a theoretical justification. And that's why you can get him having wonderful theoretical justifications for completely different things."[62] Joseph Ellis attributed Jefferson's multiple legacy to his "disarming ideological promiscuity."[63] Anyone with almost any point of view can claim a piece of Jefferson. Herbert Hoover and Franklin Roosevelt, for example, would both invoke Jefferson as they laid out policy in response to the Great Depression. But his contradictions make him perhaps the most human of the Founding Fathers, and the most accessible. They also make him the most controversial. Through the years his standing has risen and fallen, with the volatility of a tech stock, while Washington's has shown the stability of a low-yield bond. And, in the past decade, Jefferson's morality has been questioned in connection with his alleged relationship with Sally Hemings.

In the end, Jefferson's enduring mystique and appeal among the Founding Fathers may stem from the fact that he is most like us. His romantic ideals are who we want to be; his pragmatism, his flaws, are who we are.

# III

# JOHN TYLER

## *The Accidental President*

Fletcher Webster rode all night. The previous day, April 4, 1841, the twenty-eight-year-old chief clerk of the State Department and son of Secretary of State Daniel Webster hastily mounted his horse with orders from his father to go from Washington to the home of Vice President John Tyler with an urgent message from President William Henry Harrison's cabinet. At daybreak, at around 5 o'clock, after riding more than 150 miles with U.S. Senate assistant doorkeeper Robert Beale at his side, he arrived at Francis Street in Williamsburg, Virginia, and pounded at the door of the vice president's colonial brick town house. Tyler himself, still in his bedclothes, opened the door, whereupon the weary young man gave him the news he was dispatched to deliver: The president was dead.

Harrison, had been battling pneumonia for a week and had succumbed to it the day before, a month to the day after becoming president. The evening prior to his death just before midnight, Harrison uttered the words, "Sir—I wish you to understand the true principles of government. I wish them carried out. I ask nothing more." Those present assumed them to be an appeal to Tyler, who had been at home in

Williamsburg since just after Harrison's inauguration.[1] Tyler had been
informed two weeks earlier that the president was ill in another message
dispatched from Webster, but his most recent news on Harrison's condition came from an article in the *National Intelligencer* just days earlier, reporting that Harrison's health had "much improved."[2]

Two hours later—after changing out of his long white nightshirt, eat-
ing a quick breakfast, packing his bags, and borrowing money from a
friend to tide him over for the journey—Tyler set out by horseback and
boat for Washington, where he would become the country's tenth and, at
fifty-one, its youngest president.

Or would he? No sitting president had ever died in office before, and
the Constitution was hazy on what the death of an incumbent meant for
his successor. Its Article II, Section I read simply:

*In case of the removal of the president from office, or of his death, resignation,
or inability to discharge the powers and duties of the said office, the same shall
devolve on the vice-president.*

The crux of the matter was rooted in what "the same" meant. The same
duties? The same office? Therefore, it was a matter of interpretation as
to whether he would be president or simply an acting president, a stand-
in for his deceased predecessor. The bureaucrats waiting for Tyler in
Washington had varying opinions on the subject, but Tyler's own view
was clear, clear enough that he didn't believe he even needed to take an
oath to confirm it: Upon Harrison's death, he *was* the president.[3]

That Tyler had achieved the vice presidency had little to do with his
ideological compatibility with Harrison. It was a marriage of conve-
nience between the Whig Party and Southern Democrats, who bolted
the Democratic Party to join the Whigs shortly after the party was
formed. With Southern Democrats in tow, the Whig Party was united
not along policy lines—indeed, members disagreed on pivotal issues like
slavery and nationalism versus states' rights—but in its desire to unseat the

Jacksonian Democrats, personified by Andrew Jackson. Jackson had served as president for two terms ending in 1837, after which his vice president and chosen successor, Martin Van Buren, carried on Jacksonian democracy after winning the presidency in his own right.

The backlash against Jackson escalated in 1832, when he vetoed a congressional bill to recharter the Second Bank of the United States, the constitutionality of which he questioned along with the bank's unholy alliance with big business. Those opposed to Jackson saw him as dictatorial, branding him "King Andrew I." In response they formed the Whig Party, led by Senators Henry Clay and Daniel Webster, taking the name of the British political faction that stood in opposition to Royalists. Tyler, the leading voice of Southern Democrats against Jackson, left the Democratic Party and joined the Whigs in 1834, bringing others with him.

The Whigs had tried in vain to defeat Van Buren in 1836, formulating a regional strategy in which the party ran different candidates from the North, South, East, and West. The tactic was meant to prevent Van Buren from securing a majority vote in the Electoral College, which would force the contest to be decided in the House of Representatives, where one of the regional candidates might secure an upset win. It backfired, and Van Buren went to the White House.

In choosing a presidential candidate to go up against Van Buren in 1840, the Whigs went with William Henry Harrison, who had been the party's Western candidate four years earlier. Harrison had spent much of his career in the Midwest in what was then the Northwest and Indiana territories. He served a dozen years as governor of the Indiana territory, making a name for himself as the "hero of Tippecanoe," an 1811 Kentucky battle in which he led a thousand troops to drive off a confederation of Shawnee violently resistant to the western advancement of white settlers. Almost two hundred men were killed or wounded in the battle, but while attacks from the Native American confederacy diminished for the moment, they were back within a year.[4] Still, Harrison's stand against them was enough to earn him national acclaim.

Tyler's selection as the vice presidential nominee provided geographic balance to the ticket, giving it broader appeal in the South. The fact that

Tyler's views as a strict states' righter were in conflict with the nationalis-
tic views of Whig Party leaders—Clay, Webster, and indeed, Harrison,
among them—seemed to matter little. At least, it mattered little at the
time.

A longtime presidential aspirant, Clay had made a strong run for the
presidential nomination and had the unquestioned support of a group
within the party known as Clay Whigs, whose loyalty to him went beyond that of party. The Clay Whigs included Harrison, who was cast
under Clay's spell shortly after his 1816 election to the House of Representatives, where Clay served as speaker. But Clay's staunch proslavery
stand ruled out support from Northern Whigs. Harrison's nomination
was the next best thing for Clay, providing as it did an electable candidate whose strings Clay and others in the party leadership could pull to
their own ends. Harrison would prove just as compliant when it came to
the manipulation of his image for voter consumption.

Well over a century before the Marlboro Man squinted in the sun
with a cigarette between his lips, and Keebler Elves baked cookies in a
hollow tree, the Whig Party created a brand image around William
Henry Harrison that would have done Madison Avenue ad men proud.
A patrician who hailed from an upper-crust Virginia family, Harrison
had studied with private tutors before attending Hampden-Sydney
College, where he took up the classics and enjoyed a life of rarefied
privilege—even if it meant living in debt. But the Whigs cast "Old
Tippecanoe" as a humble and homespun war hero, with a "just folks"
image much like that of Andrew Jackson, "Old Hickory." The Demo-
crats unwittingly played into the strategy. "Give him a barrel of hard cider and settle a pension of two thousand a year on him," wrote a
Democratic newspaper, "and take my word for it, he will sit the remainder of his days in a log cabin." Turning the insult into an advantage, the
Whigs embraced the image of Harrison as the "Log Cabin and Hard
Cider" candidate who was born in a simple log cabin and lived in one
still—never mind that Harrison actually dwelled in a mansion in the
Ohio Valley. The masses, hungry for a populist hero, swallowed the image of Harrison the blue blood as "Old Tip" the redneck as easily as they

did the cider and whiskey, contained in cabin-shaped bottles, no less, handed out at campaign rallies.[5]

The Whig ticket's catchy campaign slogan, "Tippecanoe and Tyler Too," proved just as irresistible, as in their popular campaign song:

> *What has caused the great commotion;*
> *Motion, motion, Our country through?*
> *It is the ball a rolling on.*
> *For Tippecanoe and Tyler too—Tippecanoe and Tyler too.*

The "ball" was a giant sphere, ten feet high, made of paper and tin and covered in a score of campaign slogans for the Whig ticket, which party members rolled from town to town (inspiring an addition to the American lexicon: "keep the ball rolling"). With each revolution of the ball, it seemed, the momentum for the Whig ticket escalated.

The incumbent Van Buren, meanwhile, a serviceable president, was depicted as a short, effete, city-dwelling elitist, as in another Whig campaign song:

> *Old Tip he wears a homespun coat*
> *He has no ruffled shirt-wirt-wirt*
> *But Mat has a golden plate*
> *And he's a little squirt-wirt-wirt*

Translation: Harrison, real man. Van Buren, girlie man.[6]

The Democrats tried in vain to counter the lowest-common-denominator tactics of the opposition, getting an Indian woman to appear at Whig rallies claiming she had borne Harrison's child. When they tried to beat the Whigs on political issues, it proved even less effective. The electorate seemed as indifferent to where the Whigs stood on the policy—the western expansion of slavery and the status of statehood for Texas chief among them—as the candidates were in articulating it.

As the Whigs' slogan suggested, the "Tyler Too" part of the ticket was little more than an afterthought to the electorate, just as his nomination had been to the Whigs. The vice presidential candidate himself had no desire to rub elbows with the rabble who were imbibing free whiskey and whooping their support for Old Tip; his strong stand against voting rights for men without property hardly made him a man of the people. One rally, at the scene of Harrison's military triumph, the rural Tippecanoe battlefield seven miles north of Lafayette, Indiana, attracted a crowd of sixty thousand. Wary of "mob rule," Tyler was content to sit out most of the campaign in the comfort of his Virginia home.[7]

An astounding 80 percent of the electorate showed up at the polls on Election Day. Though the popular vote was close—with the Whigs capturing 53 percent to the Democrats' 47 percent—the Electoral College vote was 234 votes for the Whigs, 60 for the Democrats. Van Buren didn't even capture his home state of New York. The Whig ball had rolled over its opponents.

Fifty thousand supporters showed up at Harrison's inauguration in March, where the nation's oldest president, at sixty-eight, took the oath of office and then gave a rambling speech for over ninety minutes in the frigid cold wearing neither hat nor overcoat, an oversight that would give him a lingering cold and lead to pneumonia.[8] Tyler drew far less attention. After taking the vice presidential oath in the Senate chamber of the Capitol, and giving a gracious three-minute speech to the dignitaries assembled, he departed Washington for Williamsburg, where he expected to spend the better part of an uneventful tenure.

A month later, with an early morning rap on his front door, Tyler would discover his duties would now be a bit more taxing.

Tyler arrived in Washington before dawn on April 6. By noon, fifty-three hours after Harrison's death, he was sworn into office by William Branch, chief justice of the U.S. Circuit Court of the District of Columbia, at his residence at the Brown's Indian Queen Hotel on Pennsylvania Avenue. The simple ceremony took just five minutes.[9] Though Tyler believed no oath was required to confer upon him his new responsibilities, Daniel Webster and others convinced him that it was necessary as a symbol to confirm his appointment in the minds of the public.[10] They were right. Taking the oath may have been the wisest action Tyler took in his presidency, representing the swift, orderly transfer of power without lingering doubt as to who would fill the leadership void left in Harrison's wake. This decisive precedent was Tyler's gift to future vice presidents who would find the presidency thrust upon them with the death of the incumbent.

If there were further doubts about his legitimacy, Tyler issued a written address to the nation three days later. Reworking language from the Constitution, he notified Congress and the American people that for the first time in the country's history an elected vice president "has had devolved upon him the Presidential Office." Several references to himself as "President" and "Chief Magistrate" further underlined the notion that he had now rightfully taken up the job.[11]

Harrison's funeral was conducted in the East Room of the White House, with the new president in attendance, the day after Tyler arrived back in Washington. But while Harrison was put to rest, questions surrounding Tyler's presidential authority in Harrison's place were not. Some simply doubted his ability. John Quincy Adams, the sixth president and now an esteemed member of the House of Representatives representing his district in Massachusetts, gloomily anticipated Tyler's reign. He described Tyler as "a political sectarian, of the slave-driving, Virginian, Jeffersonian school, principled against all improvement, with all the interests and passions and vices of slavery rooted in his moral and political constitution—with talents not above mediocrity, and a spirit incapable of expansion to the dimensions of the station upon which he has been cast for the hand of Providence, unseen through the apparent agency of chance. No one ever thought of his being placed in the executive chair."[12]

There were at least a few among Harrison's cabinet who saw Tyler as a presidential surrogate. Largely out of respect for the late president, Tyler made the decision—ill-fated he would soon discover—to keep Harrison's cabinet intact. All the members were strong partisans of the Whig cause as defined by Whig boss, Kentucky senator Henry Clay, just as

Harrison had been. Clay viewed Tyler as a "flash in the pan" who would keep the presidential chair warm until he could fill it upon the next election, and expectations were that Tyler would toe the line.[13] In his first act as president, Tyler brought his cabinet together, at which point Webster informed him that Harrison had made his decisions by committee, where cabinet officials each exercised a single vote along with the president. Tyler patiently heard Webster out before carefully responding. "I am president," he told the group coolly, "and I shall be held responsible for my administration. I shall be pleased to avail myself of your counsel and advice. But I can never consent to being dictated to as to what I shall or shall not do. When you think otherwise, your resignations will be accepted." It was a rocky beginning. Tyler's intransigence alienated his cabinet—and would soon draw Clay's fury.[14]

Stubbornness was as much a part of Tyler's character as his Old Dominion heritage. Like Harrison, Tyler hailed from Charles City County, where he enjoyed the advantages of the state's ruling class. One of eight children of John Tyler, an affluent tobacco planter, and his wife, Mary, Tyler was born at the family's Greenway Plantation on March 29, 1790. His mother died of a stroke when he was seven. His father looked after his twelve-hundred-acre plantation while pursuing a life in politics, serving as a U.S. circuit court judge, speaker of the Virginia House of Burgesses, and governor of Virginia (a post also taken up by Harrison's father). After a youth plagued with illness, the younger John Tyler attended the College of William and Mary, where he graduated at seventeen, then returned home to study law with his father. His schooling, at the college and with his father, a friend of Thomas Jefferson's, included the doctrine of states' rights prevalent among the Virginia gentry, which would define Tyler throughout his own political rise.[15]

As a practitioner of that doctrine, Tyler protected the economic interests of the Southern elite and, intrinsically, the institution of slavery that fueled them, mechanically rejecting the national policies—mostly from the Northern elite—that threatened them.

Two years after passing the bar at nineteen, Tyler was elected to the Virginia legislature (the House of Burgesses) in 1811 and went on to serve in the U.S. House of Representatives in 1816. While there, he fiercely espoused a states' rights policy in the face of a growing national-ist movement.[16] In 1821, he resigned from the body in disgust over the Missouri Compromise, which restricted slavery in certain states while granting it in others. Compromise was not much in Tyler's nature. He was back in the Virginia legislature shortly afterward, served as gover-nor for two one-year terms, then was elected to the U.S. Senate in 1826. But once again, in 1836, he resigned over principle when the Virginia legislature asked that he renounce a vote to censure President Jackson he had made three years earlier. While he believed that he, as a senator, served at the behest of the legislature, he also believed that overriding his own vote was unconstitutional.

During his years in Washington, Tyler engaged in an active social life as a capital insider, leaving his large family at home at Greenway Planta-tion, which Tyler had inherited upon his father's death in 1813. The beautiful former Letitia Christian, a Virginian of comparable upper-class stock whom he had married the same year on his twenty-third birthday, had little interest in being a political wife and was content to tend to their five daughters and two sons while her husband was away in Washington for long stretches. (The Tylers had eight children, one of whom died in childbirth.) In all his time in Congress and in the vice presidency, she visited the White House only once for an extended stay during Washing-ton's winter social season.[17]

Lean and tall, at just over six feet, with close-set eyes, thin lips, and an extended Roman nose that matched his long ears, Tyler had an aristocratic appearance that suited his background. Though pigheaded ideologically, he was every inch the Southern gentleman. Even political enemies conceded his impeccable manners, charm, and grace, but those qualities were not enough to keep them—or those of his own party, for that matter—at bay.[18]

Though Tyler had taken the presidential oath and asserted his leader-ship with his cabinet, many remained unconvinced of his position. He would spend much of his presidency battling the notion that he was a pre-tender to the throne. Newspapers commonly referred to him as "acting president," and seven weeks after he took office, an act of Congress was introduced by a Pennsylvania congressman attempting to downgrade his title to "Vice President Now Exercising the Office of President." It was quickly defeated, but denigrating nicknames such as the "Accidental President" and "His Accidency" dogged Tyler throughout his administration. He, in turn, made certain that letters sent to the White House addressed to "Acting President Tyler," "Vice President Acting as President," or other such dubious titles were promptly returned to the sender unopened.[19]

Clay had been among those opposed to Tyler taking on the full authority of the presidency, but he soon changed course. Initially he worked closely with Tyler in hopes that the president would help him enact his American System agenda, which included many of the national policies Tyler had opposed as a congressman, including measures to develop a national infrastructure that Clay saw as imperative to the growth and prosperity of the country.

He would soon find his hopes dashed. The two men came to a showdown just weeks into Tyler's tenure over one of the major issues on Clay's agenda: the reestablishment of a strong national bank. When Clay proposed the Bank of the United States, a central bank to be located in Washington, in a special session of Congress in May 1841, he implored the new president to support it. Tyler, in adherence to his states' rights leanings, was in favor of a weaker national bank, where individual states could decide for themselves if they wanted to be associated with the central institution. He told Clay he would need more time to consider the matter. Imperious and impatient, Clay informed the president that a delay was unacceptable, to which the president responded, "Go you now then, Mr. Clay, to your end of the avenue, where stands the Capitol, and there perform your duty to the country as you shall think proper. So help me God, I shall do mine at the end of it as I shall think proper."[20]

Over the next several months, a cooler head prevailing, Clay watered down his bank measure and resubmitted the bill to Tyler. The response he got from Tyler's "end of the avenue" was a veto issued on constitutional grounds as a breach of states' rights. When Congress sent another bill to Tyler, this one designed to address the president's specific objections, Tyler again didn't budge. He sent back another issue on September

5.[21] The apoplectic Clay was at his wit's end. In retaliation, hoping to force Tyler's resignation in a crisis of confidence, he exerted his influence with Tyler's cabinet: By September 11, five of Tyler's six-member cabinet had submitted their resignations. Daniel Webster, a longtime interparty rival of Clay's, was the lone holdout. Webster had supported Tyler's assumption of the role of president and now resisted the pull of Clay away from Tyler, despite the knowledge his stand would sever his own ties to the Whig Party. In a meeting at the White House the same evening, Webster met with the president to determine his future. "Where am I to go, Mr. President?" he asked.

"You must decide for yourself," replied Tyler.

"If you leave it to me," Webster said, "I will stay where I am."

"Give me your hand on that," Tyler said, rising from his chair and extending his own hand, "and now I will say to you that Henry Clay is a doomed man."[22]

Tyler had overstated it, for it was not clear who was doomed. But one thing was certain: For the remainder of his term, Tyler was, as Clay put it, "a president without a party." The Whigs summarily turned their backs on him. In retrospect, Tyler's inflexibility may have been as short-sighted as Harrison's lack of winter garb on Inauguration Day. Tyler and his presidency were now openly under siege. In a recurrent battle with Clay, Tyler continued to use the veto as a primary and an effective means of parrying Clay's thrusts. Throughout his term he would issue a total of ten, almost all on constitutional grounds, a record exceeded only by Andrew Jackson over the first seventy-five years of the presidency.[23] After Tyler vetoed two Whig-sponsored bills calling for higher federal taxes, the Whigs took their revenge by initiating impeachment proceedings despite the fact that Tyler eventually signed a bill after making his own changes. The politically motivated movement soon fizzled; the Whigs settled for censuring Tyler through a Whig-directed congressional committee.

Burned in effigy in Washington and throughout the country after killing Clay's second national bank bill, Tyler was the first president to actively receive assassination threats throughout his tenure. While Congress gave Tyler as little as possible, it did see the need to offer a permanent

White House security force in light of the threats. In 1842, it allowed for a four-man security detail referred to as "doormen," precursors to the Secret Service.[24]

Despite the onslaught, Tyler conducted his affairs with aplomb. Equanimity and stoicism, qualities becoming a Southern gentleman, were, like stubbornness, endemic to his nature. In Tyler's second year in the White House, the celebrated young Charles Dickens, thirty years old and visiting the United States from London for the first time, called on the president and recognized those qualities in a diary passage capturing their first meeting:

> We had not waited in this room many minutes, before the black messenger returned, and conducted us into another of smaller dimensions [probably the president's office], where at a business-like table covered with papers, sat the President himself. He looked somewhat worn and anxious,—and well he might: being at war with everybody,—but the expression of his face was mild and pleasant, and his manner remarkably unaffected, gentlemanly and agreeable. I thought that in his whole carriage and deemanor [sic], he became his station singularly well.[25]

Although Dickens was impressed with Tyler's bearing under the circumstances, he was not struck by the White House itself. The mansion was in a deplorable state, with walls in dire need of painting and scores of spiders visibly dwelling in the creases of its ceilings. One newspaper described it as "a contemptible disgrace to the nation," suggesting that some of its furniture would be unsuited even for a brothel. But refurnishing, renovations, and repair would have to wait. Congress, in no mood to offer comfort to the enemy, flatly rejected Tyler's request of $20,000 for those purposes.[26] Perhaps as a refuge from the dreary confines of the mansion and the strain of his presidency, Tyler purchased a plantation near Richmond in early 1842, including a simple Georgian-style house built around the time of his birth. Though cash poor and beset by persistent debt that his $25,000 annual salary hardly abated, he ordered expansions and renovations to the home, turning it into a bastion of Old

Virginia civility to which he would retire when the opportunity presented itself.[27] Tyler called the estate Sherwood Forest, a nod to his "outlaw" status in Washington. Relief may also have come from another development in the year. In the midterm elections in November, the Whigs lost their majority hold on Congress to the Democrats, a decisive development that Tyler saw as a public reckoning. But the president's troubles with Congress were hardly over.[28]

As Tyler clung to his tenuous hold on the presidency, his wife, who had made the move to Washington shortly after her husband's inauguration, was confined largely to the White House's second floor. Though she was "still beautiful in her declining years," in the words of her admiring husband, a stroke in 1839 had left her an invalid at age forty-nine.[29] Shunning White House social duties, which the introverted Mrs. Tyler might have avoided anyway, she presided over family activities and tended to her knitting upstairs while leaving the White House social calendar in the hands of her twenty-four-year-old daughter-in-law, Priscilla, the wife of her eldest son, Robert.[30] She appeared in public only once as first lady, to attend the White House wedding of her daughter Elizabeth. On September 10, 1842, Letitia Tyler died after suffering another stroke, a damask rose clutched in her hand.[31] As the White House was "hung with black, its walls echoing with sighs," according to her daughter-in-law, Mrs. Tyler was buried at her family's plantation in Virginia.[32]

While Letitia Tyler left the White House tragically, others left willfully—and with alarming incidence—adding to the president's woes. The exodus of five of his six cabinet members in 1841 would be followed by ten more resignations of cabinet members, mostly conservative Democrats, during the course of his one term. In just under four years, he would see twenty-two cabinet appointees rotate through its six seats. But Webster would hold on for just over half of Tyler's term and would help him amass a respectable record in foreign affairs in spite of manifest adversity.

In a chapter devoted to Webster in *Profiles in Courage,* John F. Kennedy described him as "a great man—he looked like one, talked like one, was treated like one and insisted he was one."[33] The son of a New Hampshire farmer and eight years Tyler's senior, Webster had demonstrated his courage by remaining in Tyler's cabinet as his Whig colleagues fled. But his greatest accomplishment in Tyler's service came with the Webster-Ashburton Treaty, which he negotiated with Britain's foreign secretary Alexander, Lord Ashburton, settling the long-lingering, and at times provocative, question with Great Britain over the American-Canadian border. Though the Treaty of Paris ending the Revolutionary War had allowed for boundary lines between the United States and Canada, clashes had arisen over areas on the northern tip of Maine where the borders were nebulous. Military skirmishes over the disputed territory underscored the need to resolve the matter. Webster and Ashburton settled the issue by splitting the ambiguous territory—7,015 square miles for the United States and 5,012 for Great Britain—while clearly defining the border along the Great Lakes and the Lake of the Woods at Minnesota's northern edge.[34] (The issue of the Oregon border was tabled for a later date.) With other outstanding issues settled and rolled into the treaty as well, the Webster-Ashburton Treaty, signed in August 1842, allowed for a clean slate between the two nations and put to rest the underlying threat of war.

But Tyler and Webster, the principal ally of his administration, would eventually part company—amicably—over Tyler's greatest achievement: the annexation of Texas. Early into his term as president, in spite of all the upheaval, Tyler began thinking about ensuring his place in the presidential pantheon, while concerning himself with the practical matter of how to get reelected in 1844. In securing statehood for Texas, he believed he could achieve both. In the fall of 1841, he addressed the issue with Webster in a letter, inquiring rhetorically, "Could anything throw so bright a lustre around us?"[35] The notion of bringing Texas into the union had been kicked around since Texas had declared its independence from Mexico in 1836, under the leadership of its president, Sam Houston. But with it came the incendiary question of the expansion of slavery, which threatened to tip Congress's sectional balance.

A slave owner himself, albeit a decent master by all accounts, Tyler favored a gradual end to slavery.[36] He saw the institution simply petering out as it exhausted its economic utility. As such, he believed slavery to be a nonissue in bringing Texas into the union. Instead he promoted the benefits of Texas statehood: establishing a virtual monopoly in the cotton industry and the continual realization of manifest destiny with America's continental push westward.[37] But the implications of the expansion of slavery were enough to disaffect Webster, an abolitionist with the antislavery views of his New England constituency to think about. He resigned his post in 1843, with Tyler's gratitude for his loyal service of just over two years.

Pressing fellow Virginian Abel Upshur into service as the new secretary of state, Tyler and Upshur began secret negotiations with Houston. As progress was being made with Houston in negotiating a treaty, however, Upshur was killed in a freak accident. Rumors that Upshur would be succeeded by John C. Calhoun, South Carolinian firebrand and a fierce defender of slavery, were enough to drive the hope of Texas statehood off the rails for the moment. Tyler was forced to appoint Calhoun against his wishes rather than risk stirring up the South, and with Calhoun now steering Texas annexation forward, the issue of slavery stood front and center, resulting in a divided Senate, where ratification of the treaty needed a two-thirds majority.[38]

Tyler would eventually see Texas annexation, but it would come at a cost. Attempting to secure the presidential nomination of the Democratic Party, where he had successfully courted the conservative wing and made headway with his "Tyler and Texas" platform, he was usurped by dark horse candidate James K. Polk, who had co-opted annexation in his own platform. Tyler agreed to drop out of the race if congressional Democrats supported ratification of the treaty, but it failed to secure the necessary two-thirds vote.

Polk would go on to defeat Clay, the Whig's candidate, 170 electoral votes to 105. After Polk's election, Tyler, now a lame duck, continued to press annexation as mandated by Polk's win at the polls. Here an uncharacteristic lapse in Tyler's constructionist principles served him, just as it had for Jefferson with the Louisiana Purchase: He dodged the Constitution's requirement of a two-thirds majority vote by serving up Texas statehood as a joint resolution of Congress, entailing a simple majority vote. The resolution passed—barely—and Tyler signed the bill on March 1,

1845, just three days before leaving office, giving him the "crown in [his] public life."[39]

Texas statehood may have been his crown, but Tyler scored other accomplishments of note in foreign affairs in the latter part of his administration. Looking ever westward, he extended the principle of the Monroe Doctrine beyond the Western Hemisphere to include the Hawaiian Islands, recognizing it as an independent kingdom and warning the British against imperial designs.

In a besieged presidential tenure of forty-seven months, Tyler had shown himself to be nothing if not resilient. Domestically, too. Five months after his wife's death, he began courting Julia Gardiner, a New York socialite known as the "Rose of Long Island." A smitten Tyler proclaimed her "the most beautiful woman of the age"—and age itself didn't seem to be an issue. At twenty-three, Miss Gardiner was thirty years Tyler's junior. The May-December romance took hold, and the pair married at a White House wedding in June of 1844. When a friend suggested that his fifty-three years might make him a bit old for his wife, Tyler responded, "Oh pooh. Why, my dear sir, I am just in my prime." The seven children the second Mrs. Tyler would bear throughout the course of their eighteen-year marriage may have proved him right.[40]

Several weeks prior to their departure from the White House, Tyler's newlywed bride threw a farewell gala attended by more than three thousand guests—"as thick as sheep in a pen," according to one—where champagne flowed and political tensions were forgotten for the moment. Looking out over the meticulously planned affair, Tyler declared, perhaps with some defiance, "They cannot now say that I am a president without a party."[41]

Tyler gave the office over to Polk on March 4, but not before one final slight from Congress. On his penultimate day in office, the body overrode his veto of a maritime bill, the first time Congress had ever superseded a presidential veto.

The Tylers retreated to Sherwood Forest, where the former president oversaw the slaves who cultivated his wheat and corn crops as he tended to his young wife and their growing brood, the last of which he fathered at age seventy. An elder statesman of sorts, Tyler was called on by the Democratic Party sixteen years after his departure from the White House to be the presiding officer at a Peace Convention in Richmond in February 1861, a last-ditch stab at averting civil war. Afterward, described by poet and Lincoln biographer Carl Sandburg as "a tottering, ashen ruin," Tyler met with President-elect Abraham Lincoln at Washington's Willard Hotel to present him with the convention's resolutions.[42] A moderate among Southerners, Tyler was opposed to secession as long as slavery was protected as the sovereign right of Southern states. But when Lincoln did not act on the convention's motions, he openly joined the Confederacy, accepting election to the new House of Representatives of the Confederate States of America. He died of a stroke on January 12, 1862, before taking his seat.

Tyler's body was taken to lie in state in Virginia's Capitol in Richmond, his coffin draped with a Confederate flag. No services observing the tenth president's passing were held in Washington, the only time in the nation's history that a president's death has gone unrecognized.[43] A year later, in January 1862, Sherwood Forest was overrun and vandalized by Union soldiers who saw Tyler as a traitor to the American cause.


Almost 150 years after Tyler's death, Sherwood Forest is still owned by the Tyler family. The manor house endured its assault in the thick of the Civil War and stands intact, a relic of things past. Tyler's grandson, octogenarian Harrison Tyler, presides over the former plantation, which is available to the public to rent for weddings and private parties. Reflecting on his grandfather's legacy, Tyler called him a "positive president" who "accomplished things in spite of great obstacles."[44] Though bias typically runs the way of bloodlines, Mr. Tyler has a point. First and foremost, John Tyler strengthened the presidency by resolutely assuming the reins of executive power after Harrison's death, patently disregarding those who questioned his constitutional authority. Additionally, he chalked up some noteworthy accomplishments in foreign policy, including the Webster-Ashburton Treaty, while giving Texas its statehood. Not bad for a president without a party.

But while Sherwood Forest survived the scars inflicted by Union troops, its "outlaw" former owner is forever branded by his association with the Confederacy, a fact his grandson concedes. Though Tyler wished for a vaunted place in history, his states' rights doctrine, which implicitly clung to the outdated precept of slavery during his presidency and led to his stand for secession in 1861, would soon be washed away by history's sweeping tides. With them went any chance for Tyler to achieve a meaningful place in its annals.

# IV

# ABRAHAM LINCOLN

## *"The Union is unbroken"*

The Capitol building stood unfinished as Abraham Lincoln went
through the rites of his presidential inauguration on a temporary
wood platform erected over the steps of its east portico, the fourth day of
March, 1861. The first president, George Washington, had laid the
building's cornerstone in 1793, and since then it had borne witness to
much of the nation's turbulent history. Only a chance thunderstorm
saved it from being engulfed by flames as the British overtook it, setting
it ablaze two years after the War of 1812 had begun. The following year
work on its completion resumed in fits and starts as plans for its edifice
broadened with America's westward expansion. As Lincoln prepared to
recite the oath that fifteen others had taken, the Capitol's massive ro-
tunda, still under construction, remained unenclosed, looking more like
a coliseum than a dome, its floor vulnerable to the elements, which fell
unfettered from the sky above. In the coming weeks work would be suspended as war erupted between the Confederate states in the South and
the Northern states that made up the balance of the Union. Soon afterward the building would be called upon to house Union troops and serve

as a hospital for the war's sick and wounded.[1] But on this day, Abraham Lincoln began his presidency with the distant hope that civil war could be averted.

"Tall and ungainly," in the words of a newspaper reporter from the Associated Press, Lincoln wore "a black suit, a black tie beneath a turn-down collar, and a black silk hat. He carried a gold- or silver-headed walking-cane. . . . He drew from his breast pocket the manuscript I had seen him reading at the [Willard] hotel, laid it before him, placing the cane upon it as a paperweight." He removed his hat, adjusted his steel-frame reading glasses, and began reading to a crowd of ten thousand the speech he had prepared for an anxious nation, his voice "high pitched, but resonant."[2]

"I have no purpose, directly or indirectly, to interfere with the institution of slavery in the states where it exists," he quickly assured his apprehensive countrymen in the Southern states. "I believe I have no lawful right to do so, and I have no inclination to do so." At the same time, he made clear his constitutional authority prohibiting the secession of individual states:

> *No state upon its own mere motion can lawfully get out of the Union. . . . You have no oath registered in heaven to destroy the government, while I have the most solemn one to "preserve, protect, and defend it." . . . I therefore consider that in view of the Constitution and the laws the Union is unbroken, and to the extent of my ability, I shall take care, as the Constitution itself expressly enjoins upon me, that the laws of the Union be faithfully executed in all the states. . . . In doing this there needs to be no bloodshed or violence, and there shall be none unless it be forced upon the national authority.*

He ended his address with a poetic appeal to the reason of those who would defy the Constitution in secession.

> *I am loath to close. We are not enemies, but friends. We must not be enemies. Though passion may have strained it must not break our bonds of affection. The mystic chords of memory, stretching from every battlefield and patriot*

*grave to every living heart and hearthstone all over this broad land, will yet*
*swell the chorus of the Union, when again touched, as surely they will be, by*
*the better angels of our nature.*

But the scene around the capital belied Lincoln's ostensible optimism. Military men stood on guard throughout the city, more than just ceremonial ornaments as they had been in inaugurations past. Two batteries of artillery were stationed in the shadow of the Capitol, while the cavalry was posted at intersections throughout the city and sharpshooters patrolled vigilantly from the rooftops of low buildings.[3] The federal government braced for conflict.

On December 20, 1860, a little over a month after Lincoln's election, the South Carolina legislature, in a secession convention in Charleston, declared "the union now subsisting between South Carolina and other States under the name of the United States of America is hereby dissolved," raising the din in the drumbeat for secession throughout the South.[4] By February, other states in the Deep South followed—Alabama, Florida, Georgia, Louisiana, Mississippi, and Texas—forming, along with South Carolina, the Confederate States of America. Their secession was more than a political statement; as the states broke away from the union, their militias took over the federal armories and forts that fell within their borders in the name of the Confederacy. In the months before Lincoln took office, several Southern forts—Fort Pickens in Pensacola, Florida, and the forts around Charleston—remained in federal control. But on January 9, South Carolina's militia fired on a Union ship, the *Star of the West*, as it attempted to bring supplies and troop reinforcement to Major Robert Anderson at Fort Sumter. Unable to carry out its mission, the ship reversed course, leaving Anderson stranded in what was now clearly enemy territory. Resolving Anderson's plight would involve the first major decisions of the Lincoln administration.

A month before his inaugural, as Lincoln traveled by rail to Washington from his hometown of Springfield, Illinois, a plot to assassinate him was exposed in the pro-Southern city of Baltimore before his train passed through. At the urging of his security detail, the president-elect—concealed by his overcoat, which was draped like a loose cape over his shoulders, a felt kossuth hat replacing his trademark stovepipe—boarded a train incognito in Harrisburg, Pennsylvania, where he was booked into a room designated for an "invalid passenger" and transported furtively into Washington's Union Station.[5] By then the die was cast: Well before the pacifying remarks made at his inaugural, the South had largely made up its mind about Abraham Lincoln and his intentions.

Toward the end of his life, Thomas Jefferson likened the American institution of slavery to holding a wolf by the ears. "We can neither hold him, nor safely let him go," he wrote a friend. "Justice is on one scale, and self-preservation in the other."[6] The nation had had the "wolf" tenuously in its grasp since the first African slaves had been brought as cargo to American shores in 1619. Slavery grew in proportion to a rising economy, almost entirely in the South, where the cotton industry thrived, creating a Southern power bloc among plantation owners around protecting the status quo. When Washington assumed the presidency in 1789, half a million slaves resided in the United States, producing a thousand tons of cotton a year. By the time Lincoln became president, four million American slaves produced a million tons of cotton.[7]

While Jefferson high-mindedly invoked justice as a deciding factor against slavery, the issue of abolition had more to do with the clash of regional economic interests. For much of the nineteenth century, the South had resisted the expansionist economic policies of the North marked by national programs allowing for free land to broaden the nation's settlement, free labor, and a free-market economy. All were threats to the safeguarding of slavery and the way of life enjoyed by the Southern ruling class.[8]

A number of legislative compromises had been made to ensure harmony between North and South, and the preservation of the union, including the Northwest Ordinance of 1787, the Missouri Compromise of 1820, and the Compromise of 1850. But it was a judicial ruling that brought the long-heated issue of slavery to a boil, rendering those compromises moot. In 1857, the Supreme Court's decision in the case of Dred Scott, the slave of a former army surgeon, who sued for his freedom with the argument that he had lived in the free territories of Illinois and Wisconsin before returning to the slave state of Mississippi, resounded throughout the union. The court was divided, its justices rendering decisions that fell along political and sectional lines, though it was the opinion of Chief Justice Roger B. Taney that would prevail. Taney, a former slave owner from Maryland who would issue Lincoln's inaugural oath, included in his opinion that black men are "so far inferior that they had no rights which the white man was bound to respect," and maintained that Scott shouldn't be recognized by the Court at all, since Scott, as a slave, was not a person but property. He further held that the congressional compromises that made certain states throughout the union "free" despite earlier legislation were unconstitutional. Challenging the Declaration of Independence's phrase "all men are created equal," Taney wrote, "It is too clear for dispute, that the enslaved African race were not intended to be included, and formed no part of the people who framed and adopted this declaration."

The country's leading African-American voice of the time, Frederick Douglass, saw opportunity in the decision, proclaiming, "Never have my hopes been brighter."[9] Douglass's optimism was well placed. The case provoked a debate in America around the issue of slavery, weakening the Democratic Party, whose Northern and Southern wings were polarized, while giving momentum to the Republican Party, which had sprung from the ashes of the Whig Party, and to the emergence of Abraham Lincoln on the national political scene.[10]

A year after Taney rendered his opinion, a U.S. Senate race played out in Illinois between the Democratic incumbent Stephen Douglas and his Republican challenger, Lincoln, a former one-term U.S. congressman, which put the issue of slavery front and center. Over the course of the campaign, the two men engaged in a series of seven debates throughout Illinois. The contest gained national attention in addition to capturing the interest of the state's electorate, which turned out in droves to watch to the candidates spar. Douglas was known as the "Little Giant," a moniker that captured not only his diminutive size—he was five two—but also his imposing stature. Although he had failed to gain his party's nomination for the presidency in 1852 and 1856, and had designs on it for 1860, his prodigious career in the Senate and gift for oratory made him one of the most famous men in the country. By contrast Douglas's opponent, who stood a solid but lanky six four, was a virtual unknown outside political circles in Illinois and had pursued a life in politics punctuated by a string of losses. But his deeply held views on slavery and eloquence in the debates would make him a national figure. The country would know him soon enough.

Lincoln was the product of hardscrabble frontier life, born unpromisingly in a lowly one-room, dirt-floored log cabin in the rough country of Hardin (now Larue) County, Kentucky, on February 9, 1809. His father, Thomas Lincoln, was an illiterate farmer and carpenter whose hard work, like his aspirations for his son, added up to little. His mother, Nancy Hanks Lincoln, an illegitimate child by Lincoln's own account, died when he was nine. "All that I am or even hope to be," Lincoln once said, "I owe to her," a sentiment pointedly not applied to his father. A year after his wife's death, Thomas Lincoln married Sarah Bush Johnson, a widow who brought her three children to live with the Lincolns and treated young Abraham and his sister, Sarah, two years older, like her own. (Lincoln's brother, Thomas junior, three years younger, died in infancy.) During Lincoln's time under his father's roof, the elder Lincoln moved his family four times to other rural outposts: first to another location in Kentucky, ten miles from Lincoln's birthplace, then, "partly on account of slavery," as Lincoln later maintained, to the free state of Indiana, and finally on to Macon County, Illinois.[11] Though there was always food on the table, poverty doggedly followed them throughout.

Books provided Lincoln an escape from the dreariness of backwoods life. He read voraciously—Parson Weems's *The Life of George Washington* was a favorite—firing his imagination and, one imagines, stirring the young man's ambition, which Billy Herndon, his friend and law partner, later described as "a little engine that knew no rest."[12] One of the earliest writing samples from the future president, a poem etched in his classroom copybook among a schoolboy's scrawls, provides a glimpse of his youthful aspiration:

*Abraham Lincoln*
*his hand in pen*
*He will be good*
*But God knows when*[13]

Though he lacked clear direction growing up, his father provided a reference point for what he did not want to be. In the words of biographer William Lee Miller, Lincoln ran from farming "as fast as his long legs would take him."[14] He promptly left home at nineteen, when the owner of a flatboat offered him a job on board taking produce down the Mississippi River. Upon delivering the goods in New Orleans, he got a firsthand look at the brutality of slavery, leaving a deep impression on him. At age twenty-two, in 1831, he set off as if in a Horatio Alger tale, settling in the small Illinois town of New Salem, where he went on to try his hand at almost every other occupation available to backwoods frontiersmen except farming, including stints as a store clerk, handyman, postmaster, soldier, store owner, surveyor, lawyer, and politician.[15] The last two vocations stuck. Over time, Lincoln made a name for himself in New Salem, and later in Springfield, the capital, where he moved in 1837. While he considered himself "uneducated," with formal education not much beyond "A.B.C. schools," his own study of law resulted in his passing the bar in 1836 and going on to become one of the state's most successful lawyers.[16]

Lincoln's character and talents complemented his ambition. Tales of his physical strength, a particularly important attribute on the frontier, grew to legend. A neighbor in Indiana called Lincoln "a strong man, physically powerful; he could strike with a maul a heavier blow than any man."[17] His might and capacity for hard work later contributed to his homespun "rail-splitter" political image, though Lincoln confessed that while he had split rails earlier in life to earn extra money, he had done so only so that he would never again have to split rails.[18] Clients and fellow lawyers acknowledged Lincoln's remarkable work ethic, which would be manifest in the White House.[19] The nickname "Honest Abe" also pointed to a virtue recognized and respected by his peers. Lincoln considered honesty to be paramount in the practice of law and was never known to lie.[20] Stephen Douglas called Lincoln "as honest as he is shrewd."[21]

Wit was another of Lincoln's attractive qualities; one friend claimed Lincoln could "make a cat laugh." Often his humor was self-deprecating. During his debates with Douglas, his rival accused him of being "two-faced." "I leave it to the audience," responded Lincoln. "If I had another face, do you think I would wear this one?"[22] Indeed, his looks were not a strong suit. Even friends described him commonly as "homely." A description of Lincoln from Billy Herndon does not paint a pretty picture:

> *His hair was dark—almost black and lay floating where the fingers or winds left it, piled up at random. His cheek-bones were high—sharp and prominent. His eye brows heavy and jutting out. Mr. Lincoln's jaws were long up curved and heavy. His nose was large—long and blunt, having the tip glowing in red, and a little awry toward the right eye. His face was long—sallow— cadaverous—shrunk—shrivelled—wrinkled and dry, having here and there a hair on the surface. His cheeks were leathery and flabby, falling in loose folds at places, looking sorrowful and sad.[23]*

Sorrow and sadness. Those were also intrinsic parts of Lincoln's makeup, as plain in his demeanor as his stovepipe was on his head. As a fellow Illinois lawyer, Henry Whitney, put it, "No element of Mr. Lincoln's character was so marked, obvious and ingrained as his mysterious and profound melancholy."[24] Depression shrouded Lincoln, coloring his often gray view of life. Twice in his early adulthood, at twenty-six and thirty-two, he thought of suicide.[25] He warded it off, at least in part, due to the nagging realization that he had yet to leave a meaningful mark on the world. In 1841, reeling over his aborted engagement to Mary Todd, whom he would marry the following year, he told his friend and law partner Joshua Speed that he would willingly die but for the fact that he "had done nothing to make any human being remember that he had lived."[26]

Politics would offer that prospect. A devotee of Whig Party boss Henry Clay, Lincoln spent the bulk of his political career in the Illinois state legislature, where he served as a representative of his district for four consecutive two-year terms beginning in 1834, bookended by vain attempts to win the same seat in 1832 and 1842. He served one two-year term representing Illinois's Seventh District in the U.S. House of Representatives beginning in 1847, declining to run for another term to be with his young family in Springfield. After a tumultuous courtship, he married the diminutive, fiery Miss Todd, nine years his junior, in 1842. A year later, Mrs. Lincoln gave birth to their first child, Robert, producing three more boys—Eddie, Willie, and Tad--over the course of the next decade. Mary Lincoln would spur her husband's ambition through her unwavering faith in his abilities. "Mr. Lincoln may not be a handsome figure," she said of him when he was compared to his rival, and one of her former Springfield suitors, Stephen Douglas, "but the people are perhaps not aware that his heart is as big as his arms are long."[27]

After a four-year respite from elected office, Lincoln was back in the state legislature in 1854, which he resigned the same year to make a failed run for the U.S. Senate. Nonetheless, as a favorite son of Illinois, his name was placed in nomination for the vice presidency after he joined the Republican Party in 1856, along with other Conscience Whigs who opposed slavery.[28] Two years later he was back as a candidate for the Senate, taking on the redoubtable Douglas.

Lincoln's views on slavery were well established by the time he squared off against Douglas in 1858—and so were his opponent's. The Kansas-Nebraska Act, forged by Senator Douglas in 1854, effectively annulled the Missouri Compromise that prevented slavery in the Northern states, putting the decision on slavery in the hands of the people to determine through "popular sovereignty." The Republican Party, composed of an alliance between the antislavery wings of the Whig, Democratic, and Free-Soil parties, formed as a result with an aim toward curtailing slavery's westward expansion. Even so, abolition would be a tough sell in Illinois, where much of the population had, like the Lincoln family, migrated north from Southern states, and where just a decade

earlier 70 percent of voters supported a constitutional amendment ban-
ning black inhabitants in the state.[29]

That explained Lincoln's balancing act on the slavery issue throughout the debates. A lifelong opponent of slavery, Lincoln wrote in 1864, "I
am naturally anti-slavery. If slavery is not wrong, nothing is wrong. I can
not remember when I did not so think and feel."[30] Political pragmatism,
though, dictated a more conservative approach to the matter in areas of
the state where a dimmer view of race was more expedient. In Charleston, Illinois, he professed "a physical difference between the white and
black races which I believe will forever forbid the two races living together on terms of social and political equality"; in more open-minded
Chicago, he declared the races to be equal.[31] But his stand on the preservation of the union—whether slave or free—was unequivocal. He stated
at the Republicans' state convention in Springfield earlier in June, in
what became known nationally as the House Divided speech:

> *"A house divided against itself cannot stand." I believe this government cannot
> endure permanently half slave and half free. I do not expect the Union to
> dissolve—I do not expect the house to fall—but I do expect it will cease to be
> divided. It will become all one thing, or all the other. Either the opponents of
> slavery will arrest the further spread of it, and place it where the public mind
> shall rest in the belief that it is in course of ultimate extinction; or its advocates
> will push it forward till it shall become alike lawful in all the States, old as
> well as new, North as well as South.*

Douglas derided Lincoln's speech as a "slander upon the immortal
framers of our Constitution," who had allowed for free and slave states
through state sovereignties.[32] He occasionally stooped to demagogic
tactics, asserting his belief that the Founding Fathers formed the government on a "white basis . . . for the benefit of white men and their
posterity forever."[33] Lincoln rebutted that it was Douglas who was guilty
of slandering the Founding Fathers, for "the entire records of the world,
from the date of the Declaration of Independence up to within three
years ago, may be searched in vain for one single affirmation, from one

single man, that the negro was not included in the Declaration of Independence."[34]

Voters braved wet, raw November weather to go to the polls in high numbers—higher than even the presidential election two years earlier. The Republicans, although taking the popular vote by some four thousand ballots, failed to gain control of the state legislature, which remained in the hands of the Democrats, who sent Douglas back to the Senate as Lincoln licked the wounds of another defeat.[35] Rationalizing afterward, Lincoln wrote a friend that the race "gave me a hearing on the great and durable question of the age, which I could have had in no other way; and though I now sink out of view, and shall be forgotten, I believe I have made some marks which will tell for the cause of civil liberty long after I am gone."[36] Lincoln would hardly "sink out of view." His national exposure during the contest brought with it notoriety; he would spend the next sixteen months on a speaking tour throughout the North supporting other Republican candidates and continuing to sound his message on the "great question of the age."

As the Republican National Convention of 1860 neared, Lincoln began to gain the support among members of the party, many of whom were indebted to him for his campaign efforts on their behalf. Slowly momentum began to build for Lincoln as the party's presidential nominee. Lincoln confessed "the taste *is* in my mouth a little" for the nomination and gently stoked the fire by lining up delegates where possible.[37] When the party assembled in Chicago in May, he dramatically secured the nomination on the third ballot, as the favorite for the nomination, former New York governor and sitting U.S. senator William Seward, was passed over due to his uncompromising antislavery position, which would play poorly in swing states like Pennsylvania, Indiana, Iowa, and Illinois.[38] With the Democratic Party split along regional lines, the GOP saw its chance to prevail in the election and was taking no chances. Maine senator Hannibal Hamlin, a former Democrat, was chosen as Lincoln's running mate, a nod to New England. Returning to one of the themes of the Lincoln-Douglas Senate contest, the party's platform included an assertion of the principles of equality inherent in the Declaration of

Independence, while spelling out policy to ban slavery in the territories and allow its continued existence in the slave states.

The Democratic Party meanwhile divided into Southern and Northern factions and held separate conventions, with the former nominating as its presidential candidate John C. Breckinridge of Kentucky, while the latter turned to Lincoln's previous rival, Stephen Douglas. Further fracturing the electorate would be a fourth candidate, John Bell of Tennessee, who represented a party composed mainly of former old-line members of the Whig and Know-Nothing parties called the Constitutional Union Party—though the Republicans scoffed at them as "Do-Nothings."[39]

When Election Day came on November 6, 1860, Lincoln, while earning just 40 percent of the popular vote, a million fewer than the other three candidates combined, took 180 of 303 electoral votes to win the presidency. He carried every Northern state except New Jersey, which he split with Douglas. The South, though, was a far different story; aside from a handful of votes in the border states and in northern Virginia, not a single Southern vote was cast for the Republican ticket.[40] Lincoln's hometown of Springfield erupted jubilantly over the news of his victory. "Our city is as quiet as a young lady who has just found out that she was in love," the local *Journal* wrote.[41] But from the South, far darker commentary: "Let the consequences be what they may," wrote the *Confederacy* in Atlanta, "whether the Potomac is crimsoned in human gore, and Pennsylvania Avenue is paved ten fathoms deep with mangled bodies, or whether the last vestige of liberty is swept from the face of the American continent, the South will never submit to such humiliation and degradation as the inauguration of Abraham Lincoln."[42]

Awaiting Lincoln when he settled down to work the day after his inauguration was a report from Major Robert Anderson on the dire situation he faced at Fort Sumter, as the Confederacy demanded its evacuation. Anderson informed the president that he had only six weeks' worth of provisions left; without reinforcement, he would have to surrender to the Confederacy. He further reckoned that twenty thousand troops would be needed to secure the fort.[43] Though resolution to the standoff was critical in setting policy for the new administration, Lincoln took no immediate action, signaling no clear direction to the country. In the words of Lincoln biographer David Herbert Donald, he was "temperamentally averse to making bold moves. It was his style to react to decisions made by others rather than take initiative himself."[44]

Just as indiscernible as Lincoln's policy was the logic around his cabinet choices. Lincoln had a firm idea upon his election whom he would select, refraining from making announcements only due to his anticipation that he would be "teased to insanity to make changes."[45] Given the eclecticism of his choices, which included an array of formidable Republicans of every stripe—three former Whigs and three former Democrats—he was almost certainly right. William Seward, Lincoln's opponent for the Republican nomination and the most prominent of the conservative wing of the party, was tapped as secretary of state, while another opponent for the nomination, the most prominent among the radical wing, Salmon P. Chase of Ohio, was chosen as secretary of the treasury. Gideon Welles of Connecticut was given the post of secretary of the navy, and Simon Cameron of Pennsylvania was named secretary of war (to be replaced in 1862 by Edwin M. Stanton, who had served as attorney general to Lincoln's predecessor, James Buchanan). None had been openly supportive of Lincoln—or each other, for that matter. The result was an extraordinary collection of men the historian Doris Kearns Goodwin called "a team of rivals." "To surround himself with all of his disappointed antagonists seemed to be courting disaster," maintained another Lincoln biographer, Benjamin P. Thomas. "It was a mark of his sincere intentions that Lincoln wanted the advice of men as strong as himself or stronger. That he entertained no fear of being crushed or overridden by such men revealed either surpassing naïveté or tranquil confidence in his powers of leadership."[46]

"They will eat you up," an aide warned Lincoln about the men he had chosen. "They will just as likely eat each other up," Lincoln replied.[47]

Seward presented the first challenge. Eight years Lincoln's senior, stooped, slight, and hawk-nosed, Seward deemed Lincoln to be too inexperienced to be president, particularly given the challenges that awaited, and believed himself to be the true leader of the party, despite Lincoln's mandate. He pondered whether he could do more good outside Lincoln's cabinet before opting to accept his post as secretary of state. But, on the eve of Lincoln's inauguration, upon hearing that his rival Salmon Chase had been selected as secretary of the treasury, he informed Lincoln that he would have to withdraw his name given the irreconcilable differences between himself and Chase. "I can not afford to let Seward take the first trick," said Lincoln to his secretary, John Nicholay, shrewdly managing the situation and keeping in their designated posts both Chase and Seward, who remained so as not to "leave the country to chance."[48]

To that end, Seward quickly moved to assert himself in his new role—and to reach beyond it. Uncomfortable with the president's vacillating, and thinking himself to be more qualified to lead the country forward, Seward, less than a month into the administration, fired off a letter to Lincoln remonstrating with him for his lack of direction. He advised shifting focus from slavery to unionism by abandoning Fort Sumter but bolstering other military strongholds in the South, and to divert attention from the crisis with the Southern states, he suggested starting a war with France or Spain. If Lincoln didn't want to do these things himself, Seward proposed to take care of it for him, implicitly making himself a sort of American prime minister.[49] Lincoln handled Seward's extraordinary impertinence with relative aplomb. *He*, as president, would carry out the duties of the executive office, he informed Seward, adding, "Still . . . I wish, and suppose I am entitled to have, the advice of all the cabinet."[50] Giving Seward the benefit of the doubt under the strain of the new administration, he kept Seward's communiqué under wraps, sparing him the damage his reputation would suffer if it saw the light of day. Seward, for his part, would soon come around to respecting and admiring his chief. "Executive force and vigor are rare qualities," he wrote his wife in New York two months later. "The President is the best of us."[51]

Decisions on policy would be forced on Lincoln soon enough. Shortly after Seward's letter, in the hours before dawn on April 12, the Confederacy opened fire on Fort Sumter. Thirty-four hours later, Major Anderson surrendered the garrison. Lincoln's response was swift: He called for seventy-five thousand volunteers—which he felt was just the start—and ordered a blockade around the South. The president's actions were followed within weeks by the secession of Virginia, Arkansas, North Carolina, Tennessee, and Texas, which joined the burgeoning Confederacy. The lines had been drawn; the country was at war.

Like Muhammad Ali picking the round in which a foe would fall, the North put forth brash predictions of a fast Union victory. Seward thought it would take ninety days; the *New York Times* guessed no more than a month.[52] Sentiments of members of the business community were captured by the *New York Herald*, which declared their "demand that the war shall be short, and the more vigorously it is prosecuted the more speedily will it be closed. They cannot endure a long, uncertain and tedious contest."[53] The numbers, like the odds, lined up in the North's favor. Four million of its 22 million inhabitants were men of combat age; in the South, a population of 9 million had just 1.2 million men of combat age. Plus the North's advanced industrial infrastructure meant a greater ability to manufacture weapons and ship them by rail.[54] Still, Lincoln had his doubts that victory would come either quickly or easily.

The outcome of the first major engagement in the war, the Battle of Bull Run, waged on July 21, just twenty miles away from Washington in Manassas, Virginia, confirmed Lincoln's instincts. The Confederate army scored a decisive blow against the Union, showing them to be ill prepared and outmaneuvered. Lincoln attributed the upset to poor leadership, replacing his commander, General Irvin McDowell, with General George B. McClellan the following day. Lincoln bowed to the opinions of many in selecting the thirty-four-year-old West Point graduate—"Little Mac" or "The Young Napoleon" as he became known—who looked and acted the part of a leader of men and was possessed of a cocksureness that crept into vainglory, as Lincoln would soon discover.[55] At McClellan's request, Lincoln gave his new commander until the end of the year to train his men for the long campaign to come.

McClellan, though, was not Lincoln's first choice for the post. At the strong recommendation of Winfield Scott, Lincoln's seventy-five-year-old general-in-chief, Lincoln first offered the command to Robert E. Lee,

another West Point graduate of indisputable ability. Lee declined the offer in deference to his loyalty to his home state of Virginia. He resigned
from the U.S. Army on April 20, and three days later accepted the command of the Confederate army under Jefferson Davis, former U.S. senator from Mississippi and secretary of war for Franklin Pierce, who became
president of the Confederacy. Other accomplished, battle-tested military
officers from the Southern states also put their state allegiances first,
leaving Lincoln with a leadership void that would gnaw at him throughout the war—and keeping the Confederate cause afloat well after it
might have sunk.

    In the early days of his presidency, Lincoln set a new tone and style
for the office, one marked by manifest egalitarianism. The new president
spent the first months in office besieged by visitors, who consumed the
bulk of his time as well as that of his beleaguered staff, notably his devoted secretaries John Hay and John Nicholay. He admitted later that he
was "entirely ignorant not only of the duties, but of the manner of doing
the business" of the president. During business hours, the White House
teemed with petitioners of every station who queued up in lines that often
extended beyond the stairs to the front entrance. Lincoln saw as many as
he could, patiently hearing them out. Most were office seekers aiming for
a job in the administration. Others were there to air complaints or to appeal to him to right a wrong as they saw it. Though the environment
around the White House was chaotic, the president's willingness to see
all comers had a positive effect: His patience, wisdom, and paternal concern earned him the nickname "Father Abraham" and a standing
throughout the North as a true man of the people. Wholly devoid of pre-
tension, he had a reputation for classlessness that also extended beyond
his own color. Frederick Douglass recognized Lincoln's "entire freedom
from prejudice against the colored race." Still, doubts about Lincoln's
ability to succeed in his role as president prevailed.[56]

    He was not presidential by traditional standards. Certainly, he looked
different from his predecessors, all of whom were born in the original
thirteen American states, half of them in Virginia. He seemed almost
freakishly tall, taller still with the ubiquitous top hat perched on his

head. He also became the first president to wear a beard, which he'd grown in a Quaker style during the 1860 campaign at the suggestion of an eleven-year-old Massachusetts girl, Grace Bedell, who maintained in a letter that "all the ladies like whiskers and they would tease their husbands to vote for you."[57] At fifty-two, Lincoln was relatively youthful—only John Tyler had been younger, at fifty-one—and became the first presidential father to bring young children into the White House.

Ten years separated the Lincoln boys. Robert, the oldest, was seventeen and enrolled at Harvard by the time his father took office. The Lincolns' second child, Eddie, died at age three in 1850, the same year their third son, Willie, was born. Their youngest, Tad, was born three years later, in 1853. The two younger boys had the run of the White House, making mischief and running roughshod over the White House staff, while capturing the imagination of the American public, who sent them gifts in abundance including two small goats, Nanko and Nanny, which became fixtures on the White House lawn. Neither parent was inclined toward discipline. Their father, amused by their antics, played with them when he could, but his prodigious work ethic and the enormous task at hand meant little time for being the attentive parent.

If the boys provided a lighthearted relief for Lincoln as he struggled with the burden as President, Mary Lincoln often added to it. The fourth of the seven children of Robert Todd, a merchant and lawyer, Mary Todd was born and raised in her husband's native Kentucky but enjoyed a privileged background. She was attended to by the family's slaves and sent to private schools, including four years of boarding school.[58] Her mother died when she was six, leaving her to a childhood that was, by her own word, "desolate."[59] Strained relations with her stepmother led her to leave her family home in Lexington at age twenty-two, in 1839, for an extended visit to her married sister, Elizabeth Edwards, in Springfield.

The vivacious Miss Todd soon became a bright light of Springfield society. Plump and pretty at five feet two, with a round face, striking blue eyes, and chestnut brown hair, Miss Todd attracted no shortage of suitors with her glow. Among them was Stephen Douglas, to whom she was erroneously reported to be engaged. But it was Abraham Lincoln who won her heart with his decency, ambition, and potential. She was "the first aggressively brilliant feminine creature who had crossed his path so that he lost his head," according to Carl Sandburg, and Lincoln was smitten with her.[60] After a tempestuous on-and-off three-year courtship made stormier by Lincoln's cold feet, the couple married in 1842, as Mr. Lincoln, as she often called him, placed a ring on her finger engraved with the words "Love is eternal." True enough, they were a devoted couple, their love strengthened by their bond as parents. But just as Mary Lincoln endured her husband's bouts with melancholy, he put up with her ill temper and erratic nature that regularly beset their marriage with tempests. Often Lincoln found himself on the other end of his wife's irrational tirades. Hay and Nicholay, used to seeing unseemly displays of Mrs. Lincoln's temper, took to calling her "Hell-cat."[61]

Mary Lincoln's palpable ambition, which helped propel her husband into the White House, came with an attendant agenda as wife of the president. Her mission upon entering the White House, which the Lincolns found in a dilapidated and deplorable state, was to restore its luster, making it the pride of the nation. Congress appropriated $20,000 for the undertaking, to be spent over four years. After extravagant shopping expeditions to New York and Philadelphia, she soon far exceeded the allowance. When Lincoln learned of his wife's reckless spending spree—after her vain attempts to keep the news from him—he was apoplectic. How could she possibly go through $20,000 to spruce up the executive mansion when "the poor and freezing [Union] soldiers could not have blankets?"[62] He vowed to pay off the debt himself before practicality dictated soliciting Congress for additional funds to cover the overage. It did, however, cost him politically.

While patience proved a necessary virtue for Lincoln in his personal life, he also needed it in dealing with McClellan on the war. In November, Lincoln boosted McClellan to general-in-chief, forcing the resignation of the aging and overweight Winfield Scott. "I can do it all," Little Mac assured the president, a boast that fell as short as Little Mac's five-foot-four frame.[63] As Union troops swelled from 50,000 to 165,000, McClellan showed himself an able organizer, effectively training his men and readying them for battle.[64] But when it came to actual combat, Lincoln thought him to have a case of "the slows."[65] The two men disagreed on battle strategy, with Lincoln yielding to McClellan's plan to march on Richmond, the Confederate capital. When, in January, Lincoln called for a Union offensive in his first order of the war, McClellan obstinately ignored it. By March, with no progress made, he demoted "the Young Napoleon," giving him command only of the Army of the Potomac, while, in July, making General Henry Halleck his general-in-chief. The first hope for the Union army came in early February as General Ulysses S. Grant toughed out a win on the Tennessee River to capture Fort Henry, then went on to take Fort Donelson, just outside Nashville, ten days later.

Lincoln's pleasure over Grant's triumph was soon overshadowed by an enormous blow. After fighting a cold and typhoid fever, eleven-year-old Willie Lincoln, thought to be his father's favorite, died on February 20. Polluted water, which flowed into the White House directly from the Potomac River, was the likely culprit. The Lincolns were devastated. Mrs. Lincoln took to her bed for three weeks after his death, so overcome with grief that she couldn't bring herself to attend the boy's funeral. She wore mourning black well into the following year and never again entered the White House bedroom in which Willie died or the Green Room where he was embalmed.[66] Lincoln went back to the grim work of preserving the union but often withdrew alone into rooms in the mansion where he could weep in solitude.[67]

The year 1862 would see no end to Lincoln's suffering; his son's death did not abate the torrent of pressure that leached from the war, or the burden it heaped upon its commander in chief. It came from all sides. The war continued inconclusively well after those in the North had imagined it would be won. No clear war strategy emerged from the White House or from Lincoln's commanders, including the recalcitrant McClellan. Lincoln's micromanagement of the war, alongside Secretary of War Edwin Stanton, proved ineffective.[68] War casualties mounted at alarming rates; and the number of desertions among Union soldiers was high, reducing troop levels and morale. The border states—Delaware, Maryland, Missouri, and Kentucky—teetered precariously toward possible secession, requiring constant concessions. Special-interest groups lobbied tenaciously for their causes. Many across the country called for peace at any price, while abolitionists—notably Massachusetts senators Charles Sumner and Ben Wade, *New York Tribune* editor Horace Greeley, and Frederick Douglass—demanded an immediate end to slavery and the unconditional surrender of the South. And animosity and disparate views and agendas divided the members of Lincoln's cabinet.[69] Lincoln slogged through it all.

Though Lincoln had sworn to uphold the Constitution in his presidential oath, invoking that duty in his inaugural address, its parameters took a backseat to the presidential activism he deemed necessary to save the country. It made little sense, he reasoned, "to lose the nation and yet preserve the Constitution." Desperate times, it seemed, called for desperate measures. The war itself had begun without a declaration of war and congressional consent.[70] Critics railed at Lincoln as he trampled on the law, ordering the arrest and detention of suspected traitors, the blockade of Southern ports, and the closing of post offices to "treasonable correspondence." When judges invoked the writ of habeas corpus to interfere with the draft of Union soldiers, Lincoln resolved to have them jailed and exiled. After a debate with his cabinet, which counseled him to be less extreme, Lincoln simply had the writ suspended.[71]

Lincoln's approach to war was just as unyielding: The faster the South was crushed—through soldiers killed on battlefields, homes and businesses destroyed, and earth scorched—the more lives would be saved by the war's end.[72] In order to achieve his ends, he insisted that his commanders fight relentlessly. When they didn't share his sense of urgency, he had no compunction in changing the guard. During the war's course, four generals commanding the Army of the Potomac would come and go, each one fired when he came up short of Lincoln's expectations. To one of them, George Meade, he wrote: "Be sure to fight; the people demand it of the Army of the Potomac." He further promised that if Meade advanced on the enemy "with all the skill and courage, which he, his officers and men possess, the honor will be his if he succeeds, and the blame may be mine if he fails."[73]

As a result of Lincoln's steadfastness, and that of the Confederate army to preserve the Southern way, the war was bloody beyond the imagination of any Unionist or Confederate when shots were first fired at Fort Sumter. One out of every five of its soldiers would die from battle or disease.[74] Grant, eventually Lincoln's favorite general due simply to the fact that "he fights," recalled the carnage in the wake of his victory at Shiloh: "I saw an open field . . . so covered with dead that it would have been possible to walk across the clearing, in any direction, stepping only on dead bodies without a foot touching the ground."[75] Lincoln's hope was that the fierce military advance, while exacting a heavy price in human life, would soon bring the war to a close. "Hold on with a bulldog grip," Lincoln encouraged Grant by telegram in 1864, "and chew and choke as much as possible."[76]

When it came to the enemy's breach of the commonly recognized laws of war, Lincoln handed down an eye-for-an-eye policy. After hearing that the Confederates had threatened to shoot captured African-American soldiers, he issued an order stating "for every soldier of the United States killed in violation of the laws of war, a rebel soldier shall be executed; and for every one enslaved by the enemy . . . a rebel soldier shall be placed at hard labor on the public works."[77]

But Lincoln's resolve was balanced by compassion. He often applied his weary presidential signature—*A. Lincoln*—to pardons for men who deserted their posts or faced other criminal charges that otherwise could mean the gallows, rarely failing to apply moral justice when it was in his power. (In most cases, he believed deserters to be "leg cases," so called because God had cursed them with cowardly legs that ran from battle.)[78] Pettiness and revenge were beneath him. Although his position on the war meant never acknowledging the legitimacy of the Confederacy, he recognized enemy prisoners as citizens of an independent nation, allowing them to escape execution or long-term imprisonment on charges of treason.[79] Moreover, he never blamed his enemies for their transgressions. As he put it in a letter to a Unionist in Louisiana in the summer of 1862, "I shall do nothing in malice. What I deal with is too vast for malicious dealing." Indeed, as Herndon said later, Lincoln was "a very poor hater."[80]

Lincoln's fortitude in the course of the war was more remarkable given the forces he battled in his own psyche. How did a man whose "melancholy" during periods of his earlier adult life kept him bedridden for weeks on end and drove him to thoughts of suicide endure when circumstances were so unimaginably dark? Joshua Wolf Shenk, whose book *Lincoln's Melancholy* explores the recesses of Lincoln's depressive condition, asserted, "When a depressed person [gets] out of bed, it's usually not with a sudden insight that life is rich and valuable, but out of some creeping sense of duty or instinct for survival. If collapsing is sometimes vital, so is the brute force of will."[81] Hopelessness and despair thus surmounted by a profound sense of purpose, Lincoln was, as he could only have imagined as a boy reading Weems's biography of Washington, able to make his mark on the world. His desire "to impress himself upon [his times] as to link his name with something that would redound to the interest of his fellow man," in the words of his friend Joshua Speed, gave his suffering meaning.[82]

Much meaning would come for Lincoln in putting an end to slavery. The abolitionist movement had been in America since 1683, when four linen weavers of the Germantown Society of Friends in Philadelphia—Derrick Up de graeff, Abraham Up den graef, Gerret Hendricks, and Daniel Pastorious—drafted a clumsily translated protest "against the traffik of men-body." But in spite of the moral high ground taken by this small band of noble Quakers, the former three of whom were among the first thirteen German families to settle in America, their bid to end slavery languished in committee due its sheer "weight."[83] The weight of the issue would continue to derail the efforts of abolitionists for nearly 180 years, as slavery's contribution to America's burgeoning economy presented an overpowering counterpunch. During the summer of 1862, though, things would change as Lincoln began giving serious thought to the institution's abolishment—despite his earlier claims that the war was being fought solely to preserve the union. The war itself, which gave him the power as commander in chief to free the slaves of the conquered enemy, afforded Lincoln an opportunity to eradicate the scourge that had tainted America almost since its colonization.

George Washington in Gilbert Stuart's famous portrait and in an illustration depicting his first inauguration in New York City's lower Manhattan on April 30, 1789. As the nation's first president, Washington saw "clouds and darkness" in the task ahead. A crippling debt and lingering antagonisms with the British were among the burdens he faced. What's more, the success or failure of the new republic and its untested Constitution—and the audacious notion of egalitarian liberty itself—rested largely on his shoulders. Each step he made toward a stable government would set the standard for those who succeeded him. "There is scarcely any part of my conduct which may not hereafter be drawn into precedent," he observed. *Portrait by Gilbert Stuart, courtesy of the U.S. National Archives*

The presidential election of 1800, pitting the Federalist candidate, incumbent President John Adams, against the Republican candidate, incumbent Vice President Thomas Jefferson, marked the formal emergence of two parties in the electoral process. Fears of a dual-party system leading to, in Washington's words, "riot and insurrection" were well founded. Never in world history had a nation seen one party peacefully yield power to another. Though the election was perhaps the most scurrilous in American history, no blood was spilled, signifying that the country and its ideological underpinnings were strong enough to sustain opposing viewpoints. But it fell to Jefferson to unite the country under his Republican leadership. *Portrait of John Adams by Gilbert Stuart, circa 1800–1815, and portrait of Thomas Jefferson by Rembrandt Peale, circa 1805. Courtesy of the National Archives*

Dubbed "His Accidency" by detractors, John Tyler (top) became the first vice president to succeed to the presidency, on April 6, 1841, after the death in office of William Henry Harrison. Given the Constitution's ambiguities, it was a matter of interpretation as to whether Tyler would be president or simply acting president. Official Washington had varying opinions on the matter, but Tyler's own view was clear: Upon Harrison's death, he was the president. His determination to be his own man put him at odds with his own party, the Whigs, led by Kentucky senator Henry Clay, and doomed his presidency. *Courtesy of the U.S. National Archives*

Abraham Lincoln visiting General George B. McClellan in Antietam, Maryland. Lincoln's approach to the Civil War was unyielding: The faster the South was crushed—through soldiers killed, homes and businesses destroyed, and earth scorched—the more lives would be saved by the war's end. He insisted that his commanders fight relentlessly and changed the guard when they didn't. As a result of his steadfastness in preserving the Union, and that of the Confederates in trying to preserve the Southern way, the war was bloody beyond imagination. One out of every five of its soldiers would die from battle or disease. *Photo by Alexander Gardner, courtesy of the U.S. National Archives*

A portrait of Lincoln by Matthew Brady, circa 1863. Lincoln's strength throughout the war was joined with compassion after the South's surrender in April 1865. "With malice toward none, with charity for all," he had said in his second inaugural address a month earlier, "let us strive to finish the work we are in, to bind up the nation's wounds." *Photo by Matthew Brady, courtesy of the U.S. National Archives*

Franklin D. Roosevelt relaxing in Warm Springs, Georgia, in October 1932, two weeks before his election as president. As he took office five months later, the Great Depression, the worst economic calamity ever to befall the nation, was in full throttle. With his manifest optimism and ebullience, Roosevelt would become a much-needed buoy for struggling Americans. *Courtesy of the Franklin D. Roosevelt Library, Hyde Park, New York*

FDR, flanked by members of his cabinet, visits a Civilian Conservation Corporation (CCC) camp in Virginia's Shenandoah Valley, August 1933. Over three million men eighteen to twenty-five enrolled in the CCC, one of many New Deal programs the federal government put in place to alleviate the Depression's suffering in the prodigious first 100 days of Roosevelt's activist administration. "If [a method] fails, admit it freely and try another," Roosevelt asserted. "But above all try something." *Courtesy of the Franklin D. Roosevelt Library, Hyde Park, New York*

Harry S. Truman, in the Oval Office in his first year as president. He took office on April 12, 1945, upon the death of Franklin Roosevelt. As World War II wound down, a number of urgent matters requiring monumental decisions would cross Truman's desk. Many saw him as a little man out of his depth. "We should be less than candid at this grave moment," wrote *The Washington Post*, "if we did not recognize the great disparity between Mr. Truman's experience and the great responsibility that has been thrust upon him." *The White House, courtesy of the Harry S. Truman Library*

The "Big Three"—Winston Churchill, Truman, and Josef Stalin—met in Potsdam, Germany, on July 25, 1945. Stalin's breaches of agreements with the Allied leaders would lead to the beginnings of the cold war as he made clear his designs on expanding the Soviet Union's sphere in Eastern and Central Europe. By March 1946, Churchill would warn, "an iron curtain has descended across the continent." Containment characterized Truman's foreign policy in the face of the threat, setting a resolute tone for America's position in the cold war. *United States Signal Corps, courtesy of the Harry S. Truman Library*

John F. Kennedy in his first presidential press conference, January 25, 1961. While Kennedy's elegant first days in office put him on the right foot to lead the nation, he soon stumbled. In May 1961, three months after taking office, he approved the Bay of Pigs invasion in Cuba. The botched operation emboldened the opportunistic, ambitious Soviet Union, led by Nikita Khrushchev, who saw the president as "not strong enough. Too intelligent and too weak." *Abbie Rowe, White House, John F. Kennedy Presidential Library and Museum, Boston*

Kennedy (far left) conferring with advisers in the Cabinet Room of the White House at the height of the Cuban Missile Crisis, October 27, 1962. Standing firm against the Soviet threat in Cuba without pushing Khrushchev to the brink of nuclear war would become the central trial of Kennedy's presidency—and the darkest hour of the twentieth century's latter half. During the crisis, Kennedy coolly outmaneuvered Khrushchev while he kept his own hawkish military advisers at bay, successfully preserving the peace as the Soviet ships retreated. *Cecil Stoughton, White House, John F. Kennedy Presidential Library and Museum, Boston*

Gerald and Betty Ford bidding good-bye to Richard and Pat Nixon after Nixon's resignation on the morning of August 9, 1974. At noon, Ford became the nation's first unelected president under the provisions of the Twenty-second Amendment. As the country got to know its new president, Nixon's imperial shadow began to recede. A simple image of Ford toasting his own breakfast English muffin on September 5 bore reassuring testimony to the public that he was "just like us." But his pardon of Nixon, granted on September 9 as a means of putting an end to the Watergate saga, saw his approval rating plummet. Though it likely cost him the election of 1976, the public would eventually come around to appreciating Ford's wisdom—and political selflessness—in granting the pardon. *Photo at top, courtesy of the U.S. National Archives; photo at foot by David Hume Kennerly, courtesy of the University of Texas*

Regardless of Lincoln's moral aversion to slavery, its abolition within the context of the war made sense for a variety of political reasons. Principally, it would keep England and France at bay by appealing to the antislavery opinions held by most Europeans, lessening the threat that either nation would come to the aid of the Confederacy. And it would mollify the radicals in his administration and in Congress.[84] In July, he announced to his cabinet his intention to issue an Emancipation Proclamation. "Things had gone from bad to worse [in the war]," he recalled later, "until I felt that we had reached the end of our rope on the plan of operations we had been pursuing; that we had about played our last card, and must change our tactics, or lose the game!"[85] His cabinet advised waiting for a material Union win so that the proclamation didn't look like an act of desperation. Lincoln agreed.

An opening came when McClellan's forces met Lee's along Antietam Creek in Maryland. In the war's bloodiest day, the Union thwarted the Confederacy's northward push, achieving what could be spun as a Union victory—even though McClellan didn't exploit the chance to pursue the enemy as it retreated. Unsure if another win would be forthcoming, Lincoln announced on September 22 that if the Confederate states did not step down by the first day of 1863, he would issue a presidential decree abolishing slavery throughout the Confederacy but allowing it to continue in the Union states and in those areas in the Confederate states held by the Union.[86]

On January 1, 1863, Lincoln made good on his promise, signing the Emancipation Proclamation. The previous month he justified the decree in a message to Congress as a means to save the union: "In giving freedom to the slave, we assure freedom to the free—honorable alike in what we give, and what we preserve. We shall nobly save, or meanly lose, the last, best hope of earth."[87] While Lincoln considered the proclamation an "act of justice," there was no shortage of critics—including members of his cabinet—who felt it didn't go far enough.[88] "The principle is not that a human being cannot own another, but that he cannot own him if he is not loyal to the United States," one newspaper commented, referring to the preservation of slavery in the border states.[89] Lincoln rebutted that while his powers as commander in chief allowed him to legally abolish slavery in enemy territory, doing so in the Union required an act of Congress.

The president's proclamation to end slavery throughout the Confederacy did not, however, mean an end to the war, which dragged on along with Lincoln's continuing troubles with his generals. Fed up with McClellan, who stubbornly stayed put in Maryland rather than give chase to Lee's forces in Virginia, Lincoln sent the general packing, replacing him with Ambrose Burnside. After a humiliating defeat in December against Lee in Vicksburg, Virginia, in which Union troops far outnumbered their Confederate counterparts, Lincoln replaced Burnside in January with Joseph Hooker. In late June, Hooker, also not aggressive enough in the eyes of his commander in chief, was fired in favor of George Meade. Meade, on the same measure, would also soon lose the command.

After his victories in Virginia, Lee led his entire Army of Northern Virginia into southern Pennsylvania, to the small, quiet town of Gettysburg. There, on the first day of July, his forces met Meade's in the definitive confrontation of the war. In three days of fierce battle under a blazing summer sun, Meade's army fended off Confederate attacks, taking out a third of Lee's troops. By the battle's end, twenty-eight thousand Confederate and twenty-three thousand Union soldiers were dead, wounded, or missing.[90] Lee retreated back to Virginia on July 4, thwarted in his progress by the flooded Potomac River as Lincoln's order to pursue Lee and destroy the remnants of his army went unheeded by the cautious Meade. Meade missed his chance when the waters of the Potomac receded and Lee escaped, keeping the remainder of his troops intact, and, in Lincoln's view, prolonging the war "indefinitely."[91] Again, Lincoln was disappointed in the timidity of yet another Army of the Potomac commander. But the war, for the first time, seemed in the Union's grasp.

On November 19, Lincoln traveled to Gettysburg to help dedicate a national cemetery on the battlefield where more than five thousand soldiers—blue and gray—met their last hours. The president was slated to offer remarks along with an orator of greater renown, Edward Everett, whose speech preceding Lincoln's consumed the better part of two hours. Lincoln followed Everett's verbosity with disarming brevity, giving an address of a mere 266 words, which would become among the most hallowed in American history.

*Fourscore and seven years ago our fathers brought forth upon this continent a new nation, conceived in liberty and dedicated to the proposition that all men are created equal. Now we are engaged in a great civil war, testing whether that nation or any nation so conceived and so dedicated can long endure. We are met on a great battlefield of that war. We have come to dedicate a portion of that field as a final resting-place for those who here gave their lives that that nation might live. It is altogether fitting and proper that we should do this.*

*But in a larger sense, we cannot dedicate, we cannot consecrate, we cannot hallow this ground. The brave men, living and dead, who struggled here have consecrated it far above our poor power to add or detract. The world will little note nor long remember what we say here, but it can never forget what they did here.*

*It is for the living rather to be dedicated here to the unfinished work which they who fought here have thus far so nobly advanced. It is rather for us to be here dedicated to the great task remaining before us—that from these honored dead we take increased devotion to that cause for which they gave the last full measure of devotion—that we here highly resolve that these dead shall not have died in vain, that this nation under God shall have a new birth of freedom, and that government of the people, by the people, for the people shall not perish from the earth.*

The day after the dedication, Everett wrote Lincoln, "I shall be glad if I could flatter myself that I came as near to the central idea of the occasion in two hours as you did in two minutes."[92]

November brought more good news from Grant, whose advance on Confederate troops in Chattanooga resulted in claiming Tennessee for the Union. This after he had led forces to take Vicksburg, Mississippi, in a pivotal victory that effectively cut the Confederacy in two parts, east and west. In Grant, Lincoln had found a general who would "take re-sponsibility and act." He could be counted on to fight skillfully and un-hesitatingly, vanquishing the enemy without being squeamish about the toll it would exact.[93] By April 1964, at age forty-two, he would gain com-mand of the Union armies and earn the title of lieutenant general, the first to hold the rank since George Washington.

Grant had come a long way in a few short years. Before the war, the former West Pointer had fallen on hard times. In the late 1850s he had been forced to resign from the army due to his excessive drinking while serving on frontier posts on the West Coast, losing himself in a bottle as he pined away for his family back home in Ohio. Stripped of his commis-sion, he returned to his native Midwest to a series of failed business ven-tures and menial jobs—a peddler of firewood, a rent collector, and finally a clerk at his brother's leather goods store in Galena, Illinois—before answering Lincoln's call for volunteers at the war's outset in 1861. In less than five years, he had gone from being a derelict former officer to the hero of the Union army. The war was like that. It transformed lives just as it ended them: losers became winners, rich men were now poor, brides became widows, and enslaved men and women gained freedom. Few would be the same afterward. "The contest touches everything and leaves nothing as it found it," wrote the *New York Times*.[94]

As the election of 1864 neared, Lincoln's nomination by his party was by no means assured. Republican Party radicals searched for alterna-tives to "the Rail-Splitter." Grant was one possibility, but the general flatly dismissed the notion. It was "as important for the [Union] cause that [Lincoln] should be elected," he said adamantly, "as that the army should be successful in the field."[95] Salmon Chase, who had resigned his post as Lincoln's secretary of the treasury in the summer of 1864, emerged as Lincoln's biggest threat. Chase and Lincoln had struck up an effective but often strained working relationship, with Chase self-righteously sub-mitting his resignation twice due to Lincoln's political interference on treasury appointments. Exasperated, Lincoln accepted his third. Chase had his own frustrations with Lincoln. He saw the president's stance on slavery the same way Lincoln viewed many of his commanders, believing Lincoln to be too slow, too cautious. When Supreme Court chief justice Roger Taney, shriveled and antiquated, died at eighty-seven, Chase was the logical choice as his successor. Lincoln thought about nominating him for the post on the condition that he surrender his presidential ambitions until he realized that exacting the promise could be used by his enemies as evidence of his abuse of executive power.[96] Instead, Lincoln cannily waited until after the presidential election to nominate Chase to head the Court.

At the party's Baltimore convention in June, Lincoln clinched the nomination as Andrew Johnson, the military-appointed Democratic governor of Tennessee, was named to replace Hannibal Hamlin as his running mate. But not all Republicans rallied around the ticket. Just a week earlier, a group of renegade Republicans held their own convention in Cleveland, nominating John Frémont as their standard-bearer. Frémont, the "Pathfinder," had earned national fame as an army commander leading expedition parties in parts of Oregon and California through much of the 1840s. Though their parties' platforms differed, both conventions included a commitment to support a Thirteenth Amendment to the Constitution abolishing slavery.

Meanwhile, the Democrats nominated as their presidential candidate George McClellan, who had resurfaced to once again become a burden to Lincoln. The Democratic platform called for a negotiated peace with the South, a compelling proposition to Northerners as the war dragged on, and McClellan became an early favorite to carry the election.

Even Lincoln had doubts that he would prevail. In fact, he thought it "exceedingly probable" that he would be passed over in favor of McClellan.[97] Others agreed. Before the election, Horace Greeley, editor of the *New York Tribune,* believed Lincoln to be "already beaten."[98] American voters weren't in the habit of reelecting presidents; that hadn't occurred since Andrew Jackson's reelection in 1828. But, as always, Lincoln's honor rose above political pettiness. In preparation for his own defeat and in the hope of a smooth transition, he drafted a letter for McClellan, though he thought it highly unlikely that his former general, who had disdained Lincoln since the war, would pay it any mind.

"General," he wrote, "the election has demonstrated that you are stronger, have more influence with the American people than I. Now let us together, you with your influence and I with all the executive power of the Government, try to save the country."[99] He asked all the members of his cabinet to sign it along with him.

Progress in the war, however, altered Lincoln's fate. On September 2, General William T. Sherman, who had fought with the ferocity of Grant, took Atlanta for the Union, leaving much of the city, and the state of Georgia, in flames. The end of the war was in sight, and so too was another term for Lincoln as Frémont dropped out of the race and McClellan backpedaled on a negotiated settlement. The Republicans took no chances, introducing the absentee ballot for military personnel, banking on the hope that the troops would cast their votes for their commander in chief so as not to see their efforts in vain. On November 8, Lincoln glided to a smooth victory, with the electorate yielding to the Republican slogan, "Don't swap horses in the middle of the stream." The president won 55 percent of the popular vote, and a lopsided 212 electoral votes to McClellan's 21. Though McClellan had been a popular general with his troops, Lincoln took nearly 90 percent of the military vote.

After Lincoln's reelection, the Union armies continued to make progress. Sherman turned his troops northward, where they marched on the Carolinas, leaving scorched earth in their path much as they had in Georgia, coming closer to Lee's forces in Petersburg, Virginia. As the war played out its last gasps, slavery drew its last breath. On January 31, 1865, the House of Representatives met to vote on the proposed Thirteenth Amendment. The amendment had passed in the Senate the previous April but had failed to secure the two-thirds vote needed in the House. Anticipating a close vote, Lincoln prevailed on Congressman James Ashley of Ohio to do some horse trading with congressmen whose votes were in doubt. The amendment passed with only three ballots to spare, inspiring a thunderous reception in the crowded House chamber and a one-hundred-gun salute outside the Capitol.

Four years after his first inauguration, in which he expressed to the country his hope of preventing war, Lincoln, on March 4, 1865, offered words in his second inaugural address in anticipation of its long-awaited end:

> With malice toward none, with charity for all, with firmness in the right as God gives us to see the right, let us strive on to finish the work we are in, to bind up the nation's wounds, to care for him who shall have borne the battle and for his widow and orphan, to do all which may achieve and cherish a just and lasting peace among ourselves and with all nations.

By spring, the last hope for the Southern cause began to fade as Union troops from all sides began surrounding Lee's forces in Petersburg, choking off supplies of food and ammunition. Believing it would do his commander in chief good to get away from the pressures of Washington and to see the progress the Union was making, Grant invited Lincoln to army headquarters in City Point, Virginia, as the war was in its final stages. Just a week earlier, Lincoln had held a cabinet meeting from his bed, so ravaged physically from the toll of the war that he was unable to get up.[100] He readily accepted Grant's invitation, leaving on March 23 aboard the steamship *River Queen,* which served as floating war headquarters for Grant, accompanied by Mary Lincoln, Tad, a maid, and two bodyguards.[101]

As the boat worked its way down the Potomac with the president on board, Lee sent word to Confederate President Jefferson Davis that he should abandon Richmond, the seat of the Confederacy, which was about to be captured by Union soldiers. A day after Union troops took Richmond on April 3, Lincoln and a small party made their way unannounced to the city. Without ceremony or fanfare, Lincoln discharged the boat and walked slowly through the dusty, devastated streets of Richmond, flanked by a dozen sailors who acted as bodyguards. A small band of African-American workmen spotted him. "Bless the Lord, there is the great Messiah! Glory, Hallelujah," exclaimed its leader, a man of sixty-some years, who threw aside his shovel and rushed toward Lincoln. Joined by others, he fell to his knees and tried to kiss Lincoln's feet. "This is not right," Lincoln said. "You must kneel to God only, and thank him for your freedom." As word spread of Lincoln's appearance, hordes of other former slaves, now emancipated, descended on him, some shouting with joy, "Bless the Lord, Father Abraham come," others silent and rapt, as former Confederates watched impassively from their windows.[102]

The following day, the president and his family made their way back to Washington on the *River Queen*, leaving the captured Confederate capital in its wake. "Do not allow [Jefferson Davis] to escape the law," Mary Lincoln reminded her husband of the Confederate president, now a fugitive. "He must be hanged!" "Judge not, that ye not be judged" came his quiet reply.[103] That sentiment was reflected in his policy, which he had articulated in a meeting with his commanders, Grant, Sherman, and Admiral David Porter, on board the *River Queen* during the journey. Simply put, Lincoln's order regarding the vanquished enemy was, "Let 'em up easy." There would be no retribution or reprisals; that was not Lincoln's way. Rather, with all due speed, he wanted the Confederate army disbanded and soldiers back on their fields and in their shops, and with civil governments reestablished in the Southern states. As much as possible, he wished the reunited country to get beyond the war and to establish sure footing for its future. He gave Grant and Sherman leeway to negotiate with the enemy on those terms, while expecting that all considerations requiring political nuance—including the readmission of the Southern states into the union and the restoration of civil and political rights—would be turned over to him.[104] Sherman, who had met Lincoln only once before, in 1861, and had thought him to be a hack politician out of his depth, came away from the meeting with a very different impression of his commander in chief. "Of all the men I have ever met," he wrote later, "he seemed to possess more of the elements of greatness and goodness than any other."[105]

Upon arriving back in Washington on April 9, Lincoln got word of a telegram received by Secretary of War Gideon Welles from Grant. "General Lee surrendered the Army of Northern Virginia this morning on terms proposed by myself," Grant wrote. "The accompanying additional correspondence will show the conditions fully."[106] Earlier in the day, Grant had met Lee at the home of William McLean, on the edge of Appomattox village, ninety-five miles west of Richmond. Lee was impeccably attired in his gray general's uniform, while Grant arrived in muddy boots and a borrowed private's uniform adorned with three stars to mark his rank.[107] Grant apologized to the silver-haired Lee, who at fifty-eight was fifteen years Grant's senior, allowing that he had come directly from the battlefield and hadn't had a chance to change his clothes.[108] They talked briefly about their experiences in the Mexican War years earlier, before Grant, acting on Lincoln's instructions, offered Lee the Union's generous terms of surrender. Confederate officers would be paroled and free to go home, able to keep their sidearms and horses, which many would now need to plow the fields of their farms.[109] "This will have the best possible effect upon [my] men," said Lee as he signed his name to the terms Grant had written out in pencil. After hearing that Lee's soldiers were hungry, Grant ordered that they be given rations, and later sent out a directive among his own troops forbidding any demonstrations of jubilance in the Union victory.[110]

But the sound of celebration over the war's end could be heard in impromptu celebrations in cities, towns, and hamlets throughout the North. The diary entry of Caroline Cowles Richards, a twenty-three-year-old resident of Canandaigua, a farming village in New York State's Finger Lakes region, captures the elation felt by Americans as they heard the news. "Lee has surrendered! and all the people seem crazy in consequence. The [church] bells are ringing, boys and girls, men and women are running through the streets wild with excitement; the flags are all flying, one from the top of our church, and such a 'hurrah boys' generally, I never dreamed of. . . . No school to-day. . . . Every man has a bell or a horn, and every girl a flag and a little bell, and every one is tied with red, white and blue ribbons."[111]

At the White House, Tad appeared at an upstairs window where his father often greeted the public, waving a captured Confederate flag to a mass of celebrants teeming on the front lawn below. Too tired to make a formal speech, Lincoln addressed the crowd extemporaneously.[112] "Finding themselves at home," he said of the fallen states of the South, "it would be utterly immaterial whether they had ever been abroad. Let us all join in doing all the acts necessary to restoring the proper, practical relations between these states and the union."[113]

April 14, 1865—Good Friday—began much as any day in Lincoln's White House. The president awoke early, had a light breakfast with his wife, Tad, and Robert, who had graduated from Harvard and now served as an army officer under Grant, an apprenticeship of sorts arranged by his father. Afterward, he met with some of the callers who were beginning to fill up the reception rooms. At 11:00 A.M., he convened his cabinet and Grant, who had arrived the previous day from Virginia. The primary subject was bringing the Southern people back into the union. Lincoln felt strongly that there be "no bloody work" in picking up the pieces after the war, no vengeance. Too much blood had been spilled already. More than 600,000 Americans had been lost in the war—360,000 in the North; 260,000 in the South. It was time to move on.[114]

Gaunt and thirty pounds underweight, Lincoln had only an apple for lunch before returning to his office to see to the day's business. He signed a pardon for a young soldier who was sentenced to death for desertion, opining, "He will do us more good above the ground than below it." When a weary former slave appeared at the White House gates asking to see the president regarding a stop in her husband's Union army pay, she was turned away crying before Lincoln himself appeared at the front portico and motioned her in. Lincoln saw to it that her husband's pay would be issued the following day before sending her away with a bow.[115]

At 4:00 P.M. he treated himself to a quiet carriage ride through Washington with Mrs. Lincoln, who was taken aback by his cheerfulness. "And well I may feel so, Mary," he told her. "I consider *this day*, the war, has come to a close." As they enjoyed the warm spring weather, he allowed himself to anticipate happiness and serenity ahead. "We both must be more cheerful in the future," he said. "Between the war and the loss of our darling Willie, we have both been very miserable."[116] But when he arrived back at the White House and walked to the War Department with his bodyguard, James Crook, a more somber thought surfaced. "Crook," he said as they passed a group of drunken men, "do you know I believe there are men who want to take my life? And I have no doubt they will do it. . . . I know no one could do it and escape alive. But if it is to be done, there is no way to prevent it."[117]

That evening the Lincolns went to Ford's Theatre accompanied by Major Henry Rathbone and Clara Harris—the stepson and daughter of Ira Harris, senator from New York—for its presentation of *Our American Cousin,* an insipid comedy of little note about an American country girl who goes to England to claim an inheritance from a wealthy relative. In the third act, John Wilkes Booth, a Southern sympathizer and tragedian actor of some repute, entered the president's box armed with a pistol in one hand and a large hunting knife in the other. He pointed the gun at the back of Lincoln's head and pulled the trigger as the president jolted forward, a fifty-caliber bullet now lodged just off his right eye.[118] Rathbone tried to apprehend Booth and was met with his knife, which slashed his arm with its seven-inch blade. Booth then leaped from the box onto the stage, breaking his shinbone as he fell. He waved his knife at the audience and, in an actor's melodramatic tone, shouted the motto of the state of Virginia—*"Sic semper tyrannis,"* thus always to tyrants. Confusion among the crowd was quickly followed by chaos as cries that the president had been shot filled the theater.

In the ensuing hours, the nation would learn more about the deranged twenty-six-year-old Booth, who had led a conspiracy to kill not only Lincoln but also Vice President Andrew Johnson and all of Lincoln's cabinet. Ultimately, aside from Lincoln, only Seward was targeted. Seward, in bed recovering from a carriage accident, was brutally stabbed by one of Booth's accomplices who had forced his way into the secretary of state's home. Though he was severely wounded, Seward would survive the attack. Booth, who fled Washington into the northern Virginia countryside on horseback, lasted twelve days before members of the Sixteenth New York Cavalry killed him in a standoff at a farm near Bowling Green.

Unconscious and breathing erratically, Lincoln was carried by soldiers across the street from the theater to the small home of a tailor, William Petersen, where he was taken to a back room, stripped of his clothes, and laid diagonally across the bed, which was not long enough to contain his massive frame. Cabinet members and congressmen jammed the room as doctors tended to Lincoln, though there was little to do but make him comfortable. Mrs. Lincoln sat beside her fallen husband "kissing him and calling him every endearing name," according to one witness, before being led away to a front room sobbing as his breathing began to fade further.[119]

The magnificent spring weather of the previous day had given way to a cold rain, which began falling on Washington at dawn on the 15th. At 7:22 A.M., Lincoln's heart ceased to beat. Coins were applied to the lids of his eyes, and a white sheet was drawn over his head, before word went forth that the president was gone.

A tree is best measured when it's down.[120] So it was with Lincoln. "No one who personally knew him but will now feel that the deep, furrowed sadness of his face seemed to forecast his fate," wrote *Harper's Weekly* just after his death. "It is small consolation that he died at the moment in the war when he could best be spared, for no nation is ready for the loss of such a friend. But it is something to remember that he lived to see the slow day breaking."[121] Over the years, regard for Lincoln has only grown. In a joint session of Congress after the publication of his biography of Lincoln in 1954, American Poet Laureate Carl Sandburg bore testimony to the sixteenth president's greatness. "Not often in the story of mankind," he said, "does a man arrive on earth who is both steel and velvet, who is both as hard as rock and soft as drifting fog, who holds in his heart and mind the paradox of terrible storm and peace unspeakable and perfect."[122]

The Lincoln Memorial, which stands at the base of the Mall in Washington, is a temple of sorts, with a statue of Lincoln at its center, his hands resting on the arms of his chair—one clenched in strength, the other open and outstretched empathetically—his wise, steady gaze toward the gleaming white Capitol dome in the distance. Over the years it has become a place where Americans go emblematically to seek inspiration, justice, unity. In the 1939 Frank Capra movie *Mr. Smith Goes to Washington,* Jimmy Stewart's title character, a naïve freshman congressman, goes there after he has been framed by corrupt House peers to reaffirm American ideals and prepare to defend himself against those who would betray them. The same year, Marian Anderson, the African-American concert singer, sang angelically on its steps on Easter Sunday after she was denied permission to perform at Washington's Constitution Hall because of her color. And it was there that Martin Luther King Jr. shared his dream for racial harmony almost a quarter of a century later. Even Richard Nixon left the insular confines of the White House in the wee hours of a restless night during the Vietnam War to reach out to student protesters who had congregated there—though he ended up talking to them awkwardly about football. If George Washington stands God-like at the head of the presidential pantheon as America's chief creator, Lincoln is beside him as its Christlike savior.

Iconic ubiquity comes with the territory. Twenty-first-century incarnations of "Honest Abe" abound, from doppelgängers at used-car dealerships on Presidents Day to ads serving up a sleep remedy that have the sixteenth president palling around with a talking beaver. Lincoln would have been amused by that. Just as his melancholic mind would have brightened at the knowledge that the nation he rescued in the face of blistering adversity a century and a half ago stands today—despite outsized imperfections—as the envy of the world.

# V

# FRANKLIN D. ROOSEVELT

## *Nothing to Fear*

On March 8, 1933, his third full day in office, President Franklin Delano Roosevelt bucked social tradition and left the White House to call on an august local resident of advanced years at his home on I Street. There, Oliver Wendell Holmes, retired U.S. Supreme Court justice who had served on the high court for nearly thirty years, was celebrating his ninety-second birthday with two of his former secretaries. Holmes was lucky to have survived past early adulthood. At twenty, he had left Harvard University after graduation to heed Abraham Lincoln's call for seventy-five thousand volunteers after the first shots were fired at Fort Sumter, marking the beginning of the Civil War. During his three years with the Twentieth Massachusetts Volunteers, the "Harvard Regiment" as they were known, he had been seriously wounded in battle three times. Holmes and the new president, a fellow Harvard alumnus forty-one years his junior, chatted amiably during their brief visit before Roosevelt asked the old judge if he had any advice for him in the colossal job he had taken on. Holmes harkened back to his days in the war long gone. "No, Mr. President," he replied. "The time I was in retreat, the army was in retreat in disaster, the thing to do was stop the retreat, blow your trumpet, [and] have them give the order to charge. And that is what you are doing."[1]

The Civil War was the only domestic crisis America had faced greater than the one that now confronted Roosevelt. Four days earlier, the newly inaugurated president sounded his trumpet, and his administration had been charging ever since. On March 4, he had taken office as the Great Depression, the worst economic calamity ever to befall the nation, was in full throttle. The United States had weathered various kinds of economic slumps before, but never had a downturn taken hold with such fury. "Now is the winter of our discontent the chilliest," wrote the editor of *Nation's Business*. "Fear bordering on panic, loss of faith in everything, our fellow man, our institutions, private and government. Worst of all, no faith in ourselves, or the future. Almost everything ready to scuttle the ship, and not even women and children first."[2]

Since the stock market's precipitous crash on October 29, 1929, the country's gross national product had tumbled by half, with world grain prices at a three-hundred-year low. More than ten thousand banks had folded since the Depression began, with thousands of businesses, unable to secure loans and credit, closing their doors in their wake. Twelve million people, a quarter of the workforce, were unemployed according to government statistics, though the actual number could have been twice that high. In Toledo, Ohio, unemployment stood at 80 percent. Other industrial cities suffered similar levels of joblessness. The farm states throughout the Great Plains were just as devastated, the soil dried up and useless from sustained drought, causing a migration of inhabitants westward for the idle promise of something better. Homelessness, despair, and misery suffused the nation, with few invulnerable to a turn of fate as conditions worsened. In the summer of 1932, when the economist John Maynard Keynes was asked if anything in history compared to the Great Depression, he answered, "Yes, it was called the Dark Ages, and it lasted for four hundred years."[3] As Roosevelt would later put it in a Fireside Chat, "the country was dying by inches."

In June 1932, as he accepted his party's nomination at the Democratic National Convention at in Chicago, Roosevelt had promised the country a "new deal for the American people." He gave few specifics, but even in the abstract, it was a welcome alternative to the raw deal most Americans believed they had gotten with Roosevelt's predecessor, Herbert Hoover. Hoover had ridden out much of the Depression thinking the worst had passed, disinclined to use the government to mitigate its ills to the extent that he could have, fearing that doing so would trample on core American values of individualism and self-reliance.[4] "Partial regimentation cannot be made to work," he held, "and still maintain live democratic institutions."[5] As the plight worsened, Hoover became a scapegoat, a symbol of passivity and indifference.

His fate was sealed in June of 1932, when the Bonus Army, a group of twenty thousand military veterans and members of their families, encamped in Washington to demand bonuses earmarked for 1945. Hoover ordered the Bonus Army camps evacuated, mobilizing the army under Douglas MacArthur to clear them out. MacArthur had their camps burned, leading to riots that killed two veterans. Roosevelt was disgusted at Hoover's handling of the situation, maintaining, "There was nothing left inside [Hoover] but jelly. Maybe there never had been anything."[6] Most of the country shared Roosevelt's outrage at Hoover, and a hint of anarchy lingered in the air. Arthur M. Schlesinger Jr. observed that more than seventy years after the fact most people "have forgotten how close we were to revolution in the days before FDR."[7] Indeed, for the first time since the Civil War, heavily armed military guards stood in front of all the major public buildings on the day of Roosevelt's inauguration.[8]

Roosevelt's inaugural oration, given with measured self-assurance in a booming voice that pointedly defied the circumstances, charted a new course.

*This is preeminently the time to speak the truth, the whole truth, frankly and boldly. Nor need we shrink from honestly facing conditions in our country today. This great nation will endure as it has endured, will revive and will prosper. So, first of all, let me assert myself in my firm belief that the only thing we have to fear is fear itself—nameless, unreasoning, unjustified terror which paralyzes needed efforts to convert retreat into advance. In every dark hour of our national life a leadership of frankness and vigor has met with that understanding and support of the people themselves which is essential to victory. I am convinced that you will again give that support to leadership in these critical days.*

*We do not distrust the future of essential democracy. The people of the United States have not failed. In their need they have registered a mandate that they will want direct, vigorous action. They have asked for discipline and direction under leadership. They have made me the present instrument of their wishes. In the spirit of the gift I take it.*

His words were imbibed by many desperate Americans as a tonic. The collective relief of most of the nearly one hundred thousand souls who crowded around the steps at the northeast end of the Capitol to witness Roosevelt's ascendance was palpable. Some wept openly.[9] What's more, Roosevelt's words were backed up by action as the wheels of the president's New Deal started turning almost at once.

The first "Hundred Days" of Roosevelt's administration began with immediate measures to alleviate the banking crisis that had escalated in recent weeks. Within eight hours of a special session of Congress, the Emergency Banking Act was passed on a voice vote based on a plan Roosevelt had scribbled on a napkin.[10] It was signed the same evening by the new president. Given the fiscal complexities of the plan, it was a good bet many of the congressmen giving a yea vote didn't understand it fully, but urgency was the order of the day given Roosevelt's mandate. The act entailed a federally instituted three-day bank holiday during which each institution was evaluated to ensure its solvency. Those that passed muster could reopen their doors; the others would remain closed.[11] It also included a temporary suspension of the gold standard and gave the government the power to demand that gold be sold to the government at $20.67 an ounce while making the importation of gold illegal. Within a month, 70 percent of U.S. banks were back in business, with deposits amounting to $31 billion.[12] The creation of the Federal Deposit Insurance Corporation, protecting private bank deposits, would follow later in the year.

On March 12, just over a week after taking office, Roosevelt revived a practice he had begun as New York governor, giving his first radio Fireside Chat, so called because Roosevelt gave them as though he were talking to a few people at home in front of the fireplace.[13] In plain language, he explained the measures the administration was taking toward stabilizing the banks, before turning to a recurrent theme. "There is an element in the readjustment of our financial system more important than currency, more important than gold, and that is the confidence of the people," he said. "Confidence and courage are the essentials of success in carrying out our plan. You people must have faith; you must not be stampeded by rumor or guesses. Let us unite in banishing fear. We have provided the machinery to restore our financial system; it is up to you to support and make it work. It is your problem no less than it is mine. Together we cannot fail." We're all in this together, he was saying, it's up to everyone to do his or her part—even if it's just having a little faith.

Regular communication became one of the hallmarks of the administration. By talking often to the American people—he would give thirty-one Fireside Chats during his tenure—Roosevelt would become a household voice in the living rooms across the country, offering updates on the affairs of state while raising confidence and prevailing on citizens to help where they could. Ronald Reagan, who cast his first vote for Roosevelt, followed by three more, wrote in his memoirs, "During his Fireside Chats, [Roosevelt's] strong, gentle, confident voice resonated across the nation with an eloquence that brought comfort and resilience to a nation caught up in a storm and reassured us that we could lick any problem. I will never forget him for that."[14]

Roosevelt also dominated the headlines and became his own public relations director by talking regularly to the news media, holding his first press conference two days after taking office, and thereafter meeting with journalists about twice a week. In his first term, he held five times the number Hoover had staged in his entire term in office.[15] About two hundred reporters, all men, would crowd around FDR's desk in the Oval

Office and shoot questions at the charismatic man in charge behind it. Though the sessions had an informal air about them—the previous practice of having questions submitted in advance had been scrapped—the White House kept tight control over the resulting material. Follow-up questions, or "cross-examinations" as Roosevelt called them, were verboten, and direct quotes from the president required White House approval.[16] Still, the shrewd and charming president gave "the boys" the impression that they were getting what they wanted. "I never met anyone who showed greater capacity for avoiding a direct answer while giving the questioner a feeling that he had been answered," the author John Gunther recalled.[17] By working the press effectively, Roosevelt was able to offset the anti–New Deal biases held by many wealthy newspaper owners and publishers.[18]

After getting the banks back on track, the administration addressed other crises. The remaining hundred days saw a virtual alphabet soup of remedies cooked up by FDR and his Brain Trust of advisers, almost all of which sailed through an obliging Congress with the rapidity of machine-gun fire. The Civilian Conservation Corps (CCC) was aimed at putting young men eighteen to twenty-five back to work, mobilizing them to rural areas to work on conservation projects like reforestation, for which they were paid $1 a day. More than three million men would enroll in the program, sending most of their earnings back to their families for relief.[19] Farmers were subsidized through the Agricultural Adjustment Administration (AAA), which paid them to limit the harvest of agricultural products as a means of preventing price deflation due to overproduction. Though the plan drew criticism for destroying produce and livestock when so many in the country were going hungry, it was successful in boosting the income of the nation's farmers and helping them to stave off debt.

The Federal Emergency Relief Act (FERA) allocated $500 million for the immediate relief of those most in need, marking the beginning of the welfare system. And the Tennessee Valley Authority (TVA) provided cheap hydroelectric power along the Tennessee Valley River basin, which flowed through seven states and some of the most impoverished parts of the country, improving the basic necessities of its inhabitants while creating jobs. The TVA also included reforestation of the area, and the creation of dams and recreational lands, while offering farmers fertilizer and better methods to increase crop yields. The idea, in Roosevelt's words, was to create "a corporation clothed with the power of government but possessed of the flexibility and initiative of a private enterprise."[20]

The prodigious first hundred days ended climactically with the passage of a centerpiece of the New Deal—and one of its most controversial programs. The National Industrial Recovery Act (NIRA), which the president called "the most important and far-reaching [act] ever enacted by Congress," was created as a means of revitalizing and reforming private industry. NIRA would spawn two new agencies: the National Recovery Administration (NRA) and the Public Works Administration (PWA). In exchange for abiding by the NRA's guidelines on limited working hours, minimum wages, and safe working conditions, businesses received government subsidies. It also encouraged collective bargaining power for unions. In his third Fireside Chat, just after the flurry of legislation in his first hundred days had ended, Roosevelt explained the act this way: "If all employers in each competitive group agree to pay their workers the same wages—reasonable wages—and require the same hours—reasonable hours—then higher wages and shorter hours will hurt no employer. Moreover, such action is better for the employer than unemployment and low wages, because it makes more buyers for his product. That is the simple idea which is the very heart of the Industrial Recovery Act."

The NRA went further in establishing a code system designed to promote fair competition in every industry, backed up by law and exempt from antitrust provisions.[21] Participation in the program became a movement of sorts. Demonstrations and parades were held to rally the cause as businesses adhering to its provisions displayed a banner graced by a blue eagle, which amounted to a government endorsement. The idea was that the NRA would be a catalyst for self-regulation among private enterprise.[22]

But the program ran into a snag two years later, when the Supreme Court—immune to Roosevelt's influence and electoral mandate, and soon to become the bane of his administration—ruled it to be unconstitutional, thus dismantling FDR's most ambitious New Deal initiative.

The PWA drew less controversy. Its purpose was to develop large-scale public works programs that would prime the economy by creating jobs and spurring orders for building materials from private industry. Soon, fueled by a $3 billion budget, projects like the construction of Miami's Orange Bowl and San Francisco's Golden Gate Bridge were breaking ground.

In just over three months, FDR's seminal New Deal initiatives—the "bloodless revolution," as Secretary of the Interior Harold Ickes called it—had not only addressed the crisis at hand but also transformed the federal government into an activist body, irrevocably increasing its role in American life. Critics would call it socialism; Roosevelt, no ideologue, saw it as pragmatism. Ultimately, it would strengthen liberty itself.

After Roosevelt's visit to Justice Holmes on March 8, Holmes reflected on the new president with his former secretaries. "You know," he said, "I have not seen Frank Roosevelt for years, but this ordeal of his with polio, also the governorship [of New York], and the presidency, have made his face much stronger than it was when I knew him."[23] Yes, Roosevelt *had* changed. He *was* stronger, and not just his face. In fact, he had been transformed in ways he himself could not have imagined just after the "ordeal" robbed him of his mobility and confined him largely to a wheelchair. The fact that he had ascended to the presidency was a testament to a relentless spirit that now buoyed the nation. But as would be the case with the United States in the grips of Depression, his ordeal was a dark night that led to a new day.

Roosevelt was born into patrician East Coast privilege at the family's estate at Hyde Park on the banks of the Hudson River on January 30, 1882. An only child, he was the center of his parents' world—and this was especially true of his doting mother. The former Sara Delano was the second wife of James Roosevelt, twenty-six years her senior, a lawyer who spent much of his time as a financier. They wed in 1880. Though the family was not as well-heeled as another prominent New York family, the Vanderbilts, the Roosevelts were Old World enough to consider the Vanderbilts to be "nouveau riche" and to turn down their social invitations for fear that they would have to be reciprocated.[24]

Growing up, Franklin made extended trips to Europe with his parents, learning French and German, before attending prep school at Groton, where a classmate described him as "nice, but colorless."[25] In 1900, the year of his father's death, he enrolled in James's alma mater, Harvard. Leaving home, though, did not mean leaving his widowed mother, who took up residence in Cambridge to attend to him. A middling student and mediocre athlete, Roosevelt found distinction as the editor of the *Crimson* but little else.

While in college, he began a courtship with his fifth cousin once removed, Eleanor, who hailed from the Oyster Bay, Long Island, Roosevelts. In spite of his mother's objections—or because of them—Roosevelt pursued the romance. Unlike her handsome suitor, Eleanor had not enjoyed a nurtured upbringing. Born in 1884, the only child of Kermit Roosevelt and the former Anna Hall, she spent much of her youth off balance and insecure. Her striking mother, who expressed open disappointment that her awkward daughter did not possess the virtue of beauty, was a distant figure in her life.[26] She died in 1892. Two years later, her father, whom she adored, died an alcoholic, failing to live up to the promise of his youth, leaving her an orphan at age ten. Eleanor was brought up by her maternal grandmother, sent to an English boarding school, and often shuttled from one set of relatives to another.

Franklin and Eleanor married in 1905, with the bride given away by her uncle Teddy, the president of the United States. Though no more secure in marriage than she had been earlier in her life, Eleanor dutifully played the role of wife and mother under the watchful and often disapproving eye of her ubiquitous mother-in-law. From 1906 to 1916, she gave birth to six children: Anna; James; Franklin Delano Jr., who died at eight months; Elliott; Franklin D. Jr.; and John. "For ten years, I was always just getting over having one baby or about to have another," she recalled later. "So, my occupations were considerably restricted." The all-consuming duties of motherhood precluded her continuing the volunteer work she had done earlier in a New York settlement house, where she had found some measure of confidence and fulfillment.[27]

As Eleanor Roosevelt was immersed in domestic life, her husband pursued a budding career in politics. From an early age he had seen power up close. When he was five, his father, on business in Washington, took him to see President Grover Cleveland. Beleaguered by his fights with Congress, Cleveland patted young Franklin on the head. "I'm making a strange wish for you, little lad," he said famously. "A wish I suppose no one else would make. I wish for you that you may never be president of the United States." But FDR was hard-wired for politics. It fired his imagination and suited his complex, compartmentalized, and often inscrutable nature. "My husband always found joy in the game of politics," Eleanor Roosevelt said later. "It was to him an interesting game, like chess—something in which you pitted your wits against somebody else's."[28]

Inspiration came from his famous distant cousin, Eleanor's uncle. Cousin Theodore had assumed the presidency at age forty-two, after the assassination of William McKinley in 1901, taking the country by storm with the sheer force of his magnetic personality, and enacting an activist agenda as chief executive that boosted the strength and profile of the office. Though a Democrat, FDR benefited from the Roosevelt brand name and family political connections. Like TR, he made his way up the political ladder starting off in New York politics, where he became a state senator in 1911, before becoming assistant secretary of the navy in 1913—a post also held by TR—where he served the Wilson administration for seven years. In 1920, at age thirty-eight, he secured the party's vice presidential nomination, sharing the ticket with former governor of Ohio James M. Cox. Though the pair went on to defeat in the national election, as Warren Harding rode into the White House with a decisive 64 percent of the popular vote, Roosevelt had established himself as an up-and-comer.

The following year, while spending a vacation at the family's summer home on Campobello Island, off the Canadian province of New Brunswick, Roosevelt contracted polio. After a brisk swim in the frigid waters of the Bay of Fundy, he retired to bed early feeling under the weather. The next morning, he awoke to the horrifying reality that his legs had ceased to function. After bouts of self-pity, he rejected the prognoses that he would never walk again and spent the next several years in rehabilitative treatment to regain the use of his legs. All in vain. Despite the intense physical regimens he endured and his high hopes of reversing the condition's course, he would never again be able to walk without leg braces and the aid of another.[29]

We are, mostly, products of our own hardship; painful episodes and the resulting scars are a part of us in ways that triumph and happiness can never be. Adversity becomes our greatest teacher. By any traditional measure, Roosevelt's polio rendered his political career over. Who had ever heard of a crippled politician? Much of political image was about strength: Washington the brave general on horseback; Lincoln the rail-splitter. Disability was associated with weakness. Roosevelt's immobility alone made running for office not only improbable but oxymoronic. Many of those of means with similar afflictions became invalids, resigned to their fates of sitting on the sidelines in their wheelchairs, watching the world go by in the hands of others. That was not in Roosevelt's nature, or so he and others would discover. He would rise above his disability, allowing it to change him without defeating him.

It changed him physically. His dashing, lithe six-foot frame was transformed. As his legs atrophied, his torso and arms bulged with new strength, and his face expanded as though it had been inflated. It made him more patient. The young man in a hurry, always looking for immediate results, would work on his condition for months on end without any visible improvements. As he later liked to point out, "If you spend two years in bed trying to wiggle your toe, everything else seems easy."[30] It also changed him emotionally. Eleanor Roosevelt, when asked later in a lecture in Akron, Ohio, if polio had affected her husband's state of mind, replied, "Yes, I am glad that question was asked. The answer is, yes.

Anyone who has gone through great suffering is bound to have greater sympathy and understanding of mankind."[31]

Those qualities enabled him to step up to the presidency in 1933. As Ted Morgan explained in his biography *FDR*, "Roosevelt's transformation through debilitating illness was analogous to the situation of the country. In twelve years of Republican rule that just about coincided with the period of his illness and attempted rehabilitation, the country went from health and prosperity to illness and breakdown. His predicament seemed to be a private expression of the state of the nation crippled by depression and unemployment, its motor cells destroyed. Out of the nation's pain would also come renewal, and the making of a more compassionate society."[32]

A new man, a better man, Roosevelt emerged from the political wilderness in 1924, as he appeared before the Democratic National Convention in New York City, to nominate New York governor Al Smith for the presidency. Although former diplomat and U.S. representative from West Virginia John Davis ultimately received the nomination, the ten agonizing steps Roosevelt had taken to the podium on the arm of his son James had brought him back into the political spotlight and party prominence.[33] Four years later, in 1928, supported by Governor Smith, Roosevelt became the party's nominee to succeed him as governor of New York, winning the election narrowly in the fall by twenty-five thousand votes. After winning the favor of the state's electorate through the legislative reforms he initiated, he was reelected by a margin of 725,000 votes two years later.

With his eyes on the presidency throughout his second gubernatorial term, Roosevelt cruised into 1932 an early favorite to gain the party's presidential nomination at its convention in Chicago. His rivals included his former backer, Al Smith, who had been the party's nominee in 1928, and House speaker John Nance Garner of Texas. The Roosevelt camp secured his nomination by offering Garner his number two spot on the ticket and picking up his delegates. Not all agreed, though, that Roosevelt was the best candidate. The columnist Walter Lippmann called him "an amiable Boy Scout" who lacked "any important qualifications for the office."[34] It hardly mattered. Once the Democratic Party had fleshed out its ticket, there was little doubt about who would prevail on Election Day in November. Hoover's acute unpopularity among the American public made his coming defeat all but certain. Roosevelt went on to take 57 percent of the popular vote, and 472 electoral votes to Hoover's 59. Luck was with the president-elect a few weeks before his inaugural when he survived an assassination attempt in Miami. A deranged Italian immigrant, Giuseppe Zangara, fired five shots that killed the mayor of Chicago and wounded four others. Roosevelt left the scene unscathed. His calm under fire won him plaudits for courage and became an early contribution to a budding heroic persona.

The role of hero fit Roosevelt to a tee, particularly in the early days of his administration. In a very short time he not only assumed the presidency but also *became* it like an actor immersing himself in his part, using power as his medium. Indeed, one admiring newsman claimed he was "all the Barrymores rolled into one."[35] The historian Erwin Hargrove wrote, "With his sensitivity to public moods, he was forthright as a leader when crisis was high and sentiment was ripe for heroic leadership. This was the case when he first entered office and embarked on the dramatic legislative leadership of his first hundred days."[36]

After his inaugural oration and the frenzied legislative activity in the initial stages of his administration, he had solidified his image as a champion of the people. They felt that he knew them, that he understood the hard times they were going through. His optimism came through in the jaunty, upward tilt of his head and ivory cigarette holder, his broad smile, and the bubbly tenor of his voice—"the best voice in radio," according to *Fortune* magazine in 1935.[37] "There is nothing either good or bad but thinking makes it so," observed Hamlet. Roosevelt chose to think positively—and to take control, something that the passive Hamlet, a poor example of a crisis manager, failed to do—and his ebullience became a much-needed buoy for the struggling nation.[38] "Meeting him is like opening a bottle of champagne," Winston Churchill would later observe of his jovial friend and ally.[39] Conrad Black wrote of Roosevelt, "He appeared amiable, cunning, well-intentioned but inscrutable, and, when necessary, inspiring. In the magazines, on newsreels, and on the radio, Americans had more exposure to him than to any other leader in their history, and the impact of his personality and persuasive talents were very great."[40] The week after he took office, he received 460,000 letters from the American people and thereafter had to employ a staff of fifty to open and answer the flood of mail that arrived at the White House daily; Hoover had managed with a staff of one.[41]

The press was complicit in helping to shape Roosevelt's image, not so much for how they covered him but by what they didn't cover. Press photographers on the White House beat refrained from photographing the president looking in any way like a cripple. In his dozen years in office, not a single press picture was taken of Roosevelt in a wheelchair, or being carried up stairs, or lifted into a car, all daily realities in his life. If a photographer tried to take a shot that revealed Roosevelt's condition, which happened on rare occasions, he could expect to have it blocked or to have his camera gently pushed to the ground by one of his peers. Nor was there any account of the routines around Roosevelt's handicap by the reporters covering the president. A code of silence was observed by everyone around him. Consequently, although the public knew of his polio, the extent of his disability was a well-kept secret.[42]

Not everyone saw Roosevelt as a hero. He was not without a whack of critics who derided him for a lack of political principles. As it happened, he had castigated Hoover in the campaign of 1932 for his profligate federal spending, making promises to the electorate to balance the federal budget. One couldn't blame Hoover for retorting that Roosevelt was a "chameleon on plaid," particularly as Roosevelt would later ask Congress to appropriate massive sums to relieve unemployment, leaving the federal budget awash in red ink.[43] Others offered harsher condemnation. The political commentator H. L. Mencken said of Roosevelt, "If he became convinced tomorrow that coming out for cannibalism would get him the votes he so sorely needs, he would begin fattening a missionary in the White House backyard come Wednesday."[44] Many conservatives could barely utter his name, using the phrase "that man" instead, the wealthier among them further cursing him as a "traitor to his class."[45]

Few of his staunchest critics would be won over during his Depression reign.

In fairness, Roosevelt, who believed in a balanced budget, may have intended to do so when he made his campaign promise. The New Deal was hardly premeditated; no rigid plan was in place when he took the helm. The historian Wilson Sullivan described it as "less a carefully formulated stage-by-stage plan than a makeshift series of experiments, some brilliantly effective, some impractical, some discriminatory and punitive if noble in vision, but all aimed directly at real problems."[46] His administration had a seat-of-the-pants air to it. "It is just common sense to take a method and try it," said the president. "If it fails, admit it freely and try another. But above all try something." Though the New Deal's centerpieces, the NRA and AAA, yielded mixed though mostly fruitful results, the preponderance of the initiatives were triumphant. FDR's budget director, Harold Smith, later recalled, "People like me who had the responsibility of watching the pennies could only see the five or six or seven percent of the programs that went wrong, through inefficient organization or direction. But I can now see in perspective the ninety-three or -four or -five percent went right . . . because of unbelievably skillful organization and direction."[47]

The administration's batting average mattered less than the psychological impact among the American people that *something* was being done. That alone created the impression of progress. "Any good idea got a hearing," wrote Hugh Sidey. "Those programs that did not work were torn up, and the young, brainy aides would start over the next day. At night, when Roosevelt gathered his band of political warriors around him, there was robust laughter and the tinkle of his martini pitcher and his long cigarette holder pointed at a rakish angle, which signaled to everybody that the U.S. was rising from its fear."[48]

Roosevelt's Brain Trust was composed of a group of academics and economists charged with coming up with solutions to the daunting problems of the times. The group's point man was Harry Hopkins, whom Roosevelt, while New York governor, tapped to head the state's Temporary Emergency Relief Administration, a Depression remedy for the state that became a precursor to New Deal relief programs. Hopkins would become a trusted aide to both the president and the first lady. (He would also become close to the Roosevelts in a literal sense. A late night at the White House in 1940 led to an invitation from Roosevelt for Hopkins to spend the night. Hopkins, a bachelor, borrowed a pair of pajamas, retired for the evening, and ended up taking residence for three and a half years; even after he married, he brought his wife to live there with him two years into his stay. One of Roosevelt's staff joked that it was Hopkins who inspired George S. Kaufman and Moss Hart to write their play *The Man Who Came to Dinner..*)[49]

Among the members of Roosevelt's in-house think tank were Louis Howe, a longtime Roosevelt aide; journalist Raymond Moley; attorney Basil O'Connor; and Adolf Berle and Felix Frankfurter, professors from Columbia and Harvard Law School, respectively. Most of their plans had been formulated before Roosevelt took office, and the group was clear about all that was at stake. "It must be remembered," wrote Berle, "that by March 4th [1933] we may have anything on our hands from a recovery to a revolution."[50] The Brain Trust never convened as a group after FDR's inaugural, though all served in official posts in the administration. Roosevelt's cabinet consisted of an equally dedicated and talented team of New Dealers, including Secretary of the Interior Harold Ickes; Secretary of Agriculture Henry Wallace, later his second vice president; and the first female appointee to a presidential cabinet, Secretary of Labor Frances Perkins.

Notably missing from FDR's team was a chief of staff. Instead, Roosevelt played the role himself, aided by confidants who, at the president's behest, trolled the West Wing surreptitiously for intelligence to keep him apprised of everything that was going on—unaware that he had asked others to do the same.[51] The president also deftly and subtly pitted his top lieutenants against each other in order to ensure that all decisions ultimately came through him.[52] His agreeable nature—Oliver Wendell Holmes famously called it "a first class temperament"—made advisers believe he had taken their side, often to discover he had chosen the opposite course. One aide cited it as Roosevelt's deceptive ability to be "pleasantly present."[53] In actuality, his ostensible openness masked often imperceptible political motivations and a character of byzantine complexities. "His smile came from the teeth out," claimed the newsman William Allen White.[54]

Eleanor Roosevelt also played a pivotal role in the administration, albeit an unofficial one. When she first took on the position of first lady, she had a modest aim: "I'm just going to be plain Mrs. Roosevelt. And that's all," she said. It didn't quite turn out that way. In Eleanor Roosevelt, the United States would find its most active and influential first lady. If she had not found fulfillment in motherhood, it came in being her husband's eyes and ears—and legs—as she doggedly traveled to the nation's most remote and impoverished reaches to get a sense of how Americans were bearing up through the crisis. Often she became his conscience, too. "I sometimes acted as a spur," she said later. "Even though the spurring was not always welcome."[55]

Earlier on, the Roosevelts' marriage had undergone a crisis of its own. In 1919, two years before her husband's polio struck, Eleanor Roosevelt discovered that her husband was having an affair with their social secretary, the pretty, sophisticated Lucy Mercer, when she happened upon a batch of letters from the lovelorn Miss Mercer in his desk. "The bottom dropped out of my particular world," Eleanor Roosevelt later wrote of learning of her husband's infidelity, "& I faced myself, my surroundings, my world, honestly for the first time."[56] The marriage survived the threat of divorce, which would have certainly compromised Roosevelt's political career—and his bank account. His mother threatened to disinherit him if he insisted on sullying the Roosevelt name. The Roosevelts' marriage went on, but thereafter any traces of romance faded; at night Eleanor Roosevelt retreated to a separate bedroom and was through with the business of conjugal relations, which she described later to her daughter Anna as "an ordeal to be borne."[57] Though there would always be love between them, their marriage became a domestic, and ultimately political, partnership. But despite Roosevelt's promise never to see Mercer again, a recent book suggests that they continued their affair throughout the remainder of FDR's life, even after she married a man twenty-nine years her senior—becoming Lucy Mercer

Rutherfurd—reflecting Roosevelt's secretive and occasionally duplici-
tous nature.[58] (Roosevelt's disability did not preclude him from sexual
dalliances, and there has been speculation, though not entirely convincing, that his affairs went beyond Mercer. What is undisputed is that Roosevelt adored attractive women, of which there were many in his social
circle, and that his admiration was reciprocated. He once mused to a
friend, "Nothing is more pleasing to the eye than a good-looking lady,
more pleasing to the spirit than the company of one.")[59]

In her first seven years as first lady, Eleanor Roosevelt, often accompanied by her companion Lorena Hickok, visited every state in the union
except South Dakota. She could be found virtually anywhere at any time:
in impoverished Appalachia, a derelict urban slum, or a small farm town
ravaged by Dust Bowl winds. A cartoon in the *New Yorker* showed two
miners deep in a quarry looking toward its opening, as one exclaims,
"For gosh sakes, here comes Mrs. Roosevelt!" If one didn't catch her live,
there was always her daily syndicated (and often frivolous) newspaper
column, "My Day," her books, or her appearances on newsreels and
radio interviews. She was, in a sense, the Oprah of her day. The first first
lady to give press conferences—she gave more than three hundred in her
tenure—Eleanor Roosevelt insisted that the reporters on her beat be
women, providing the impetus for many newspapers to hire their first
female reporters.[60] She became a powerful advocate for the poor and
disenfranchised, and a champion of civil rights. In 1939, when African-
American opera singer Marian Anderson was denied a concert appearance at Washington's Constitution Hall by the Daughters of the American
Revolution, Mrs. Roosevelt publicly condemned the organization's stance
and promptly turned in her membership. Here, though, Eleanor Roosevelt's "spurring" of her husband did not amount to much, at least legisla-
tively. No major New Deal initiative addressed the ongoing plight or the
inferior treatment of blacks throughout the country, due in part to FDR's
conscious decision not to rock the boat among Southern Democrats by
pushing for civil rights measures.

Despite her initial ambivalence about being first lady, Eleanor Roosevelt became an asset to her husband and the country, adding to the em-

pathy that flowed from the White House. Unintentionally, she offered another asset to her husband. As Ted Morgan pointed out, "No one then realized how useful Eleanor was in drawing the fire from FDR. She was a highly visible decoy that New Deal critics could snipe at."[61]

Critics notwithstanding, Roosevelt received another resounding mandate in the midterm election of 1934, reversing the general trend by picking up seats for his party in both houses of Congress. Within the year came the passage of more sweeping legislation, including the Securities Exchange Act, which placed regulations on the stock market, and the Federal Housing Administration, providing aid to homeowners. By the end of 1935, the New Deal would touch every segment of the American population as the administration continued to drift leftward in its policy.[62]

The Second New Deal, so called later by Roosevelt scholars, saw a batch of new legislation in a hundred-day period from June to August. The Social Security Act, perhaps Roosevelt's signature and most far-reaching act, brought relief to older Americans by providing pensions through joint contributions from employers and employees, while the National Labor Relations Act, more commonly known as the Wagner Act, allowed labor to organize and enter into collective-bargaining agreements. The Works Progress Administration doled out work instead of welfare checks, employing Americans for construction projects across the country. Called a "make-work boondoggle" by skeptics, the project was an investment in America's future, bolstering its infrastructure with new roads, dams, public buildings, and other large-scale production projects. The number of American roads increased by 10 percent due to the WPA, which also resulted in the creation or improvement of hospitals, schools, playgrounds, and airfields, including the construction of New York's La Guardia Airport. In addition to offering work to unemployed laborers, the act provided jobs for those in the arts, allowing them to ply their trade for between $23 and $35 per week. "Hell, they've got to eat just like other people," said the WPA's director, Harry Hopkins, of the thousands of artists, actors, musicians, photographers, and writers who benefited from the program, including

Arthur Miller, Zora Neale Hurston, Orson Welles, Jackson Pollock, Willem de Kooning, Eudora Welty, and Gordon Parks.[63]

In 1936, Roosevelt coasted to an easy win against his opponent, Kansas governor Alfred Landon, who managed to win only two states—and small ones, at that—Maine and Vermont. Roosevelt captured over 60 percent of the popular vote while strengthening the Democratic Party's rein on Congress. The party held 333 House seats to the GOP's 89, and 75 to 17 in the Senate. Roosevelt would become the first president to be sworn in through the newly enacted Twentieth Amendment, which moved the date of the presidential inauguration from March 4 to January 20. "The test of our progress," he said in his inaugural remarks, "is not whether we add more to the abundance of those who have much, it is whether we provide enough for those who have too little." To that end, Roosevelt's second-term legislative victories included a Fair Labor Standards Act, which guaranteed workers a minimum wage of twenty-five cents an hour and a maximum forty-four-hour workweek, levels that would change to forty cents an hour and a forty-hour workweek by 1945.[64]

The year 1937 would prove trying for the president. In an effort to balance the federal budget, he and his secretary of treasury, Henry Morgenthau, cut government spending, a rejection of Keynesian economics that encouraged federal spending as a stimulus during recessionary times. By modern standards, Roosevelt's federal spending, even at its height, when he borrowed $3.6 billion from the federal till the year before, was not extreme.[65] The result was a contribution of $4.1 billion in consumer purchasing power. In 1937, it dropped to less than $1 billion as income fell off by 12 percent and unemployment rose. Almost four million Americans lost their jobs, bringing the national total to just under twelve million, a level comparable to when Roosevelt had taken office.[66]

Even before the economy began to regress, the president's second term—very unlike his first—began unpromisingly. Just days after his second inaugural, still at the height of his power, Roosevelt overreached.

Since the wheels of the New Deal began turning, the Supreme Court had derailed a number of its programs, citing the abuse of federal authority. The New Deal's cornerstone, NIRA, as well as the AAA and the Railroad Act, was among the legislation that was rendered constitutionally null and void by a majority of the "nine old men" who presided on the high court, the youngest of whom was sixty-one. Octogenarian justice Louis Brandeis expressed his frustration with the administration's New Deal legislation when, after the court struck a deathblow to NIRA, he cautioned a Roosevelt aide, "This is the end of this business of centralization, and I want you to go back to the President and tell him that we're not going to let this government centralize everything. It's come to an end."[67] The warning portended the Court's probable rejection of the Social Security Act and the National Labor Relations Act, on which it had committed to rule later in its term.

Roosevelt, in turn, was just as exasperated with the Court. In his second inaugural address he stated that Americans "will insist that every agency of popular government use effective instruments to carry out their will." Shortly afterward, he sought to stack the deck in his favor, formulating a bill to increase the number of Supreme Court justices. His plan—to become infamously known as court packing—would allow for the appointment of one justice for each sitting justice over the age of seventy, and, in allowing the president to appoint like-minded justices to the new positions, would give him the majority support he needed to keep the New Deal rolling unimpeded. Hatched in secret by the administration, the bill would have created appointments for six new justices, bringing the court's total from nine to fifteen. Retiring justices over seventy would not be replaced, unless the attrition brought the Court's total number to fewer than nine.

Tongues wagged over the controversial plan throughout the first half of the year. Many conservatives howled, including Herbert Hoover, who spoke for most of them when he asserted that Roosevelt had finally shown his true dictatorial colors. Such was Roosevelt's sway, though, that the *New York Times* headlined that Congress was "expected to approve" the bill.[68] But Congress had its own mind on the issue. House judiciary chairman Hatton Sumners, a conservative Democrat from Texas, referring to his waning support of the president, told his colleagues, "Boys, this is where I cash in my chips."[69] The bulk of Sumners's peers, conservative and otherwise, agreed.

Confident he could win the support of the American people, Roosevelt gave a Fireside Chat on March 9, in which he made his case for creating a Supreme Court that could "understand these modern conditions." He cited the Court's narrow five-to-four vote in favor of the Emergency Banking Act of 1933 as an example of how one vote might have gotten in the way of maintaining the "main objectives of the Constitution to establish an enduring nation. . . . The balance of power," he said, "has been tipped out of balance by the Courts in direct contrast of the high purposes of the framers of the Constitution. It is my purpose to restore that balance." The Court, he believed, was overstepping its bounds by violating the mandate of the people. Here Roosevelt was misguided. The Supreme Court, after all, had been envisioned by the Founding Fathers as being impervious to the political passions of the day, basing its rulings solely on constitutional grounds. As such, it hardly mattered that the programs of the New Deal reflected the will of the president and the people.

Maybe the people appreciated that, too. Roosevelt's appeal didn't do much to turn the tide in his favor. In June, the Senate Judiciary Committee issued a report calling the plan "a needless, futile, and utterly dangerous abandonment of the constitutional principle . . . without precedent or justification."[70] A senate vote of seventy to twenty took the bill back to committee where, in essence, the teeth were extracted from the shark. All controversial language was removed, and in August the disenchanted president signed a watered-down version of his original plan that left the Supreme Court intact.

Still, over time he could claim some semblance of victory over the recalcitrant Court. In what was called "the switch in time which saved the nine," no New Deal program was again rejected. What accounted for the Court's sudden ideological shift—senility? self-preservation?—remains a historical mystery. The Court even ruled in favor of the Social Security Act and National Labor Relations Act, relieving fears that the programs would go the way of NIRA. The upshot was that the administration, as Roosevelt would later boast, had lost the battle but won the war. Nevertheless, the scheme cost Roosevelt some of his moral authority and much of the political capital he had built up with his two landslide elections. The spell he had cast over Congress for more than four remarkable years of legislative reform was broken.[71]

If the court-packing fiasco humbled Roosevelt, it didn't last long. In an effort to rid Congress of ten conservative Southern Democrats who had stood in the way of progress on the New Deal, Roosevelt meddled in the Democratic midterm primaries in 1938, openly supporting the more liberal opponents who were challenging them. Once again, his plan backfired. Only one of the ten members failed to win the party's primary; the other nine returned to Congress in 1939, none too pleased with the man in the Oval Office and less inclined than ever to support his agenda. They, along with other Southern Democrats, would form an alliance with Northern Republicans, further impeding Roosevelt's legislative aims. If Roosevelt's failed purge wasn't troubling enough, the midterms would yield the Republicans seventy-five seats in the House and seven in the Senate, marking the first time since 1930 the Democrats had lost ground to the GOP.

The two episodes amounted to major political miscalculations on Roosevelt's part, allowing detractors to make more plausible accusations of autocratic rule. Was Roosevelt—as was charged by the columnist Walter Lippmann—"drunk with power"?[72] No. While he may have overreached his authority, often overstrengthening the presidency as a result, he never pushed it over the edge. Like Lincoln, he forced his will for what he saw as the greater good—a cause no less vital than alleviating the suffering in a nation in which one-third of its people were in his words "ill-housed, ill-clad, ill-nourished"—not simply for the consolidation or retention of power. As Ted Morgan put it, Roosevelt always remained aware that "his power was fragile because it came from forces outside himself. It could be maintained only if he made himself the embodiment of both the collective will and the moral compact. If he lost the ability to personify the psyche of his people he would lose his power, because it was derivative."[73] Though he wielded power as masterfully as any American politician of his century, Roosevelt knew he was ultimately an instrument of the people.

But despite what may have been the purity of Roosevelt's intentions, his New Deal remedies, while alleviating many of the Great Depression's symptoms, did not cure the disease. Unemployment numbers continued to remain well into the double digits throughout the thirties, and the stock market teetered precariously. Still, there's no telling how bad the Depression might have been had it not been for Roosevelt's leadership. He renewed the dwindling faith among his beleaguered countrymen in American liberty and the capitalist foundation it was built on—which had changed in his tenure, softened by New Deal measures. One million American voters cast anti-capitalist ballots in the election of 1932, a number that fell to a mere 150,000 in 1940.[74]

Such was not the case overseas, where depressions hit after striking the United States. There dictatorship and despotism emerged out of economic hardship. In Germany, economic conditions and government instability had given rise to the fascism of Hitler, who had designs on the domination of Europe, as Japan marched into China with the goal of creating a Greater East Asia Co-prosperity Sphere under its control.[75] It took a world war set off by the truculent ambitions of Germany and Japan to put America's Great Depression in its wake. As the smoke started to belch from American factories revived with new activity from war orders after 1939, the country began to rise out of its economic depths. As it did, the New Deal slowly faded with America's entanglement in world events. The Lend-Lease Program, first broached by Roosevelt at the end of 1940 after France had fallen to the Nazis, allied the United States with Britain as it warded off assaults by the Nazi regime, which was spreading throughout Europe. While stopping short of America's direct involvement, the program gave the British the resources to wage the fight. "Give us the tools," Prime Minister Winston Churchill beseeched the American people in a radio address, "and we will finish the job."[76]

The danger of entry in the war, and his fears that the New Deal would perish without his guidance, caused Roosevelt to break the precedent set by George Washington and upheld by all his two-term successors, by running for reelection for a third term in 1940. Vice

President Garner, who had aims on his party's presidential nomination himself, was dumped from the ticket in favor of Secretary of Agriculture Henry Wallace, who had made his mark by administering the AAA. Roosevelt won with relative ease on promises to sustain the New Deal while keeping the country out of war, beating his Republican opponent Wendell Willkie, a Midwestern lawyer and utilities executive, by capturing 55 percent of the popular vote and a 449 electoral votes to Willkie's 82.

America, of course, did enter the war. Isolationism remained an all but impossible course even before the Japanese fatefully attacked Pearl Harbor on December 7, 1941. For Roosevelt, it was the case of jumping from the frying pan into the fire. After eight years of battling the Great Depression at home, he now led Allied powers to defeat enemies in Europe and Japan. "We are fighting," he said in 1936 of the Depression, "to save a great and precious form of government for ourselves and for the world."[77] The stakes were no less as America entered World War II.

The war gave cause for Roosevelt to run for a fourth time in 1944, along with his running mate, Missouri senator Harry S. Truman, who replaced Henry Wallace on the ticket's second spot as the latter's liberalism fell increasingly out of step with party regulars. Roosevelt defeated New York governor Thomas Dewey by a slightly narrower victory this time, taking just under 54 percent of the popular vote and 432 electoral votes versus Dewey's 99. But as Roosevelt entered his fourth term, the strain of leading the country through two of its worst crises took its toll. With Nazi surrender almost certain in Europe, and Japan's cause all but lost in the Pacific, Roosevelt's health began to fail him. He appeared pale and sickly at a war conference in Yalta on the Black Sea with Allied leaders Winston Churchill and Josef Stalin in February of 1945. Two months later, on April 12, as he enjoyed a much-needed two-week respite at his retreat in Warm Springs, Georgia, with a few friends, including Lucy Mercer Rutherfurd, Roosevelt died of a massive stroke. As he sat for a portrait wearing his crimson Harvard tie and navy blue cape, he complained of pain in the back of his head, then slumped back in his chair, never to regain consciousness. He was pronounced dead just over two hours later, at 3:35 P.M.

In the short term, a leader's impact can be gauged by the length of his shadow. Like John Adams and Andrew Johnson before him, Harry Truman, as he succeeded Roosevelt, would find the standard by which he would be evaluated impossible to measure up to. He was at an immediate disadvantage simply because of who he was not—FDR—just as Adams was not Washington, and Johnson was not Lincoln. The country defined leadership in the personification of Roosevelt, nothing less. Many younger Americans could not remember another president.

Longer term, even after his shadow receded, Roosevelt had left a mark on the nation rivaled only by Washington and Lincoln. The country had been transformed in his twelve years in office. By saving capitalism from itself in the midst of the Great Depression, he kept the fires of democracy burning as the nation entered the Second World War. Afterward, emergent as an international power with the defeat of Germany and Japan, America became a beacon for freedom and opportunity around the world.

In his early years in Washington, while in his post as assistant secretary of the navy, Roosevelt was the occasional guest of the historian Henry Adams—grandson of John Quincy Adams and great-grandson of John Adams—who lived off Lafayette Park, just a stone's throw from the White House. One day, as Roosevelt groused about the challenges he was facing at the Navy Department, Adams interrupted him. "Young man," he said, "I have lived in this house many years and have seen the occupants of the White House across the square come and go, and nothing that you minor officials or the occupant of that house can do will affect the history of the world for very long."[78] Adams would not live to see Roosevelt graduate from a "minor official" to the "occupant" of the neighboring mansion, nor to read a 1945 *New York Times* editorial that would gainsay his sentiments. "Men will thank God on their knees, a hundred years from now, that Franklin D. Roosevelt was in the White

House," the paper read just after Roosevelt's death. "It was his leadership which inspired free men in every part of the world to fight with greater hope and courage. . . . Gone is the fresh and spontaneous interest which this man took, as naturally as he breathed air, in the troubles and the hardships and the disappointments and the hopes of the little and humble people."[79]

# VI

# Harry S. Truman

## *"If you pray, pray for me now"*

Harry Truman presided over the U.S. Senate on the afternoon of April 12, 1945, listening to Senator Alexander Wiley hold forth on the issue of Mexican irrigation. Or rather, not listening. He was writing. "Dear Mamma and Mary," he scribbled on Senate stationery to his mother and sister back home in his native Missouri. "I am trying to write to you today from the desk of the President of the Senate while a windy Senator from Wisconsin is making a speech on a subject with which he is in no way familiar. . . ."[1]

Truman had been vice president for a little under three months and had spent much of that time tending to his official duties as the body's president. In truth, he was asked to do little else. Mostly, as he had written earlier to his family, the new job entailed meeting "Senators and curiosity people who want to see what a V.P. looks like and if he walks and talks and has teeth."[2] Since taking on the nation's number two spot the previous January, after serving as a senator from Missouri for nine years, he had had only two scheduled meetings with President Franklin Roosevelt, whom he barely knew. He didn't see Roosevelt at all until several weeks after he became vice president. Afterward, the president would occasionally make inquiries of Truman about Senate matters, and Truman would attend cabinet meetings, though not much happened in them. As Truman said later, Roosevelt "tried to do it all himself, which was one of his troubles."[3]

FDR had not been particularly collaborative with any of his three vice presidents and, as with the others, held Truman at arm's length. His first, John Nance Garner, described the vice presidency as a "warm bucket of piss," though cleaner versions of the denouncement had the last word as "spit." Either way, he didn't much like the office, and Roosevelt hadn't done anything to make it better. As the Second World War played out its last days in Europe and the Pacific, Truman was not privy in any great depth to the complex war strategy and foreign policy steps in place or being considered. Nor was he informed about a secret meeting at Yalta among the president, Winston Churchill, and Josef Stalin in early February at which the "Big Three" made momentous decisions on the structure of the postwar world they would soon determine.[4]

At four minutes before 5:00, Kentucky senator Alben Barkley called for a recess. Truman stepped down from the dais and strode at his brisk clip through the marble corridors of the Capitol to the office of House Speaker Sam Rayburn. Truman had been invited by the speaker for a meeting of the "Board of Education," an ongoing gathering of congressional insiders after the day's legislative duties to swap stories and drink bourbon and tap water. Truman enjoyed the company of his colleagues, and a good bourbon—if not the tap water. He arrived at around the top of the hour, but before he could join the dozen or so lawmakers who had convened, Rayburn told him that Steve Early, the president's press secretary, had just called and asked that he call him back right away. The vice president mixed a drink and phoned Early, who summoned him to the White House "as quickly and as quietly" as possible.[5]

Truman had never been called to the White House before, at least not urgently, though he "didn't think much about it."[6] He considered that Roosevelt might have come back early from his home in Warm Springs to attend the funeral of his friend Julius Atwood, the bishop of Arizona, and wanted him to do some liaison work with Congress. Still, he found himself running through the Capitol halls to get to his black limousine, which raced him discreetly to the White House. He arrived at 5:25 and was taken by the mansion's two head ushers to see Eleanor Roosevelt, who was waiting for him in her sitting room on the second floor.

"Harry," Mrs. Roosevelt said softly upon seeing him, putting her arm around his shoulder, "the President is dead."

Truman was dumbstruck. "Is there anything I can do for you?" he asked finally.

"Is there anything *we* can do for *you*?" she replied with characteristic empathy. "For *you* are the one in trouble now."[7]

By 7:09, Truman was standing in the Cabinet Room, with his hand on a Bible aides had scrambled to find in the East Wing. His wife, Bess, and daughter, Margaret, as well as members of Congress had been sent for and now looked on as Truman was given the presidential oath by Chief Justice Harlan Stone. It took less than a minute. Truman then kissed the Bible, a cheap Gideon version that had been found in the head usher's desk, and it was done.[8] "Lightning had struck," he would recall later, "and events beyond anyone's control had taken command."[9]

The following day, bucking tradition, Truman went from the White House up to Congress to be among friends, who gave him a private lunch. He wanted to tell them personally that he would look to them for help in the days ahead. Afterward, the new president, his eyes misty with emotion, met with members of the press who had congregated outside. "Boys," he told them, "if you ever pray, pray for me now. I don't know if you fellows have ever had a load of hay fall on you, but when they told me yesterday what had happened, I felt like the moon, the stars, and all the planets had fallen on me."[10]

Much of the world was praying for Truman, who had taken on a burden that many felt was far beyond his abilities. The small-town erstwhile failed farmer and haberdasher, whose formal education ended with a high school diploma, paled in comparison with his predecessor, who in his lifetime had achieved a cloak of greatness accorded to few Americans before the grave. Roosevelt had won the presidency an unprecedented four times and had guided the country through the Depression, one of its greatest storms, and through most of another as World War II wound down overseas on a bed of smoldering ash. Americans had taken as an article of faith that Roosevelt would always remain at the helm, strong and buoyant. For more than a dozen trying years he had always been there for them. Now he was gone. How would Truman—just a senator from Missouri a mere three months earlier—carry on in FDR's massive wake? How would he deal with the end of the war in Europe, where America's ambitious, exploitive Russian allies had designs on expanding the Communist sphere in Eastern and Central Europe? And how would he ensure a swift victory against the Japanese, who fought relentlessly in the Pacific despite all signs that theirs was a lost cause?

"We should be less than candid at this grave moment, if we did not recognize the great disparity between Mr. Truman's experience and the great responsibility that has been thrust upon him," wrote the *Washington Post* in an editorial as Truman picked up Roosevelt's presidency.[11] "What a test of democracy if it works," wrote Ray Roberts, editor of the *Kansas City Star,* of the succession of Truman, whom he epitomized in a widely circulated column as the average American.[12] But Roberts didn't know the extent of what lay ahead for Truman, and the monumental decisions that would be heaped upon his square shoulders. Nor, for that matter, did Truman.

Truman, the average American? By appearance, certainly. Harry S. Truman—the S was a parental compromise between family names Shippe and Solomon—looked more like a pharmacist or insurance salesman than a president. He stood an ordinary five feet nine, kept himself trim, and would likely have fit into his old World War I uniform at any point in his adult life. His face was marked by a sharp nose, thin lips, and blue eyes that were magnified behind his Coke bottle–lensed round-frame glasses. While he was nattily attired in double-breasted suits in his official duties, looking every bit the former haberdasher, his leisure wear—often including gaudy flower print shirts—gave him the look of a scorned American summer tourist in Europe. Then again, Truman often reminded himself and others that no one looked more presidential than Warren Harding.[13]

By background too, maybe Truman was average. He was indisputably American, born in Lamar, Missouri, on May 8, 1884, the eldest son of John and Mary Ellen Truman, by virtue of birth the next in a long line of farmers who had settled the land. From them he inherited a strong work ethic and values rooted in honesty, loyalty, duty to country, and Christian morality.[14] Before beginning grade school, Truman and his younger brother and sister lived on the family's six-hundred-acre farm in Jackson County, Missouri. By the time Truman turned six, the family moved twenty miles to Independence, ten miles from Kansas City, where Truman's father bought and sold livestock. There Truman attended grade school, meeting in his Sunday school class Bess Wallace, his popular, wellborn classmate and childhood sweetheart, she of "golden curls" and "the most beautiful blue eyes," who would become his wife almost three decades later.[15] A bespectacled bookworm at an early age, young Harry escaped the confines of small-town life by reading every book in the Independence library by age fourteen—and his family's Bible three times over—and playing the piano for up to two hours daily.[16]

Lacking good enough vision to attend the U.S. Military Academy and the funds to go to college, Truman set off to work in a number of clerical jobs—in the mail room at the *Kansas City Star,* at a railroad, and at a bank—all of which brought him back to the family's Grandview farm at his father's behest. With little success, he worked at the soil for ten years before, in 1917, his National Guard unit was called into action in the First World War, where Truman showed his mettle as a leader in the trenches of France, serving as an artillery officer for Battery D. In 1919, he returned to Independence where, at thirty-five, he married his patient fiancée, Bess, a year younger, who had promised her hand before he left for the war. Truman had been determined to make something of himself before marriage, but perhaps practicality and inevitability dictated getting on with it. They had their only child, Margaret, in 1924. By that time, the men's clothing store Truman had opened with his friend Eddie Jacobson had gone belly-up, leaving the Trumans deep in debt. (Refusing to declare bankruptcy, Truman would continue to pay off his debtors well into his career in the Senate.) The same year, Truman was introduced to Tom Pendergast, the powerful Kansas City boss, who took a liking to him and talked him into running for district judge. Truman won the political administrative post, then lost it two years later. With Pendergast's backing Truman went on to become chief judge of Jackson County, keeping himself at arm's length from Pendergast's notoriously corrupt political machine.

After a career checkered by failure, Truman had found success as an honest, competent politician who got things done. He won a U.S. Senate seat in 1934, entering Congress infamously as "the Senator from Pendergast." Eventually, he won favor among his colleagues, serving with distinction and chairing the Special Committee to Investigate the National Defense Program, later dubbed the Truman Committee for his stalwart leadership. By Truman's estimation, the committee saved taxpayers upward of $15 billion.[17] Truman's service on the committee, and strong reputation on Capitol Hill, where he had few political enemies, brought him to the attention of the Democratic National Committee, which was shopping for a running mate for Roosevelt on the 1944 national ticket. Roosevelt had decided to drop his incumbent vice president, Henry Wallace. Wallace, a utopian liberal with no great congressional clout, had taken a bad turn with the increasingly conservative party after denouncing *Time* magazine founder Henry Luce's vision of the "American Century" in favor of a "Century of the Common Man."[18] Leftists cheered while party regulars distanced themselves from Wallace, who would be relegated to secretary of commerce. In his place, Roosevelt and the committee thought Truman fit the bill, notwithstanding the fact that Truman had removed himself from consideration, throwing his support to James Byrnes, head of the Office of War Mobilization and Reconversion. A phone call from Roosevelt to committee chairman Bob Hannegan during the party's convention convinced Truman otherwise. Truman, who was with Hannegan at the time, heard FDR's robust voice on the other end of the line: "Bob, have you got that fellow lined up yet?"

"No, not yet," Hannegan replied. "He's the most contrariest Missouri mule I've ever dealt with."

"Well, you tell him, if he wants to break up the Democratic Party in the middle of a war, that's his responsibility," said the president.

That's all it took. "Oh, shit! Well, if that's the situation," Truman told Hannegan after the call, "I'll have to say yes. But why the hell didn't he tell me in the first place?"[19]

In the days of Abraham Lincoln, Truman's rise from humble, up-from-the-bootstraps beginnings and his down-to-earth deportment might have made him a folksy "man of the people" or, as we might say today (as if a new concept), "authentic." But in the days after Roosevelt rolled as a giant onto the world stage, it made him everyday by comparison. Roosevelt and Churchill, in the words of the historian David Mc-Cullough, "saw the history of their times as Homeric drama and they the lead players, two professionals perfectly cast and at the top of their form."[20] Truman, who privately believed Roosevelt to be an "egotist" and a bit of a phony, had no such illusions.[21] Or maybe it was just a lack of imagination. "I yam what I yam," he seemed to exude, Popeye-like; to present himself as anything more than who he was would be, as he might say in his flat Midwestern tone, "a lot of hooey." With Roosevelt as the standard, any man would appear less than presidential. Truman even confided to Eleanor Roosevelt months after taking office that he still thought of FDR as the president.[22] But despite appearances, Truman's extraordinary character made him anything but average. And, in the muddled aftermath of the war, character may have meant more than playing a heroic role in an epic historical drama.

"I felt as if I had lived five lifetimes in those first days as president," Truman recalled later.[23] One of his first moves was to retain Roosevelt's cabinet. Harry Hopkins, a key aide to Roosevelt, had advised against it, noting that the members might compare Truman unfavorably to Roosevelt and might not accept his changes in policy. Truman disagreed. "Harry," he said. "I am not gonna fire anybody. Those fellows have been working their heads off. There's a war going on, and I'm gonna keep the same outfit. Whenever they want to quit, why, they can."[24] At the same time, he rejected Roosevelt's loose administrative approach in favor of a greater discipline at the executive level, and at his first cabinet meeting "made it clear that I would be the President in my own right. And I would assume full responsibility for such decisions as should be made."[25] Truman was nothing if not decisive. He made decisions big and small without hand-wringing or lost sleep, and moved on. That would help in the days and months ahead, when crucial decisions were required.

Truman began his tenure like a college student cramming for exams as he strove to understand all that had transpired in the war, reading so much that he feared his weak eyesight would fail him further. His White House nights were spent poring through files and memos in preparation for a conference with Churchill and Stalin in Potsdam, just southwest of the devastated German capital of Berlin, in July. Trust between the United States and the Soviet Union had steadily eroded as the war wound down. Roosevelt had treated the Russians as an ally, and Stalin as a friend, a posture the Soviets perceived as softness to be exploited. FDR's performance at Yalta, where he was clearly ailing, had many wondering why he had conceded so much to Stalin. Truman saw things differently. "Force is the only thing the Russians understand," he contended, foreshadowing his intractability as the cold war loomed.[26]

Tensions soon arose over Soviet breaches in the agreements carved out by the Big Three at Yalta, in particular Poland's political fate after Russian troops had driven out the Nazi regime in February. The Yalta accords called for a broadly based Polish government, which would eventually hold free elections. But it was ambiguously conceived. The Russians construed it to mean a government in the Soviet mold, while Truman and Churchill thought it to be a Western-style democracy. Truman, in his feisty "give 'em hell" manner—a marked departure from his predecessor's diplomatic subtlety—took a firm position on the matter, pursuing it as a pivotal showdown in determining the future of East-West relations. In a harsh exchange with Vyacheslav Molotov, the Soviet foreign minister, less than two weeks after Truman took office, the president insisted that Poland be "free and independent." "I have never been talked to like that in my life," Molotov sulked after the haranguing. "Carry out your agreements and you *won't* be talked to like that," Truman snapped back, before abruptly dismissing him. "That will be all,

Mr. Molotov. I would appreciate it if you would translate my views to Marshal Stalin."[27]

If Truman had given Stalin an indirect "one-two punch to the jaw" through Molotov, it had little effect. Soon afterward, Stalin would assert the Soviet Union's grip on Poland, imprisoning sixteen of the twenty anti-Communist Polish leaders who had returned home from exile in London, after accusing them of inciting resistance to the Soviet military presence. In their place, he installed a puppet government loyal to the USSR. The Soviet premier had made his intentions in Eastern Europe clear and had the military might to bring them to bear regardless of Truman's tough posturing. The battle lines of the cold war were beginning to be drawn.[28]

From July 17 to August 2, Truman attended the conference at Potsdam—his first and last face-to-face meetings with Stalin—with knowledge of a development that gave the United States a decisive advantage in the budding conflict with the Soviets and that offered an immediate solution for ending the war with Japan. On the evening Truman became president, after a somber, impromptu reception he and Mrs. Truman held for members of the cabinet at their Washington apartment, Roosevelt's seventy-seven-year-old secretary of defense, Henry Stimson, stayed behind to inform him that the United States was in the final stages of developing "the most destructive weapon in history."[29] He said little else, but in the coming days Truman would learn of the full extent of the Manhattan Project and its implications. Truman had already known "something was going on" from the work he had done as chairman of the Truman Committee. When committee investigators had stumbled on the clandestine program to develop a major weapon, Stimson asked Truman to let it go, indicating that the project would be in jeopardy if it was made public. Knowing that Stimson was a man he could trust, Truman "called off the dogs." After Truman became vice president, James Byrnes, who headed the administration's war mobilization and reconversion efforts, informed him of a "tremendous explosive that would surely end the war." Beyond that, Truman knew very little.[30]

Going into Potsdam, though, Truman was fully aware of the nuclear advantage the United States now boasted—verified by the successful test of the weapon at Alamagordo, New Mexico, less than two weeks earlier—and it gave him the confidence to stand tall against Stalin. As Churchill recalled, "When Truman got to the meeting after having read the report [on the test], he was a changed man. He told the Russians just where they got off, and generally bossed the whole meeting."[31] And yet Truman ended up liking Stalin. "He is straightforward," he wrote Bess Truman from the conference. "Knows what he wants and will compromise when he can't get it."[32] As an ally in the war, Truman felt obliged to disclose to his Soviet counterpart the existence of a bomb but said as little as possible and in the vaguest of terms. He neglected to mention it was atomic. Unsurprised, Stalin said only he was glad to hear the news and hoped the United States would make "good use of it against the Japanese."[33] He didn't pursue the subject further. He didn't need to. Soviet spies had already briefed him on the program.

But having the bomb and using it were two different things. While at Potsdam, Truman came to the conclusion that he would order the bomb to be dropped on parts of Japan if the Japanese did not lay down their arms. His rationale was the toll the war was taking on American troops. Each day the war went by meant the loss of more soldiers. At the same time, the prospect of Japanese surrender was dim. The very concept was anathema to the Japanese, meaning as it did utter humiliation and disgrace. The fact that not a single Japanese unit surrendered to Allied forces during the war's course was a reflection of the stigma attached to yielding to the enemy. Death before surrender was the honorable course.[34] Consequently, as the Japanese plight in the war became increasingly desperate, their fighting intensified. In the three months Truman had been president, the United States had suffered almost half as many casualties in the Pacific as it had in the three years prior.[35] Something big was needed to make Japan change course, to bring the nation to its knees. In that sense, using the bomb was not much different from the scorched-earth policy ordered in the Civil War by Lincoln, who rationalized that the sooner the conflict ended, the more American lives—blue and gray—would be saved.

By the estimates of his military advisers, an invasion of Japan would result in as many as 250,000 American casualties and would draw the war out for another year or more.[36] "It occurred to me," Truman said a few months after the bombs had been dropped on Hiroshima and Nagasaki, "that a quarter of a million of the flower of our young manhood were worth a couple of Japanese cities, and I still think they were and are."[37] At Potsdam, Truman issued an ultimatum to the Japanese: Surrender or face "prompt and utter destruction." Truman's diary entry on the evening of July 25 offers the most revealing glimpse of the moral dilemma he might have wrestled with as he considered the use of the military's new weapon against the enemy. "We have discovered the most terrible bomb in the history of the world," he wrote.

*This weapon is to be used against Japan between now and August 10th. I have told Sec. of War, Mr. Stimson to use it so that military objectives and soldiers and sailors are the target and not women and children  Even if the Japs are savages, ruthless, merciless and fanatic, we as the leader of the free world for the common welfare cannot drop this terrible bomb on the old Capitol [Kyoto] or the new [Tokyo, where the Imperial Palace has been spared thus far].*

*[Stimson] and I are in accord. The target will be a purely military one and we will issue a warning statement asking the Japs to surrender and save lives. . . . It seems to be the most terrible thing ever discovered, but it can be made the most useful.[38]*

On Truman's order, the *Enola Gay*, a B-29 Army Air Force bomber, dropped the atomic bomb on Hiroshima, an urban center of Japanese industry. Shortly after it was done, Stimson sent Truman a wire: "Big bomb dropped on Hiroshima on 5 August at 7:15 P.M. Washington time. First reports indicate complete success which was even more conspicuous than earlier test."[39] An estimated seventy thousand people—mostly civilians despite Truman's rationalization—died instantly. Many more would die in the aftereffects in the days to come. As the Japanese high command, composed of half a dozen men, deliberated on conditions for surrender—a concept unthinkable earlier—a bomb was dropped on Nagasaki, another industrial center, on August 9. Thirty-nine thousand more Japanese citizens perished.[40] Five days later, the Japanese surrendered, marking an end to the war.

Dropping the bombs may have been the most fateful decision made by any U.S. president. Perhaps none has been more scrutinized—and rightfully so. In an essay titled "Victory" in *Time* magazine's August 20, 1945, issue, published just after the bombings, James Agee foretold the consequences of the newly opened nuclear age:

> *The greatest and most terrible of wars ended this week in the echoes of an enormous event—an event so much more enormous that, relative to it, the war itself shrank into minor significance. The knowledge of victory was as charged with sorrow and doubts, as with joy and gratitude. More fearful responsibilities, more crucial liabilities, rested on the victors even more than on the vanquished. . . . The rational mind had won the most Promethean of its conquests over nature, and had put into the hands of common man the fire and force of the sun itself.*

By inference, Truman's popularity in the wake of the bombings shows strong support from the public. A little under two months after Japan's defeat, a Gallup poll reflected an approval rating of 82 percent among Americans, inflated no doubt by patriotic fervor and relief from the weariness of war. But reevaluation is a part of historical analysis. Through the years Truman's decision has been supported and maligned as it has been questioned. Should the president have given the Japanese leadership greater and more specific warning about the awesome power of its new weapon before unleashing it on them? Should he have given them more time to consider surrendering after the devastation of Hiroshima, before dropping the second bomb on Nagasaki? "[Truman's] decision has been viewed increasingly through a mist of might-have-beens," wrote Lester Bernstein, a World War II veteran, in a 1984 *New York Times* op-ed piece, on the centennial of Truman's birth. "Those who write history have the gift of revision; those who make it get only one chance. Truman had to deal with the realities confronting him in the summer of 1945."[41]

For his part, Truman never looked back. Often in his postpresidential years, he lectured to students—by his count, as many as two hundred thousand in total. Almost invariably, he was asked why he ordered the bombings; just as invariably, his answer remained consistent. "The atom bomb was no great decision," he told students at Columbia University in 1959. "It was used in the war, and for your information, there were more people killed by firebombs in Tokyo than dropping the atom bombs accounted for. It was merely another powerful weapon in the arsenal of righteousness. The dropping of the bombs stopped the war, saved millions of lives. It is just the same as artillery on our side. Napoleon said that victory is always on the side of the artillery. It was a military decision to end the war."[42]

With one war over, another—the cold war—began. "If it explodes, as I think it will, I'll certainly have a hammer on those boys," Truman said of the Russians before the atomic bomb tests went off in New Mexico.[43] Having "a hammer" may have explained Truman's cockiness—or at least his brimming confidence—at Potsdam. But afterward it didn't deter the Soviets from pursuing their ambitions—just as brimming—in Eastern and Central Europe and Asia. They looked upon the American nuclear advantage as something the United States would use only as a final solution in an all-out war.[44] Otherwise, it was just a veiled threat. By late 1945, Stalin was muscling his way into Romania and Bulgaria, while taking a part of eastern Poland and giving the Polish government part of Eastern Germany in return. Additionally, the Soviets had established themselves in what would become North Korea, despite Western efforts to reunite the country after the war. Defiance of the West was the order of the day for Stalin, who shunned participation in the World Bank and the International Monetary Fund, while rejecting an international bid from the United States to grant the United Nations authority over the development of atomic weaponry. Instead, Stalin ordered the development of his own nuclear program, aided by spies who had extracted America's atomic secrets. By early 1946, Truman had had it. "Unless Russia is faced with an iron fist and strong language another war is in the making," he told Secretary of State James Byrnes. "Only one language do they understand—'how many divisions have you?' . . . I'm tired of baby-ing the Soviets."[45]

In February of the same year, Truman, accompanied by former British prime minister Winston Churchill, took a train from Washington to Fulton, Missouri—playing poker along the way—where Churchill was to speak at Westminster College. Churchill received an honorary degree from the college and gave a speech that defined the growing threat the Soviet Union posed as it encroached on neighboring countries vulnerable to its supremacy after the ravages of war. "From Stettin in the Baltic to Trieste in the Adriatic," intoned Churchill, "an iron curtain has descended across the Continent. Behind that line lie all the capitals of the ancient states of Central and Eastern Europe. Warsaw, Berlin, Prague, Vienna, Budapest, Belgrade, Bucharest, and Sofia; all these famous cities and the populations around them lie in what I might call the Soviet sphere, and all are subject, in one form or another, not only to Soviet influence but to a very high and in some cases increasing measure of control from Moscow."[46]

Containment characterized Truman's foreign policy position in the face of the threat, as he made it clear to Stalin that the "Soviet sphere" must reach no farther than the satellite countries of Eastern Europe. In 1947, Truman went to Congress to ask for $400 million in aid to thwart Soviet-initiated Communist insurgencies in Greece and Turkey. In what would become known as the Truman Doctrine, the United States would keep Soviet expansion in check by bolstering Western and Central Europe economically. His feeling was that if the Soviets' ambitions were held back as the nations rebuilt themselves, over time the internal strains in the Soviets' own system would turn into fissures.[47] Truman's unyielding posture set the tone for America's cold war strategy. Thereafter, the White House would stand at the ready to keep the Russian bear at bay. In this way, Truman broadened the powers of the presidency.

By the time Truman had handed down his doctrine, much of his cabinet had changed. Secretary of Commerce Henry Wallace, alienated by Truman's rightward push in foreign policy after the war and concerned that his militarism would lead to another war, was openly critical of the president in a speech to twenty thousand at New York's Madison Square Garden on September 12, 1946.[48] Wallace advocated acceptance of the Soviet Union's growing influence in Eastern Europe, in opposition to U.S. policy, warning, "The tougher we get with Russia, the tougher they will get with us," and adding that "the danger of a war is much less from Communism than from Imperialism." Though Truman had approved the text of Wallace's speech (with the exception of the latter statement, which Wallace had thrown in in the heat of the moment), the backlash resulted in Wallace's forced resignation. Truman had been reluctant to fire Wallace, whom he wished to retain in the cabinet symbolically as the last of FDR's New Dealers, but he was troubled by Wallace's pacifistic instincts. "He wants to disband our armed forces, give Russia our atomic bomb secrets and trust a bunch of adventurers in the Kremlin Politburo," he wrote distressingly to his mother the same month as Wallace's ouster. "I do not understand a 'dreamer' like that."[49] This was not a time for dreamers. One wonders how different the world would have been if Wallace had remained on the Democratic ticket as vice president in 1944 and had taken the presidency on Roosevelt's passing.

Secretary of State James Byrnes also fell out of favor with Truman, leading to another pink slip. Byrnes had proved to be a foreign policy freelancer who believed himself to be more capable of being president than Truman. Truman had appointed Byrnes to the position in the first months of his administration, replacing Edward Stettinius, largely a figurehead under FDR, who was his own secretary of state. But trouble with his new secretary of state started early. On the way to Yalta, Truman described Byrnes as "able and conniving."[50] Byrnes had failed to keep Truman informed of his discussions with foreign powers, and his boss was concerned over his long absences from Washington, leaving the State Department without immediate direction. A protracted visit to the foreign ministers' conference in Moscow in December was Byrnes's undoing. Senators complained that he had conceded too much to the Soviets, and on his return he called a press conference before bothering to brief Truman.

By January, Byrnes was gone, replaced by George Marshall, who had served as army chief of staff, the military's top post, from 1939 to 1945, and whom Truman revered as "the greatest living American."[51] Marshall saw eye to eye with Truman on cold war strategy, articulating in a speech at Harvard University on June 5 the essence of the Truman Doctrine. "It is logical," Marshall stated, "that the United States should do whatever it is able to do to assist in the return of normal economic health in the world, without which there can be no political stability and no assured peace. Our policy is directed not against any country or doctrine but against hunger, poverty, desperation and chaos. Its purpose should be the revival of a working economy in the world so as to permit the emergence of political and social conditions in which free institutions can exist."

The speech drew international attention, and its concept resulted in the Marshall Plan, which would bring more than $17 billion in economic relief to rebuild seventeen countries in Central and Western Europe. Truman insisted that the credit for the plan go to Marshall out of respect and practicality. "Anything that is sent up to the Senate and House with my name on it," he remarked, "will quiver a couple of times and die."[52] Regardless of the name attached to it, the plan had no assurance of passing as it implicitly invited the Soviet Union and the Eastern European satellite nations to participate. Marshall, backed by the president, sent it to Capitol Hill regardless, knowing it was the right course. As it happened, Stalin wanted no part of the plan, dismissing it as an "imperial" plot by the United States to make Europe beholden to the United States and forbidding the satellites from participating.[53] Stalin's refusal to participate helped the bill's passage in Congress, which still struggled with its staggering cost.[54] Truman rationalized the outlay with House Speaker Sam Rayburn, reminding him that the Truman Committee had saved taxpayers $15 or $16 billion, which practically made the plan a wash, a small price to pay to "save the world."[55] Congress approved the plan in March of 1948, and Truman signed the bill into law on April 3. Within several years, Western Europe would raise itself out of the debris of war and once more contribute to the world economy while, in Truman's words, "lift[ing] it from the shadow of enslavement by Russian Communism."[56] Churchill called the plan "the most unsordid act in history."[57] It may also have been one of the wisest.

Well after leaving the presidency, Truman reflected on the qualities that make a good president. "First and most important, a president must be strong," he recorded for posterity. "That means, of course, a president who can make up his own mind, who isn't afraid of controversy. . . . And when he makes up his mind that his decision is correct, he mustn't let himself be moved from that decision under any consideration. He must go through with that program and not be swayed by the pressures that are put on him by people who tell him his decision is wrong."[58] Those were things that ultimately made *him* a good president, particularly in his first few years in office.

But while Truman's resolute executive decisions left little doubt that he was president, and his reverence for the institution was plain, his personal style came up short of presidential, at least in the estimation of the public. He lacked charisma as a speaker, giving, in the view of former White House speechwriter and political columnist William Safire, "solid and workmanlike speeches, fact-filled and frank, delivered in a stilted, hurried way that made it seem as if the speaker wanted to get it over with."[59] His off-the-cuff remarks, often impetuous, could be damaging. In a profession in which thick skin is as obligatory as a face mask to a hockey goalie, he was acutely sensitive to criticism of himself, family, and friends.[60] The most notorious example of this is Truman's 1950 letter to *Washington Post* critic Paul Hume after the latter wrote a scathing review of a singing performance given by Truman's daughter, Margaret. "Some day I hope to meet you," wrote the president. "When that happens you'll need a new nose, a lot of beefsteak for black eyes, and perhaps a supporter below!" While most fathers could hardly blame Truman for his protective instincts—Bill Clinton, a protective father himself, has a framed copy of Truman's letter in his office—and executive temper tantrums from the Oval Office were nothing new, their public expression and others were a blow to presidential restraint and dignity.[61] Furthermore, his loyalty to a number of friends from the past, several of dubious character, resulted in appointments to White House staff positions, minor scandal eruptions, and legitimate charges of cronyism. "To err is Truman" went one popular phrase of the day.

Sam Rayburn famously put Truman's shortcomings this way: "He was right in the big things, but wrong in the small ones."[62] Falling short on the small things, which added up, reinforced the impression of Truman as the little man out of his depth. His deficiencies belied his strength, which, in the opinion of Truman biographer Alonzo Hamby, was "based in a temperament that he was unable to exhibit in an attractive way." Here was a man of sound judgment and character, devoid, for the most part, of pettiness, but he got in his own way. He was, as Hamby wrote, "a strong chief executive who managed to look weak."[63]

It didn't help that Truman was dealt a tough hand not only abroad but also at home as Americans put the war behind them and tried to get on with the business of feathering their nests. Converting the economy from war mode to peacetime proved a formidable challenge that likely would have bedeviled any president. As Americans contended with the scarcity of consumer goods and escalating prices, despite the wartime price controls Truman kept in place to curb inflation, the blame fell squarely on him. Frustrated over the administration's efforts to keep prices in check—and getting in a few private digs at FDR—he wrote to his wife in June 1946, the "Office of Price Administration is a mess, brought on principally by the pinheads who have administered it. It seems the late President had a positive genius for picking inefficient administrators. I've come to the conclusion that he wanted to do everything himself and get all the acclaim for successful accomplishments and then have a dumb cluck take the blame for what failed."[64]

Organized labor presented another problem. Unions, now unaffected by the no-strike laws of the war and facing a rising cost of living, struck for higher wages. The economy slowed as workers in key sectors—steel, coal, auto, railroads, shipping—walked off their jobs, leaving production lines inactive and store shelves and showrooms depleted.[65] Truman took a firm hand with the unions in resolving the strikes, in some cases mandating arbitration for the good of the country. In a bitter clash with John L. Lewis, president of the United Mine Workers of America, that made headlines throughout much of 1946, Truman seized the coal mines when four hundred thousand miners struck.[66] Though wages for workers increased over time, it did nothing to boost Truman's standing with labor, a key Democratic constituency. Once more venting frustration in a letter to Bess Truman regarding another dispute that had reached his desk, he wrote in September, "This seaman's strike is the most of all headaches. I'm in the middle no matter what happens. [Reporters Drew] Pearson and [Walter] Winchell are lying again. Some day I'll have to shoot 'em both."[67]

As the midterm elections of 1946 neared, Truman's approval rating had nosedived to 32 percent as doubts arose anew over his ability to lead the nation forward. A Republican campaign slogan—"Had enough?"—spoke to the dissatisfaction of many, including Democrats, congressional and otherwise. When voters went to the polls in November, Truman and his party took it on the chin. The GOP gained control of both houses of Congress for the first time since 1930, as the Democrats lost fifty-five seats in the House and twelve in the Senate.[68]

Truman's bold stand against Soviet aggression, bolstered by the Truman Doctrine, gave him a jump in popularity in 1947. By April, 57 percent of Americans approved of the job he was doing. But Truman's determination to hold the Russians in check while maintaining peace was challenged in the summer of 1948, as the Soviets made their own stand in Berlin, the former German capital.[69] Like Germany as a whole, Berlin had been carved up in the wake of the war, with each of the four main Allied powers—the United States, Great Britain, France, and the Soviet Union—occupying and controlling its own area. Berlin, though, was located deep in Soviet territory, with limited access by road and rail. But on June 24, in a test of Western resolve, the Soviets choked off access, preventing the Allied powers from entering their zones and cutting off supply lines that left two and a half million West Berliners vulnerable to starvation. Stalin's expectation was that the Allied powers would withdraw from the city. Truman, however, remained firm. "We stay in Berlin, period," he commanded his military advisers.[70] The only solution was to bring in supplies by air, which presented the possibility that Soviet guns would fire on them, instigating a war. Truman took the risk. Shortly afterward, the Berlin Airlift began, with C-47 cargo planes flying over Soviet airspace, landing in quick succession, and bringing massive supplies to residents. When a U.S. official asked a Soviet general how long Stalin intended to stand off against the Allied powers, he replied, "Until you drop plans for a West German government." It didn't come to that. In a UN-brokered settlement, the Soviets relented 321 days after the blockade had begun. By that time, one and a half million tons of food, clothing, and fuel had been delivered.[71] David McCullough called the maneuver "one of the most brilliant American achievements of the postwar era and one of Truman's proudest decisions, strongly affecting the morale of Western non-Communist Europe, and the whole course of the Cold War."[72]

Cold war boldness notwithstanding, Truman's popularity was under siege for much of 1948. In April, his capricious approval rating was back in the thirties. The chief culprit was another of the president's bold stands, this one at home. In late 1946, Truman had appointed a blue-ribbon Committee on Civil Rights to look into the virulent issue of racism in America. Their findings, published in a final report in December 1947, moved Truman to press ahead for reforms in the new year that proved as morally courageous as they were politically injurious.

There was more than a hint of irony in the thirty-third president as a catalyst for change on the issue of civil rights. Truman's grandparents from both sides of the family had been slave owners under the auspices of the Missouri Compromise, and his mother, who had been harassed by Union troops during the Civil War, never quite forgave Abraham Lincoln for letting it happen—and never again laid eyes on a "good Yankee."[73] When, in her nineties, she visited her son at the White House, he teasingly suggested that she bunk in the Lincoln bedroom. "Bess," she said to her daughter-in-law, "if you'll pack my bags, I'll leave this evening."

While Truman may have been inclined by background to see African Americans as socially inferior, he believed that racial discrimination was a wrong that needed to be made right. Upon receipt of a letter from an old friend in Kansas City, Ernie Roberts, who rebuked Truman for the progressive measures on civil rights he was considering, Truman fired back a letter that clearly presented his side of the issue. "I am going to send you a copy of the report from my Committee on Civil Rights and then if you still have that antebellum proslavery outlook, I'll be disappointed in you," he wrote his friend. "The main difficulty with the South is that they are living eighty years behind the times and the sooner they come out of it the better it will be for the country and themselves. I am not asking for social equality, because no such thing exists, but I am asking for equality of opportunity for all human beings and, as long as I am here, I am going to continue to fight." Truman then cited examples of the heinous violence that had befallen blacks in the South, showing that "something is radically wrong with the system." He concluded: "I am going to try to remedy it and if that ends up in my failure to be reelected, that failure will be in a good cause."[74]

There was little doubt that the civil rights legislation would die on the vine before it reached Capitol Hill. That didn't stop Truman from proposing it in an address to the nation that underlined its importance, and taking executive action—not subject to congressional approval and despite a lack of public support—to ban segregation in the military and outlaw discrimination in the civil service.[75] Southern opponents in Congress railed against Truman's position, which William Colmer, a Democratic representative from Mississippi, attacked from the House floor in early April. Speaking for the vast majority of Southern congressmen, Colmer claimed Truman's stance divided the country "at a time when unity is so highly desirable in a fight to the death with the enemy of free men—communism" and encouraged "the arrogant demands of these minority groups."[76] The alienation of the Southern wing of the party sent Truman's approval ratings spiraling to 36 percent the same month.

"This head of mine should have been bigger and better proportioned," Truman wrote to his wife in his first year in office. "There ought to have been more brain and a larger bump of ego or something to give me an idea that there can be a No. 1 man in the world. I didn't want to be."[77] It may not have been his plan to be president, but it was a job he wanted to hold on to as the presidential election of 1948 approached. Truman accepted his party's nomination in July, as much of the Southern wing of the party bolted, forming the Dixiecrat Party in response to Truman's civil rights push, and nominating as its standard-bearer South Carolina governor Strom Thurmond.

While Truman wanted the presidency, it remained to be seen whether

Bess Truman wanted to be first lady at all, coming, as the position did, with the glare of spotlights. When Eleanor Roosevelt suggested to Mrs. Truman that she meet with the press shortly after Truman became president, she agreed, only to abandon the idea irrevocably.[78] "You don't need to know me," she told the female reporters who covered her beat. "I'm only the wife of the president, and the mother of his daughter."[79] Throughout her tenure the only interviews she gave were written responses to questions submitted by reporters, and even then her answers were often monosyllabic if they were offered at all. When one reporter submitted a question about what she would wear to an afternoon tea, she told her secretary, "Tell 'em it's none of their damn business."[80] But she worked hard as the hostess of White House functions and, according to her husband, served as his "full partner in all transactions—political and otherwise," just as she always had throughout their close marriage.[81]

As often as possible, though, Bess Truman escaped Washington and retreated to Independence, seeking refuge at her family's seventeen-room Victorian home at 219 North Delaware Street. Her grandfather, General George Porterfield Gates, built it in 1867 as he began to amass a tidy sum milling Queen of the Pantry flour, making the Gates family among the wealthiest of Independence.[82] She and her mother and three brothers moved into the house after her father, David Wallace, who held a number of public offices, shot himself in 1903, despondent over his inability to provide adequately for his family. Her mother, Madge Gates Wallace, "the queenliest woman Independence ever produced" by some accounts, became even more queenly as a widow.[83] After their honeymoon trip to Chicago and Detroit in 1919, the newly wedded Mr. and Mrs. Harry Truman moved into the house with the overbearing Mrs. Wallace, a cliché of a disapproving mother-in-law. Mrs. Wallace never quite got past the fact that her son-in-law hailed from a family of lowly dirt farmers and that her daughter could have married better, views she often shared within earshot of her son-in-law, who always held his tongue.[84]

If it was lonely at the top for Truman as president, it got lonelier with his partner away from Washington for long stretches. "Never been so lonesome in my life," he scrawled in his diary as he brought in the first day of 1947 at the White House without her by his side. When Bess Truman was in residence, it often came with a price: Madge Wallace, then in her eighties, frequently came along for the ride to live in the White House with her daughter and her daughter's ne'er-do-well husband. Even then, she called the president simply "Mr. Truman," as she always had, and, as the presidential election of 1948 neared, was heard to remark that she couldn't for the life of her understand why in the world he was running against "that nice man," Republican presidential nominee Thomas Dewey.[85]

In fairness, Madge Wallace wasn't the only one who wondered why Truman would bother to take on Dewey. The mustached New York governor came off as more in keeping with what American presidents looked and acted like—and, in the autumn of 1948, he had the air of inevitability about him. Polls and pundits provided overwhelming evidence that Truman was on his way out. A *Newsweek* survey in its October 11 issue, three weeks before the election, showed that of fifty political writers across the country, every one predicted a Dewey victory. *Newsweek* had come to the same inescapable conclusion. "The landslide for Dewey will sweep the country," it proclaimed. Upon learning of the poll, Truman told his aide Clark Clifford, "I know every one of these fifty fellows. There isn't one of them has enough sense to pound sand in a rat hole."[86] But even Truman knew things were looking dim, conceding before the Democratic National Convention that his approval rating had ebbed. Undeterred, he hit the campaign trail hard, making a feisty marathon whistle-stop tour that covered 31,700 miles on the rails, and making 256 speeches along the way—as many as sixteen in one day. More than twelve million Americans turned out to see the president as he made tough-talking speeches lambasting the Republican-dominated "no-good, do-nothing 80th Congress," while offering pledges to key constituencies.[87] As the tour gained momentum, Truman was greeted with friendly whoops and enthusiastic cries to "Give 'em hell, Harry." Dewey, meanwhile, sat back in presidential repose and waited for the election returns to confirm what seemed to almost all except Truman to be a foregone conclusion.

Truman spent election eve at the Muehlbach Hotel in Kansas City.

After a bath and a ham sandwich and a glass of milk, he retired to bed early as the returns came in. Twice during the night he awoke and listened to radio reports that revealed that he was ahead in the popular vote—but that he couldn't possibly win. When he got up the next morning, the miracle invoked by practically every political underdog since had happened. As West Coast returns were tallied, the national vote for Truman came to 51 percent versus 46 percent for Dewey and 2 percent for Thurmond. What's more, the Democrats gained eighty-three seats in Congress to secure majorities in both houses. As Truman won the presidency in his own right—and brought back the Democratic Party's command of Congress—the gargantuan shadow of Franklin Roosevelt receded further.

Truman's triumph was followed by a second term laden with frustration and disappointment. Encouraged by his reelection mandate, he pursued a liberal domestic agenda—the Fair Deal—which he soon found was out of step with the appetites of increasingly conservative Americans. Much of his agenda was struck down by an obstinate Congress. Minor scandals erupted in the administration, none directly implicating Truman but furthering the perception of cronyism and incompetence.

Though Truman continued to take a firm stand against the Soviets, it did little to help his flagging support. By the late forties, the Soviets had an atomic bomb of their own, as the stakes in the cold war got higher. In 1950, Truman was faced with the decision of whether to go ahead with the development of an atomic weapon that had five hundred times the power of the bomb dropped on Hiroshima. In a meeting with military advisers he asked simply, "Can the Russians do it?" When told they could, Truman promptly gave the go-ahead. The meeting lasted all of seven minutes.[88] But with the Soviets now able to annihilate much of the world with the push of a button, fear of Communist infiltration pervaded the country. Demagogues like Wisconsin senator Joe McCarthy exploited the climate for political gain, fanning the flames of paranoia resulting in a culture of McCarthyism. In a historical irony, the Truman administration—in particular, the State Department—was targeted as being "soft" on communism. In fact, Truman's continued adherence to the containment strategy inherent in the Truman Doctrine led to U.S. involvement in the Korean War, as America led a UN effort to fend off an invasion by the Communist North Koreans into South Korea. American troops, fully integrated now, battled on inconclusively for three years, further dragging down Truman's popularity, before the war was resolved in a deadlock by Truman's successor, Dwight Eisenhower.

By the time Truman gave the presidency over to Ike in January 1953, after declining another run to keep the office—miracles rarely happen in pairs—the American people were more than happy to see him go, handing him, just before he left, approval ratings that had ebbed to 31 percent. He and Mrs. Truman headed by train back to Independence, though to live alone this time. Madge Wallace had passed on the previous month, leaving the Trumans to themselves in the old house. Truman lived there for almost twenty years more before succumbing at eighty-eight to old age on the day after Christmas 1972—but, naturally, not without a fight.

Well before then Truman had experienced an upsurge in popularity. The public had come around to appreciating all he had done in his crowded hour of history, and the enormous weight he carried, not always gracefully, but decisively after the presidency was thrown at him with such urgency in the spring of 1945. Historians, too. A decade after he left office, a survey of history professors headed by Arthur Schlesinger Jr. improbably ranked Truman at number six among the thirty-one U.S. presidents measured, enough to yield a "near great" rating, which has stood in recent polls.

After leaving the presidency, Truman often invoked the epitaph in a cemetery in Tombstone, Arizona, that read, "Here lies Jack Williams. He done his damndest." "I think that is the greatest epitaph a man can have," Truman said, "when he gives everything that is in him to do the job he has before him. That is all you can ask of him and that is what I have tried to do."[89] In his book *The Truman Presidency*, published in 1966, when Truman was in his winter years, the author and columnist Cabell Phillips wrote, "Harry Truman was and remains an ordinary man . . .

who must make do without any special endowments of genius, intellect or charm. His strength lay in his ability to do the best he could with what he had and not despair over what he did not have."[90] In the end, he had done better than anyone had a right to expect. Neither Jack Williams nor Harry S. Truman could have hoped for much more.

# VII

# JOHN F. KENNEDY

## *"The torch has been passed"*

The president-elect had slept poorly. The day before his inauguration, John F. Kennedy awoke on the second floor of his redbrick
Georgetown town house before sunrise to the sound of a motorized messenger bike backfiring. He tried in vain to go back to sleep before giving
up restlessly as Washington started to stir with morning bustle and news-
men began gathering outside around his front steps, lying in wait to
capture his every move.[1] Ten weeks earlier, the country had elected Kennedy president by a margin of less than two-thirds of a percentage point,
choosing him over the incumbent Republican vice president, Richard
Nixon, making him, at forty-three, the youngest president-elect in the
nation's history. Since then he tried as much as possible to pace himself
for the challenges ahead. Sleep forgone, he got on with the day, eventually making his way outside into the cold January morning for a White
House appointment with Dwight Eisenhower, the oldest president, at seventy, who at noon the following day—January 20, 1961—would pass on
to him the burdens of the presidency.

The pair met in the Oval Office, where they had the second of their transition meetings; the first had occurred a few weeks earlier. They had met only once prior to that, in Potsdam soon after the war in Europe ended, when Kennedy, fresh from his duty as a PT boat commander in the Pacific, was covering the war as a reporter for Hearst while Ike was the commander of Allied forces, though Eisenhower could not recall the occasion. The two had not come in contact at all during Ike's eight years as president despite the fact that Kennedy was a U.S. senator from Massachusetts, a tenure that was just as unmemorable. Initially, the men approached each other warily. Ike may have resented Kennedy's campaign promise to "get America moving again," implicitly suggesting that he had sleepwalked through his eight years in the White House. He viewed Kennedy's election victory over Nixon bitterly, as a repudiation of his leadership.[2] And maybe their generational differences got in the way; twenty-seven years separated them. Eisenhower referred to Kennedy as "Little Boy Blue," while Kennedy called Ike "the old asshole," a military term reserved by junior officers for the top brass.[3]

Still, their meeting was cordial, as Eisenhower instructed the president-elect on the job in a forty-five-minute private discourse. His orientation included a discussion about the "Presidential Emergency Action Documents," a black vinyl bag containing options and codes to engage nuclear missiles that would always be within the president's reach. "The Football," so called because it was handed off from one military steward to another every eight hours, would now be handed over, at least figuratively, to Kennedy. With it went the supreme power to launch a nuclear attack within minutes.[4]

In a dangerous world defined by cold war tensions between the United States and the Soviet Union, where the two superpowers battled across the globe for geopolitical advantage, the notion of nuclear war was a sobering reality. Kennedy had exploited cold war fears by campaigning as a hard-liner against communism, playing up a perceived "missile gap" between the United States and the Soviets that implicated the Eisenhower administration. Opinion polls of the 1950s showed that the majority of Americans believed a nuclear showdown would occur sometime in the near future.[5] Eisenhower's foreign policy was characterized by containment of the Communist threat, as it had been in Truman's administration when the cold war began out of the wreckage of World War II. Ike provided a steady hand in dealing with the Soviets, and peace prevailed despite the global ambitions of the Soviet premier, the pugnacious Nikita Khrushchev. But there had been setbacks.

In the fall of 1957, the Soviets launched *Sputnik*, a 185-pound satellite about the size of a medicine ball, spurring American fears of Russian technological superiority as it orbited Earth.[6] The fear wasn't much ameliorated by the creation in 1958 of NASA (National Aeronautics and Space Agency), which stumbled along throughout the balance of Eisenhower's tenure as the USSR broadened its lead in the space race. In 1959, Fidel Castro led a band of revolutionary guerrillas to drive out the regime of American ally Fulgencio Batista, resulting in huge economic losses for the United States and the creation of a Communist state just ninety miles off the coast of Florida. The following year, the Soviets shot down a U-2 spy plane as it covertly photographed Soviet missile installations. Though the Soviets had suspected the United States of conducting these missions for some time—despite U.S. denials—they had no evidence. The Eisenhower administration insisted that the downed aircraft was simply a weather plane, before the Soviets revealed to the United States and the world that its pilot, Francis Gary Powers, a member of the CIA's covert operations team, had survived the crash and was now in their custody.[7] The incident further strained relations between the superpowers along with U.S. credibility, while providing a public relations boon for the Soviets. By October, American worries that the Soviets' unstable leadership might do something rash grew as Khrushchev appeared unhinged in the United Nations General Assembly, ranting and banging his shoe on the table in protest of an anti-Soviet speech.

At home, the Eisenhower administration contended with the growing civil rights movement among the country's African-American population. Martin Luther King Jr.'s Southern Christian Leadership Conference—formed after the arrest of Rosa Parks in 1955, as she refused to give up her seat to a white passenger, leading to the Montgomery bus boycott—was gaining momentum across the South and national attention with its focus on nonviolent protest against segregation. The year prior, the

U.S. Supreme Court ruled unanimously in the case of *Brown v. the Board of Education,* partially overturning an earlier high court ruling in *Plessy v. Ferguson* that allowed for "separate but equal" public schools for the country's black and white students. Eisenhower had responded to resistance to the ruling in 1957 by sending federal troops into Little Rock to enforce the Court's order and admit nine African-American students to Little Rock High School, a move opposed by Senator Kennedy.[8]

After their Oval Office talk, the president and president-elect adjourned to the Cabinet Room for a larger meeting with the outgoing and incoming members of their administrations. Among the items on their agenda was "trouble spots." Laos dominated the discussion. The small nation in Southeast Asia was vulnerable to a Communist takeover, which might precipitate a domino effect in South Vietnam, Cambodia, and Burma. "This is one of the problems I'm leaving you that I'm not happy about," Eisenhower explained to Kennedy. "We might have to fight."[9] Another trouble spot was Cuba. Kennedy had learned before the meeting of a U.S. operation in Guatemala, where the CIA was training a band of anti-Castro Cuban exiles for an incursion to overthrow Castro's government. He asked Eisenhower if he, as president, should support it. "To the utmost," Eisenhower replied, adding his contention that the operation should be "continued and accelerated."[10] Just before the end of their meeting, Eisenhower found a moment to tell Kennedy quietly that despite his claims in the campaign, the United States held a nuclear advantage over the Russians due to Polaris submarines with nuclear-missile-firing capabilities that surrounded the coast of the Soviet Union. "You have an invulnerable asset in Polaris," he assured Kennedy, "invulnerable." By the end of their meetings, Ike had developed a grudging admiration for Kennedy—as Kennedy had for him—though he worried that the young man wasn't quite up to the job.[11]

Snow began falling as Kennedy left the White House a little before noon. As he and an aide got into the backseat of a waiting limousine and breezed through the mansion's black iron gates, Kennedy reflected on Eisenhower, who exercised power with such reflexive ease and spoke so calmly about the grave problems of the world he would soon inherit.

"How can he stare disaster in the face with such equanimity?" he asked rhetorically.[12]

Eight inches of snow blanketed the capital by the following morning, all but paralyzing Washington for Kennedy's inaugural, as the temperature peaked at twenty-two degrees. Weather and conditions notwithstanding, twenty thousand people crowded around the East Wing of the Capitol awaiting the words of the new president, who was sworn in at noon by Supreme Court Chief Justice Earl Warren. Kennedy, in a long black morning coat and gray striped pants, parted with his thick overcoat and silk top hat, and offered the nation—and the world—his address, a hardliner's view of America's position in a world in which liberty was threatened by the spread of communism by the Soviet Union.

His voice rang out against the frigid winter air in his choppy Boston brogue:

*Let the word go forth from this time and place, . . . that the torch has been passed to a new generation of Americans—born in this century, tempered by war, disciplined by a hard and bitter peace, proud of our ancient heritage—and unwilling to witness or permit the slow undoing of those human rights to which this nation has always been committed, and to which we are committed today at home and around the world.*

*Let every nation know, whether it wishes us well or ill, that we shall pay any price, bear any burden, meet any hardship, support any friend, oppose any foe, in order to assure the survival and the success of liberty . . .*

*. . . to those nations who would make themselves our adversary, we offer not a pledge but a request: that both sides begin anew the quest for peace, before the dark powers of destruction unleashed by science engulf all humanity in planned or accidental self-destruction. . . .*

*In the long history of the world, only a few generations have been granted the role of defending freedom in its hour of maximum danger. I do not shrink from this responsibility—I welcome it. I do not believe that any of us would exchange places with any other people or any other generation. . . .*

*And so, my fellow Americans: ask not what your country can do for you—ask what you can do for your country.*

*My fellow citizens of the world: ask not what America will do for you,*
*but what together we can do for the freedom of man.*

Kennedy's New Frontier had opened; the thirty-fifth president had begun his presidency auspiciously. Speaker of the House Sam Rayburn gave him high praise. "Why this Kennedy fellow, he's got a brain—and he knows how to use it," he claimed. "That speech he made . . . was better than anything Franklin Roosevelt said at his best—it was better than Lincoln. I think—I really think—he's a man of destiny."[13] The address, particularly his entreaty for activism among his "fellow Americans," struck a chord throughout the nation, marking the idealistic dawn of the sixties—despite the bellicose cold war rhetoric laced within it. Sixty-three percent of Americans said they could personally think of something they could do to better the country, according to a Gallup poll taken a month afterward, a number that spiked among younger members of the population.[14] Among them was a twenty-eight-year-old African-American air force veteran, James Meredith, who, upon hearing Kennedy's words, made the decision to challenge racial segregation by enrolling at the all-white University of Mississippi, a bold step he would take the following year.[15]

Idealism and youth—which the new president radiated from the inaugural platform despite the formal attire he hoped would make him look more mature—would become hallmarks of his administration.[16] But they were not leadership qualities seen as virtuous by the members of the Russian Politburo, who tended toward the old and oppressive. Though he would not make a face-to-face assessment of Kennedy until their first and only summit four months later, Khrushchev would ultimately size up his American counterpart as callow, "not strong enough. Too intelligent and too weak."[17] He would test Kennedy in ways he hadn't tried with Eisenhower.

The Kennedy inaugural was a family affair. Seventeen members of the clan crammed together behind Kennedy as he took the oath of office, brimming with pride and charisma, and flashing hundred-watt smiles that would light up the media throughout Kennedy's presidency. Family had always been behind Jack Kennedy.

The second child of Joseph Kennedy and Rose Fitzgerald Kennedy, John Fitzgerald Kennedy was born in the family's middle-class home outside Boston, in Brookline, Massachusetts, on May 29, 1917. The Kennedys would not remain a family of five—or in the middle class—for long. Two years after graduating from Harvard College, and a year before marrying Rose, Joe Kennedy secured a loan allowing him to take over a small bank in East Boston, the Columbia Trust Company, making him, at twenty-five, the country's youngest bank president. By the mid-1920s, he had become a millionaire by exploiting the opportunities of the times, building his fortune on real estate, the booming stock market, and bootlegging in the midst of Prohibition, in addition to turning his talents toward producing Broadway shows and Hollywood movies, cofounding RKO. His affair with actress Gloria Swanson, among others, belied his carefully crafted image as a family man. In 1926, he moved his family to New York to be nearer to the nation's financial center, but the sprawling family compound in Hyannis Port, on Cape Cod, bought around the same time, would become the Kennedys' summer retreat and the place they most associated with home.

While her husband was away in Hollywood and traveling for long stretches, Rose Kennedy, devoutly Catholic, ran the household and tended to the growing brood. By 1931, the Kennedys had nine children: five girls—Rosemary, Kick, Eunice, Pat, and Jean—and four boys—Joe, Jack, Bobby, and Ted. The elder Joe Kennedy's unbridled ambition went well beyond his own aspirations. He had big plans for his sons—particularly the older boys, Joe and Jack—and the money and connections to help fuel them. His goal for Joe, two years Jack's senior, was nothing short of getting him elected as the first Catholic president of the United States. Politics ran in the Kennedy bloodlines. Rose's father, John "Honey Fitz" Fitzgerald, was the mayor of Boston, while Joe's father, Patrick Joseph "P.J.," was a Massachusetts state senator. Though Joe never ran for elected office, his burgeoning fortune and the accompanying power gained him high-profile political appointments. His financial support of

Franklin Roosevelt earned him the ambassadorship of the United States
to Great Britain in 1938, as Europe braced for war with Nazi Germany.
But his own political fortunes died with his isolationist stance on the war
and his openly expressed view that Adolf Hitler should be appeased. As
America's entrance into the conflict became inevitable, so did his resignation.

Winning was everything to the Kennedys, whether prevailing in a
backyard game of touch football or a rough-and-tumble political election. As far as old Joe was concerned, losing wasn't an option, though it
rarely came to that. Competition ran in the family, particularly among
the boys. In a race to see who could ride his bike around the block faster,
Joe and Jack went in separate directions with neither giving way as they
approached the finish line. Their collision sent Jack to the hospital,
where he received twenty-eight stitches, while Joe walked away unscathed.[18] The boys took their rivalry into adulthood.

Joe attended Harvard, where he shined as an academic and an athlete. Jack, often sickly despite looking the picture of suntanned health,
skated through prep school at Choate and his freshman year at Princeton
on charm and gentleman's C's. After dropping out due to illness and
later following his brother to Harvard, he got a bit more studious. Published when Jack was twenty-three, his book *Why England Slept*, his senior thesis examining Great Britain's dormancy as Nazi Germany gained
strength, achieved bestseller status thanks to his father, who bought
thousands. Shortly after the United States got involved in World War II,
Joe and Jack enlisted separately in the navy. Joe became a pilot in Europe, Jack a PT boat commander in the Pacific. In August of 1943, Lieutenant Kennedy's boat, PT-109, was rammed by a Japanese warship,
breaking it in half and killing two members of his crew. He led the survi-
vors to a small island several miles away, including one, severely burned
from the crash, whom he towed to shore by clenching the victim's life
vest in his teeth.

Jack returned home with a lifelong back injury and the Navy and
Marine Corps Medal for his courage and leadership. Joe, whose plane
was shot down during a dangerous volunteer mission over Europe, didn't

make it home. With his older brother's death, Jack inherited all his father's hopes for his sons. After his discharge from the navy and a brief stint as a journalist, Jack, encouraged by his father, embarked on a political career, cashing in on his war hero status and the old man's influence to win a Massachusetts seat in the U.S. House of Representatives in 1946, which he held for three terms. In 1952, he gained election to the U.S. Senate and reelection in 1956. Neither tenure added up to much in legislative achievement, but they provided stepping-stones to a bigger political prize.

"The most eligible bachelor in the U.S.," according to the *Saturday Evening Post,* Kennedy tied the knot in 1953, wedding Jacqueline Lee Bouvier, twenty-four, in a Newport ceremony that became the social event of the season.[19] While his womanizing would not end with his marriage, he had met his match in Jackie. The former Debutante of the Year for 1947–48 provided a graceful complement to the dashing senator and a cool contrast to the raucous, playful Kennedy sisters and sisters-in-law. When her husband's bad back, compounded by the effects of Addison's disease, led to spinal surgery that threatened his life early in their marriage, she stood close by his side. Sidelined from the Senate, he penned *Profiles in Courage,* with her help and that of others, winning the Pulitzer Prize in 1957 with the aid of family string pulling. They had their first child, Caroline, the same year. Their second, John Junior, was born in 1960, as President-elect Kennedy awaited the start of his administration.

Kennedy's bid for the nation's highest office began after a near miss of the vice presidential nomination in 1956. At the Democratic Party's convention in Chicago, his name went all the way to the second ballot before Tennessee senator Estes Kefauver walked away with it. Kennedy had no intention of settling for the second spot four years later, throwing his hat in the ring for presidency in 1960. Through the course of just over a dozen primaries, he fended off Democratic rivals Lyndon Johnson and Hubert Humphrey, among others, to take the nomination in Los Angeles in July, with his former opponent, Johnson, rounding out the ticket as his running mate. The election pitted him against the incumbent vice president, forty-seven-year-old Richard Nixon. Image would play to

Kennedy's advantage. A series of televised presidential debates—the first ever—gave Kennedy the edge over his opponent. In the first, which aired in September, Nixon, gaunt and underweight from a stay in the hospital for knee surgery, refused makeup to lighten up his five o'clock shadow. He came off pasty and sinister-looking, while Kennedy, tanned from a California campaign swing, appeared healthy and confident. The event ushered in the era of television in politics, a medium Kennedy would master in the same way Franklin Roosevelt had radio.

In November, Kennedy took the election by about 113,000 of the 68 million votes cast. Nixon conceded defeat despite widely reported voter fraud in Illinois and Texas. "We won but they stole it from us," he told a friend privately afterward, choosing not to contest the election and risk throwing the country off balance within view of the Soviets.[20] Before the election, Kennedy had joked about his father's possible monetary influence on the election's outcome by reading an imaginary telegram from him: "Jack, don't buy one vote more than necessary. I'll be damned if I'll pay for a landslide."[21] After the election, Kennedy was a bit more reflective. "The margin is thin," he said, "but the responsibility is clear."[22]

When assembling his cabinet, Kennedy turned, naturally, to family. Just after his election, he offered the post of attorney general to his brother Bobby. Seven years his brother's junior at thirty-six, Bobby declined, concerned about charges of nepotism and being under his brother's thumb. Kennedy urged him to accept the position, as did his father. It was a matter of trust. "I need someone I can completely . . . rely on," Kennedy explained, "someone who's going to tell me what the best judgment is, my best interest. There's not another member of the cabinet I can trust that way."[23] After all the other cabinet selections had been made, Bobby eventually agreed, making him the youngest to hold the position in the twentieth century. Kennedy defused the inevitable controversy of the appointment with characteristic wit. "I see nothing wrong with giving Robert some legal experience as attorney general before he goes out to practice law," he said.[24]

Sargent Shriver, Kennedy's brother-in-law, was charged with helping to fill the remainder of the cabinet. "Shriver knew the kind of man Kennedy wanted," explained Harris Wofford, who assisted Shriver in the task. "More accurately, since Kennedy worked well with and respected a wide range of types, Shriver knew the kind *not* wanted: the too ideological, too earnest, too emotional, and too talkative—and the dull."[25] Kennedy was interested in Robert McNamara, the first president of Ford Motor Company outside the Ford family, after reading a *Time* magazine story on him. Though McNamara had held the post for only five weeks, he accepted Kennedy's offer to become secretary of defense. Dean Rusk, a veteran of the Truman administration, was chosen as secretary of state, while a Republican, C. Douglas Dillon, was chosen as secretary of the treasury, an olive branch to the business community. Additionally, Kennedy surrounded himself with the next best thing to family: proven family loyalists and longtime friends, including Ted Sorensen, Kenny O'Donnell, and Paul (Red) Fay.

A lack of formality and hierarchy characterized Kennedy's organizational structure. He likened himself to the hub of a wheel, with all the spokes—cabinet members and senior staff members—pointing to him. He steered clear of large meetings, reasoning, in the words of his press secretary Pierre Salinger, that their "productivity was in direct inverse proportion to the number of participants."[26] Instead, he preferred small briefing sessions in which he listened intently and immersed himself in the details of the issues before him. Memos were produced and consumed with ferocity, all in a thirst for more information. He enjoyed the battle of politics but never lost his perspective or humor. Vindictiveness was not in his nature. "After a battle was won," wrote *Time* journalist Hugh Sidey, "he picked up his adversaries, dusted them off and offered his hand."[27]

As for style, Kennedy's was unmatched by any of his predecessors. His vigor and youthful persona were fluid symbols that the country had moved on from the Eisenhower administration and that the men in the trenches of the Second World War, not the commanders, were now in the seat of power. Indeed, vigor was a trait for which he would become known, but that alone didn't account for his appeal, which was enhanced by an easy confidence, a disarming, quick wit, and boyish American good looks complemented by a thick sheaf of tousled hair and a slightly rumpled presentation that saved him from looking too manicured. Although the election did not provide the resounding mandate he had hoped for, the public was soon taken with him. By late March his popularity, according to his pollster, Louis Harris, had achieved "record heights," surpassing the numbers Roosevelt and Eisenhower had seen a few weeks into their administrations.[28] Regular televised press briefings took the form of entertainment as the public tuned in to watch him address matters of state, hardly programming that would have made for gripping television in Ike's day. "How's your achin' back?" one reporter asked him: "Depends on the climate," Kennedy responded, "political and otherwise." The president would also use television for a special message to the American people to ask that they stop sending congratulatory letters and telegrams that were overwhelming the White House staff.[29]

Shortly after taking office, Kennedy accelerated missile deployments to address the missile gap issue he had exploited in his campaign—this despite the fact that the administration could find no evidence to support a Soviet lead. Kennedy neglected to inform the public that the gap was a falsehood.[30] Was there, in fact, a crisis at all? The Russians were quiet for the moment. Khrushchev had even dangled an olive branch in front of the new president, offering to release two air force pilots who had been held captive for seven months after their RB-47 plane was shot down over the North Sea, in exchange for assurances that U.S. spy missions would not be conducted over the Russian mainland.[31] Things were going pretty well. Was the supposed immediate Soviet threat just campaign rhetoric? Or was the threat always lurking? Were the Soviets opportunists who would take advantage when they sensed weakness?

While his elegant first days seemed to put him on the right foot to lead the nation, Kennedy soon stumbled. Three months after taking office, the president green-lighted the CIA's plot that he had discussed with Eisenhower in his transition meeting, allowing the invasion of Cuba by anti-Castro Cuban exiles. The plan was to have the exiles storm the island through the Bay of Pigs, where they would attract other anti-Castro locals and gain the support of the Cuban people, who would enlist in the cause to take out Castro. Kennedy had been wary of the mission from the start, but he was encouraged by members of the military and the CIA to move forward. The president fatefully yielded to their judgment. He would find out soon enough that they had severely underestimated the Cuban dictator and the support his Communist government had gained through its reforms. Within three days, more than four hundred of the invading exiles were dead, the rest easily captured by Castro's forces.

Declassified CIA documents on the mission, opened in 2005, reveal that the CIA assumed the mission would fail without U.S. military support, particularly ample air cover, and believed the president would send relief as the invasion began to slip. But Kennedy was not told, and had made clear earlier that he would not provide military backup for the mission for fear the Soviets would use it to justify taking military action in West Berlin.

Kennedy knew little of defeat but saw it in spades as the world watched. In the Soviet Union, Khrushchev took heart in Kennedy's ignominy. "I don't understand Kennedy," he confided privately to his son, Sergei, after the failed mission. "What's wrong with him? Can he really be that indecisive?"[32] Now was the time, he thought, to meet with Kennedy—when he was weak. But he didn't expect Kennedy to agree to a summit. He was wrong. The two parties agreed on May 12 to a meeting in Vienna in early June. "Getting involved in a fight between the Communists and anti-Communists in Cuba or Laos was one thing," Kennedy explained to his aide Ken O'Donnell. "But this is the time to let [Khrushchev] know that a showdown between the United States and Russia would be entirely something else again."[33]

Still, while the president was eager to face down his Russian opponent, the Bay of Pigs was a blow to Kennedy's confidence. As Ted Sorensen put it, Kennedy "realized he didn't have the magic touch. And he realized he had been mistaken in relying on the [judgment of] the military."[34] Kennedy was still reeling from the episode—and the misjudgment of the military and CIA—weeks later. "We're not going to plunge into an irresponsible action just because a fanatical fringe in the country puts so-called national pride above national reason," he told his friend Red Fay, the assistant navy secretary, over checkers during a weekend in Hyannis Port. "Do you think I'm going to carry on my conscience the responsibility for the wanton maiming and killing of children? . . . Do you think I'm going to cause a nuclear exchange—for what? Because I was forced into doing something that I didn't think was proper and right? Well, if you or anybody else thinks I am, he's crazy."[35] But it provided a lesson he would draw on later in the most critical hour of his presidency.

Even without the Cuba debacle, April had not been a good month for the young president. Five days after the Bay of Pigs invasion began, the Russians had launched a rocket containing cosmonaut Yuri Gagarin into the heavens where he thrice orbited Earth, becoming the first man in space and furthering the Soviets' lead in the superpowers' race to dominate the cosmos. If that weren't enough, there was the crisis Eisenhower had warned him about: The U.S.-backed nation of Laos was teetering precariously toward a fall to communism. The botched Bay of Pigs mission made Kennedy skittish over sending troops to stem the Communist tide that threatened to flow over Southeast Asia. His options limited, he agreed to turn that country over to a neutral UN force, resolving to drive a stake in the ground on communism in Vietnam instead. "If we have to fight in Southeast Asia, let's fight in Vietnam," he reasoned. "The Vietnamese, at least, are committed to fight. Vietnam is the place."[36] To that end, Kennedy stepped up the U.S. involvement in Vietnam, increasing the number of military advisers the United States had committed to the nation since the mid-1950s to a total of sixteen thousand as the war worsened throughout his term, while sending in the Special Forces to train the South Vietnamese army in counterinsurgency warfare.[37]

As the administration closed its first hundred days—the benchmark established by the dizzying legislative achievements racked up in the initial days of the Roosevelt administration—the press was not kind. *Time* magazine took him to task over the failures of April, "a month-long series of setbacks rare in the history of the Republic."[38] The public was more forgiving. A Gallup poll showed an 83 percent approval rating, with only 5 percent indicating disapproval of his performance. "Jesus, it's like Ike," he joked upon seeing the reassuring figures. "The worse you do, the better they like you."[39] But he was determined to do better.

In late May, Kennedy appealed directly to Congress to step up funding for NASA, putting forth a goal of "landing a man on the moon, and returning him safely to earth" by the decade's end, maintaining that no single space project "would be more impressive to mankind." It was an audacious aim, particularly given the haplessness of NASA's efforts to that point. Perhaps it was just a ploy for celestial bragging rights over the Soviets, but there was wonder in it that played into the American spirit, which Kennedy in so many ways embodied. If the United States was to lead the world, it must ever press forward. "Those who look only to the past or the present are certain to miss the future," he would say later.[40]

Kennedy met Nikita Khrushchev in Vienna on June 2 and 3, for a summit that took on all the drama of a heavyweight championship bout. The men in the ring couldn't have been more different, ideologically or otherwise. In one corner, the young Kennedy, the urbane, graceful child of privilege; in the other, Khrushchev, twenty-four years Kennedy's senior, the bumpkin former pipe fitter and son of a Ukrainian coal miner—stubby and bald—who possessed all the grace of a human thumb. "Your job, Mr. President," French president Charles de Gaulle counseled Kennedy before he sparred with his Russian counterpart, "is to make sure Khrushchev believes you are a man who will fight. Stand fast . . . Hold on, be firm, be strong." Like others, de Gaulle had his doubts. After the Bay of Pigs he believed "the young man" to be "somewhat fumbling and overeager."[41] Veteran diplomat Averell Harriman advised Kennedy to "have fun with Khrushchev. Remember, he's just as scared as you are . . . he'll try to rattle you, frighten you, but don't pay any attention to that. . . . His style is to attack and then see if he can get away with it."[42]

True to his style, Khrushchev prodded Kennedy on subjects like Laos, Cuba, and NATO's ongoing efforts to thwart Communism, as

Kennedy, slightly intimidated, tried to hold his own. The Russian leader prided himself on his ability to box smooth, better educated Western leaders into a corner and must have taken pleasure in the chance to take on the man his son-in-law in the Soviet Foreign Ministry in Washington had sized up as a "little boy in short pants."[43] The summit had a few ironic moments. When Kennedy lit up a cigar—he smoked up to three a day—he accidentally dropped the lighted match behind Khrushchev before snuffing it out. "Are you trying to light me on fire?" Khrushchev asked him. After Kennedy insisted he was not, Khrushchev replied, "A capitalist, not an incendiary."[44] But Khrushchev saved his most aggressive assault for the issue of Berlin, which he and Kennedy addressed on the second day of their meeting. The former German capital, divided between East and West Germany, was a sore spot for the Soviets; East Germany was losing two thousand citizens a day as they sneaked over the city's border to make a better life for themselves in the West.[45] Khrushchev, believing the American president to be indecisive and easily maneuvered, issued an ultimatum on Berlin: The United States must sign a peace treaty with East Germany or the Soviet Union would close off the city to the West.[46] Kennedy made it clear that the United States would defend Berlin "at any risk," after which, according to one attendee, the meeting descended into "table banging and the talk of missiles flying." "It is up to the U.S. to decide whether there will be war or peace," Khrushchev told Kennedy sharply. "Then, Mr. Chairman," Kennedy responded, "it will be a cold winter."[47]

As the two sides parted, Kennedy gave Khrushchev a model of the USS *Constitution*, "Old Ironsides," noting that the ship's weaponry could reach only half a mile. In past generations, he reminded him, war could be fought without devastating an entire generation. There was no such certainty in the nuclear age.[48] With that the meetings—the "roughest thing in my life," Kennedy called them later—came to an end.[49]

The president left Vienna with a dim view of the state of Soviet-American relations—and respect for and wariness of his Russian counterpart as a worthy but dangerous adversary.[50] "The next ten years are going to be difficult," he predicted ominously. "I came away feeling that in view of the Russian commitment to their system in certain areas and our commitment to our system in the same areas, it was going to be a close thing to prevent war. There is heightened danger for both countries."[51] What he found particularly disturbing was Khrushchev's ostensible indifference to a nuclear war. "[I] talked about how a nuclear exchange would kill seventy million people in ten minutes, and [Khrushchev] looked at me as if to say, 'So what?'" Bobby Kennedy said later that he had never known his brother to be "so upset."[52]

On August 13, 1961, the Soviets began construction of the Berlin Wall. By the end of the month the city would be divided by a stark barrier made of concrete blocks and barbed wire that spanned the border's thirty miles, East Berlin, drab and colorless, cut off from its vibrant Western sister . . . just a stone's throw away. The wall provided the tangible metaphor for the Iron Curtain that Kennedy would draw on in 1963, when he spoke to a crowd of 120,000, with the wall as a backdrop, proclaiming, *"Ich bin ein Berliner"*—I am a Berliner—in solidarity. But in the summer of 1961, the wall also solved a problem: It sealed off the border, cutting off the steady migration from East to West, and defusing the threat of war—at least for the moment.

The summer of 1961 also saw the first couple glitter across the world stage in a European swing that included a stop in Paris. There, Jacqueline Kennedy's charm won the favor of the cantankerous Charles de Gaulle. Her impeccable style, along with her flawless French, made her the toast of Paris—and the pride of her husband who, upon arriving back in the United States, introduced himself as "the man who accompanied Jacqueline Kennedy to Paris."

Jack Kennedy and the French were not the only ones beguiled by Jacqueline Kennedy. Americans swelled with pride over their first lady. Born in Southampton, Long Island, in 1929, and raised there and in New York City, she brought a cultivated East Coast sensibility and verve to the White House, which she was determined to make into "the prettiest house in America." Congress apportioned $2 million for the undertaking, allowing her to put her touch on the mansion.

Jacqueline Kennedy, along with her husband, also put a spotlight on

American culture, inviting artists, writers, musicians, and philosophers to Washington and turning the White House into a sort of royal court rivaling those of Europe.[53] In the Kennedys' second year in residence, the *New York Times* wrote, "The palpable love affair between the White House and a jade called Culture shows signs of reaching an impassioned peak this year."[54]

The cultural influences the Kennedys brought to the White House included reading, which the president did voraciously. Using speed-reading techniques he honed as a senator, Kennedy, when not devouring newspapers, magazines, memos, and reports relating to the job, read books, everything from political biography to Ian Fleming's James Bond novels, an indication of his appetite for intrigue.

Much has been made of Kennedy's favorite book, *Melbourne* by David Cecil. The biography of Queen Victoria's first prime minister documents the life of the English ruling class in the Victorian age, defined during the week by their service and devotion to country in London and on weekends by their lustful, adulterous romps at country manor houses. Discipline and duty followed by decadence. It fit the pattern of Kennedy's own life, though few knew it at the time. His rampant sexual adventures, the revelations of which dripped out sensationally after his death, have provided fodder for endless books and tabloid stories that Kennedy was spared during his presidency. Had they gotten out at the time, there's little doubt that his leadership position would have been compromised. His mistresses famously included actresses Marilyn Monroe and Angie Dickenson; gangster moll Judith Campbell Exner, whom he shared with Chicago mob boss Sam Giancana; and Mimi Fahnestock, a nineteen-year-old White House intern. A bombshell dropped in 2008 suggests that a JFK love child was produced after a fling with a Texas beauty queen.[55] Perhaps, like the nineteenth-century British aristocracy, Kennedy felt a certain level of entitlement around his escapades. There is little question, though, that his reckless behavior lacked sagacity and reflected a bulbous blemish on his complex character.

Though Kennedy did not define it as a critical domestic issue in his presidential campaign, and made no reference to it in his inauguration speech, the civil rights movement, which had been heating up since the 1955 Montgomery bus boycott led by Martin Luther King Jr., was building toward a slow boil. If the American concept of liberty was threatened by communism throughout the world, it was also embattled at home, where Southern segregation exposed cracks in its inherent ideal of equality. A month before Kennedy set out for Vienna for his summit with Khrushchev, a biracial group of thirteen young volunteers from the Congress of Racial Equality boarded a Greyhound bus in Washington bound for New Orleans in a journey through the Deep South to show the impotence of federal integration laws and the reality of Jim Crow to all of America. These freedom riders made it through the upper South without incident, but trouble came just over the South Carolina border when two members of the party were beaten at a rest stop, and another was arrested without cause. The incidents created a stir in the national media. As the violence in the campaign intensified and the number of freedom riders grew to three hundred, so too did American awareness of virulent racism in the South. The freedom riders forced Kennedy to deal with the issue of civil rights head-on. When white hostility erupted in Montgomery, Alabama, Bobby Kennedy sent in federal marshals. The violence left a deep impression on the attorney general. "I never quite recovered from it," he said later.[56]

Though President Kennedy believed he had done more for civil rights than any of his predecessors—establishing the Committee on Equal Employment Opportunity in 1961—most in the movement did not see it that way. "The Kennedys wanted [it] both ways," maintained the activist Roy Wilkins. "They wanted to be our friends and they wanted to break the movement."[57] Before achieving the presidency, Kennedy could hardly have been considered a champion of the cause—he declined to support Eisenhower's 1957 civil rights bill, the most ambitious civil rights legislation to that point, though his stance likely had more to do with political practicality. "JFK saw [civil rights] as less a moral crusade for the soul of America, as many white liberals believed it to be," wrote the historian Robert Dallek, "than a barrier to his presidential nomination. He was mindful of the injustices of segregation but was more interested in making sure he secured white voters across the South."[58] In his presidential campaign, Kennedy had paid lip service to civil rights but offered little of substance to back it up. Still, he won the support of Southern blacks when he intervened as Martin Luther King Jr. was arrested at a sit-in challenging segregation and sentenced to four months of hard labor in a Georgia prison. Kennedy called King's wife, Coretta, to offer support while arranging to have King released within a few days. Afterward, King's father, a powerful clergyman in Atlanta, switched his support from Nixon to Kennedy. With it came, in the elder King's words, "a suitcase full of votes," which may have meant the difference for Kennedy in the close outcome of the 1960 election.[59]

In September of 1962, all hell broke loose at the University of Mississippi in Oxford, where James Meredith, a lone black man with a court order ensuring his admission, attempted to enroll. Once again, Kennedy's response was to send in the National Guard in an attempt to maintain order, if not to promote systemic change. But by the time he gave the order, the clash with white segregationists had claimed two lives and left many more—including 160 federal marshals—injured. Martin Luther King Jr. spoke for many when he claimed that he was convinced that Kennedy "has the understanding and the political skills [to address civil rights] but so far I'm afraid the moral passion is missing."[60] By all indications, it was.

The aftermath of the Bay of Pigs fiasco went beyond the carnage of the failed foray and the resultant black eye for the Kennedy administration. The Castro regime, which had not been allied with the Soviet Union prior to the invasion, slowly came together with the Soviets in a Communist embrace. Cuba held strategic importance for the Soviets: It gave them a toehold in the western hemisphere and a presence in America's backyard. And it needed to be protected. By autumn of 1962, the Soviets had committed twenty thousand troops to the island, along with 150 jets, 350 tanks, and 700 antiaircraft guns.[61] In the words of Kennedy aide Arthur Schlesinger Jr., "Moscow had calculated that the United States, with the Bay of Pigs still in the world's recollection, could not convincingly object to Castro's taking defensive precautions against another invasion."[62]

The administration did not expect nuclear missiles to be part of the plan. U.S. Intelligence experts considered the Kremlin to be too rational and Khrushchev too cautious to take a risk of that magnitude, which would certainly provoke and justify an aggressive American response.[63] Surveillance photos from a U-2 spy plane taken on October 14 proved otherwise. They showed a medium-range missile site being constructed on the western part of the island, which meant that 85 percent of the United States would be within firing range.[64] More proof would mount in the coming days of the audacious size and scale of the operation.

Kennedy knew firsthand of war's futility. He had been there, and it had shaped him and his enduring impression of the world. When a reporter once asked him about his experience in the Depression, Kennedy conceded that as a rich man's son he knew nothing of it until he read about it later at Harvard. "War is my experience," he said. "I can tell you about that."[65] It had claimed the lives of his brother, two of his closest friends, his sister Kick's husband, and many others he had known. "All war," he had written poignantly from his PT boat in the Pacific, "is stupid."[66] Standing firm against the Soviet threat in Cuba through thirteen days in October, without pushing Khrushchev to war's brink, would become the central trial of his presidency.

The president immediately put out a warning to Khrushchev that the "gravest issues would arise" if it was revealed that the Soviets were providing offensive weapons to Cuba.[67] In the agonizing days ahead, he often convened his inner circle, the men he trusted to give him advice and not to leak it to the press, to consider his options, which he considered with a detached objectivity.[68] He brought the group closer after the Bay of Pigs—in particular, his brother Bobby and Ted Sorensen—realizing the need to keep his own counsel on matters relating to foreign policy where the stakes were higher. "Domestic policy can only defeat us," he often said. "Foreign policy can kill us."[69] But keeping the peace with the Soviets meant keeping the military at arm's length, resisting their persistent calls for war. After the Bay of Pigs, open animosity existed between Kennedy and the Joint Chiefs of Staff as well as the CIA, both of which had been caught by surprise by the current buildup in Cuba. "I think

JKF's war-hero status allowed him to defy the Joint Chiefs," maintained Schlesinger much later. "He dismissed them as a bunch of old men. He thought [chairman of the Joint Chiefs Lyman] Lemnitzer was a dope."[70]

Two options were debated: Kennedy could launch an aerial assault of Cuba, which would take out the missiles but potentially lead to a nuclear exchange with the Soviets. Or he could do nothing. One meant certain war, the other capitulation. But as Kennedy and his team considered the matter, another possibility presented itself, one far more palatable to the president: The United States could form a naval blockade—or "quarantine"—around the island, preventing Soviet ships from delivering the missiles and other supplies. Once the decision was made, he spoke to the nation on October 22: "Let no one doubt that this is a difficult and dangerous effort. . . . No one can foresee precisely what course it will take or what costs or casualties will be incurred. . . . But the greatest danger of all would be to do nothing. . . . Our goal is not the victory of might, but the vindication of right—not peace at the expense of freedom, but both peace *and* freedom, here in this hemisphere and, we hope, around the world. God willing, that goal will be achieved."

While Kennedy took the issue to the nation, Adlai Stevenson, the U.S. ambassador to the United Nations, took it to the General Assembly, where he made his case in "the courtroom of world opinion." Kennedy was no unilateralist. His strategy called for keeping the world's nations on the side of the United States—or at least keeping them neutral. Stevenson exposed the Soviet mendacity in the matter in a confrontation with Soviet ambassador Valerian Zorin during an emergency meeting of the Security Council, demanding to know if the Soviets had shipped offensive missiles to Cuba. When Zorin dodged the question, Stevenson told him he was prepared to wait "until hell freezes over" for an honest response.

As the standoff was occurring off Cuba's shores, the world braced for the worst. "We all agreed," said Bobby Kennedy afterward, "that if the Russians were willing to go to nuclear war over Cuba, they were ready to go to nuclear war, and that was that. So we might as well have the showdown then as in six months."[71] At the height of the crisis, the evangelist Billy Graham gave a sermon for ten thousand in Buenos Aires on "The

End of the World." *Time* magazine's Hugh Sidey walked out of the White House after an interview with the president wondering if it would be the last day before nuclear winter.[72] "I don't think America had ever faced such a real threat of destruction as at this moment," Khrushchev later wrote in his memoirs.[73] Through it all, Kennedy was cool. "He insisted on knowing all his options and what [solutions] were possible," Sorensen recalled of the president at that moment. "He did not do anything rash. He did not panic or overreact, did not yield to the military. He was calm—never lost his sense of humor, perspective, modesty."[74]

Kennedy also kept the lines of communication open with Khrushchev, exchanging cables with him throughout the ordeal in a direct dialogue, and using Bobby as his emissary to the Soviet ambassador to the United States. It helped defuse the tension; Khrushchev understood Kennedy's desire to avoid war, while appreciating his predicament as the military continued to call on him to respond by force.[75] On Friday, October 26, Kennedy received a long cable from Khrushchev in which the Russian leader made plain his desire for peace and a plea for levelheadedness in the matter. He assured Kennedy that if he had a peace treaty stating that the United States and its allies would not invade Cuba, and the United States pulled back its ships from the quarantine, the Soviets would back off. Likening the crisis to a rope with a knot in the middle, he wrote that the more the two sides pulled, the tighter it would get. If, on the other hand, the two sides gave the rope slack, the knot would loosen and could be untied.[76] Kennedy was encouraged by the communiqué, which was a welcome contrast to Khrushchev's usual truculence.

But the following day, October 27, Kennedy became aware of another letter addressed to him from Khrushchev, this one first broadcast on Moscow radio and written in a more familiar, strident tone. The Soviet Union would pull back its missiles from Cuba only if the United States removed its Jupiter missiles from Turkey, Khrushchev demanded. The contradictory letters brought with them a paradox: Which letter should Kennedy respond to? And what did the change in terms mean? Was it, as some suspected, a signal that there was a power struggle in the Kremlin? Was Khrushchev still in power?

Kennedy was willing to entertain the notion of removing U.S. missiles from Turkey as a means of resolving the crisis. "We're gonna be in an insupportable position on this matter if it becomes [Khrushchev's] position," he told the Executive Committee of the National Security Council (ExComm) in a White House meeting. "In the first place, we tried last year to get the missiles out of [Turkey] because they're not militarily useful, number one. Number two, it's gonna—to any man at the United Nations or any other rational man, it will look like a very fair trade." Bobby Kennedy advocated a more politically advantageous solution: Respond to the first letter; ignore the second. Kennedy agreed to try his brother's plan but didn't think Khrushchev would bite since the second letter had been made public. "We can try this thing," he said, "but he's gonna come back on Turkey." But it was Kennedy who ultimately yielded on Turkey—at least privately. As Kennedy historian Sheldon M. Stern explained, Kennedy's final response to Khrushchev offered "a calculated blend" of Khrushchev's October 26 and 27 proposals, in which Kennedy "left the door open to settling broader international issues once the immediate danger in Cuba had been neutralized."[77] In a clandestine meeting with the Soviet ambassador, Anatoly Dobrynin, on Saturday evening, October 27, Bobby Kennedy warned that the United States needed assurances that work was halted on the missile bases and the nuclear warheads returned to the Soviet Union. Otherwise, the United States would have no alternative but to take military action early the following week. He offered as a concession an American non-invasion pledge contingent on a UN inspection, a willingness to talk later about NATO-related issues, and a secret commitment to withdraw American missiles from Turkey.

On Sunday, Khrushchev broadcast another letter to Kennedy in which he restated the terms in his original letter. With assurances that the United States and its allies would not invade Cuba, the missile bases would be dismantled and the nuclear warheads packed up and shipped back to the Soviet Union, all to be verified by the UN. Kennedy's pledge to remove U.S. missiles from Turkey was not publicly disclosed and would remain a secret until tapes of his meetings with Ex Comm were released

over four decades after the fact. The crisis had passed. As Dean Rusk put
it later, "We stood eye to eye, and the other fellow blinked."[78] If Khrushchev had thought Kennedy to be weak, Kennedy had proved otherwise
as the Russian fleet retreated and Khrushchev's big gamble sank into the
Atlantic. The newspaper columnist Joseph Kraft wrote that Kennedy
had finally "[won] his manhood from the Russians." Indeed, as Khrushchev would later write, "In the final analysis, [Kennedy] showed himself
to be sober-minded and determined to avoid war. He didn't let himself
become frightened, nor did he become reckless. He didn't overestimate
America's might, and he left himself a way out of the crisis."[79] Kennedy
had shown the equanimity he could only have imagined when he met with
Eisenhower in his second transition meeting. At that moment, it made all
the difference.

Kennedy wisely did not crow over the victory, which might have put
additional political pressure on Khrushchev and aroused further tension.
Khrushchev had already suffered worldwide embarrassment and lost favor with Castro, the Red Chinese, and his own Politburo, which would
orchestrate his ouster the following October. But the president allowed
himself to stand for the moment next to one of his greatest predecessors.
Referring to Abraham Lincoln, who opted for an evening out after the
Civil War had ended, he joked, "This is the night to go to the theater."[80]

Although cold war tensions had eased, the battle over civil rights in
the South continued to rage. If Kennedy did not see civil rights as a
moral imperative before, he came around to the issue in the middle of
1963, as violence in Birmingham erupted in what would become the
movement's turning point. Birmingham had been among the worst examples of the segregated South. The incorrigible racism in the city—
nicknamed "Bombingham" for the eighteen unsolved cases of bombings
in black neighborhoods, including one at a church that killed four young
girls—was epitomized by Eugene "Bull" Connor, its commissioner of public safety, who reigned supreme. When the movement, led by Martin Luther King, focused its attention on Birmingham in the spring, the media
closely documented the brutal treatment of the African-American dem-
onstrators on the front lines. High-pressure fire hoses and attack dogs

were set upon them, and truckloads were carted off to jails, which were filled to capacity. Among those incarcerated in the campaign was King, who was taken into custody on Good Friday, April 12, under a trumped-up charge of parading without a permit. For eleven days he sat in solitary confinement, where he composed his famous "Letter from Birmingham Jail" to white clergymen who urged him not to conduct the Birmingham campaign and to exercise more patience in his quest for equality. The mainstream media had expressed similar sentiments. The *Washington Post* wrote that the Birmingham campaign was "prompted more by leadership rivalry than the real need of the situation," while *Time* held that it was "a poorly timed protest."[81] In his letter, King described the "white moderate, who is more devoted to 'order' than to justice . . . who paternalistically believes he can set the timetable for another man's freedom." He might have been writing to the president.

Earlier in the year, in February, Kennedy had sent a civil rights bill to Congress, but the legislation failed to address the desegregation of public facilities. Just as lukewarm was Kennedy's support of the bill, which fell flat. Now, with shameful images of the brutality in Birmingham being broadcast throughout the world, Kennedy, urged by his brother Bobby, took a firmer hand. Resisting political advice to wait until his second term, Kennedy drew up another civil rights bill, this one aimed at outlawing segregation in all public facilities.[82] The law, he believed, would give hope to the black community across America and defuse the bent toward mob violence. Political expedience was trumped by doing what was right. Otherwise, Kennedy maintained, the South would "never reform."[83]

On June 12, he took to the airwaves to appeal directly to the American people. Much of his address was extemporaneous; a formal speech was given to him just five minutes before he went on the air. "We are confronted primarily with a moral issue. It is as old as the scriptures and as clear as the American Constitution," he said.

*The heart of the question is whether all Americans are to be afforded equal rights and equal opportunities, whether we are going to treat our fellow Americans as we want to be treated. If an American, because his skin is dark . . . cannot enjoy the full and free life which all of us want, then who among us would be content to have the color of his skin changed and stand in his place? Who among us would then be content with the counsels of patience and delay?*

*One hundred years of delay have passed since President Lincoln freed the slaves, yet their heirs, their grandsons, are not fully free. They are not yet freed from the bonds of injustice. They are not yet freed from social and economic oppression. And this Nation, for all its hopes and all its boasts, will not be fully free until all its citizens are free. . . .*

*Now is the time for this Nation to fulfill its promise. The events in Birmingham and elsewhere have so increased the cries for equality that no city or state or legislative body can prudently choose to ignore them.*

It was the show of support civil rights leaders were waiting for. Roy Wilkins recalled later, "All of a sudden, [Kennedy] brought passion to [the issue], he brought that eloquence to it, and it electrified me and all kinds of other black people."[84] Not everyone agreed—in the South or elsewhere. A Gallup poll taken in September revealed that 50 percent of Americans thought the bill pushed the issue too hard, too quickly. Kennedy responded, "This is not a matter on which you can take the temperature every week or two. You must make a judgment about the movement of a great historical event which is taking place in this country. Change always disturbs."[85] After a slow start on civil rights, Kennedy had found his voice. In August, as a quarter of a million people came to the nation's capital for a March on Washington, where King stood in the shadow of the statue of the sixteenth president at the Lincoln Memorial and gave his "I have a dream" speech, the movement—lifted by Kennedy's leadership—had hit a crescendo.

Just under a year after the nuclear standoff over Cuba, Kennedy achieved what he considered to be his greatest accomplishment in office, bringing the Soviet Union and Great Britain to the table to sign the Nuclear Test-Ban Treaty. The agreement called for a limit to the testing of nuclear weaponry and represented an important step in relieving cold war tension. "So let us try to turn the world away from war," said Kennedy in a televised address announcing the agreement to the nation. "Let us make the most of this opportunity, and every opportunity, to reduce tension, to slow down the perilous nuclear arms race, and to check the world's slide toward final annihilation."

By the autumn of 1963, Kennedy was riding high. Progress was being made in the peace process with the Soviets and on civil rights. NASA's Mercury program showed that the United States was finding its way in space after six successful missions, the last of which, in May, had astronaut Gordon Cooper in orbit for a total of thirty-four hours, during which he orbited Earth twenty-two times. The economy was humming along nicely. "Let's face it," wrote William Styron in a gushing *Esquire* profile in September, "after these many months into his office, JFK is no ordinary chief magistrate, like all those frock coated muttonchopped non-entities from bygone days, but the glamorous and gorgeous avatar of American power at the magic moment of its absolute twentieth-century ascendancy. The entire world, including even the Russians, has gone a little gaga over this youthful demigod and his bewitching consort and [this] writer has to confess that he is perhaps a touch gaga himself."[86] The forty-six-year-old president had gone through the fire and, after setbacks and mishaps, begun to deliver on the promise the nation saw at the dawn of his presidency, as it lost itself in his inaugural oratory. He had grown in his presidency, and esteem for him grew in kind.

Then, Dallas. In late November, the president made a trip to Texas to mend political fences, taking along his wife, Lyndon Johnson, and Lady Bird Johnson. Kennedy's approval in the Lone Star State had plunged from 76 percent the previous year to 50 percent, and he was pulling out all the stops to get back in its good graces.[87] On November 22, he and Jacqueline Kennedy awakened in Fort Worth to rain before journeying by air to Dallas. They landed at Love Field, then traveled by motorcade downtown, where Kennedy was to speak at a luncheon at the Trade Mart. It was a beautiful fall day, full of endless blue sky. What happened next is lodged in the collective consciousness of most Americans of a certain age, in iconic images that lead inescapably to the same outcome: the gliding open limousine, midnight blue gleaming in the

Texas sunshine, the first couple in the backseat, smiling, waving. Three shots. The president propelled forward by a bullet, his head slumped, then thrust back again by another. Panic. Chaos.

At Parkland Hospital, President Kennedy was pronounced dead at 1:00 P.M., a half hour after the shots were fired. His wife was the first to bid him good-bye. She slipped her wedding ring on his finger and whispered in his ear words long left to eternity.


"So now he is a legend," said Jacqueline Kennedy mournfully after her husband's death. "When he would have preferred to be a man."[88] Legend has a way of contorting reality, mocking the dead by magnifying truths until they are often stretched beyond recognition. In political figures, legendary status is almost inevitably followed by revisionism, which often goes to another extreme, like moving against a funhouse mirror. That has been the martyred Kennedy's fate.

His abbreviated legacy is complicated by the challenge in sorting out who he was from what he could have been—what *we* could have been. "Even Americans mindful of the limitations of John Kennedy's thousand days," wrote Tom Wicker, "and of the later revelations of his follies and fallibilities, look back upon him as to their own lost dreams. He is the most fascinating might-have-been in American history, not just for what he was in his time but for what we made of him—not because of what we were but because of what we thought we were, and know now we'll never be."[89]

In true Kennedy fashion, JFK had grand ambitions for his place in history. For his epitaph, though, he had this simple hope: "He kept the peace." While his legacy will continue to be debated, Kennedy, at his best, eloquently, gracefully gave us the elusive promise of peace. Would he have reversed his own policy and deescalated American involvement in Vietnam—despite the political fallout he would have faced—as some in his administration have suggested? After a slow start, would he have further advanced the cause of civil rights and bridged the divide between black and white? In the wake of the Nuclear Test-Ban Treaty, would he have continued to work with the Soviets toward détente in the cold war, perhaps ending it altogether? Or would his sexual indiscretions have gotten the better of him, compromising his leadership or cutting his administration short even if an assassin's bullets hadn't? Who can say? But in the darkest hour of the twentieth century's latter half, when nuclear tensions between the superpowers threatened to seethe unrestrained and unleash unimaginable horror, he coolly held his promise. He kept the peace.

# VIII

## GERALD R. FORD

### *"Our long national nightmare is over"*

The 531 members of the Eighty-first Congress first convened at the Capitol on January 3, 1949. The makeup of the body had changed substantially from the last Congress. On Election Day the previous fall, Harry Truman had defied the expectations of nearly everyone in America by holding onto the presidency, defeating his Republican challenger Thomas Dewey, who expected to coast to an easy White House victory. The feisty Truman, who campaigned heartily against the Republican-dominated "Do-Nothing" Eightieth Congress, won by the thinnest of margins as the GOP lost eighty-three congressional seats to the Democrats, which had gained the majority in both houses.

Truman was not the only one who had engineered a surprise victory the previous year. Among the few Republicans entering the House's freshman class on that early January day was Gerald Rudolph Ford, from Michigan's Fifth District, a thirty-five-year-old lawyer from Grand Rapids who was expected to be beaten handily by the popular nine-year incumbent Bartel Jonkman, a "dedicated isolationist." Instead, Ford, a "converted internationalist," walked away with two-thirds of the vote.[1]

But few who knew Ford would have counted him out in the first place. Jerry Ford was a winner. A hardworking, modest former University of Michigan football hero, Ford played to win, shaking hands and making friends afterward regardless of the numbers on the scoreboard.[2] It was hard not to like him.

After Ford was sworn in to the House with the other freshman members, the first hand extended to him was that of another young Republican representative who had been elected to Congress two years earlier. "I'm Dick Nixon from California," he said. "I welcome you here in the House Chamber."[3] They could not have known then that their political fortunes would ultimately become as intertwined as their introductory handshake.

At first glance, Jerry Ford and Dick Nixon had much in common. Both were born in 1913 from up-from-the-bootstraps beginnings. Both achieved good grades while working their way through college and went on to attend elite law schools before enlisting in the navy for service in the Second World War. And both gained election to the House of Representatives in their thirties, representing a new breed of congressman who had come off the front lines of the war. But while they were looked upon as "comers" in Washington, their ambitions differed. Ford wanted to be speaker of the House; Nixon wanted to be president. As the two were brought together in the White House a quarter of a century later under the extraordinary circumstances of Watergate—a plight that battered the American people's faith in the presidency and their government, precipitating a crisis of confidence—their differences could not have been more glaring.

The supreme political ambitions of Richard Nixon would be achieved as he and his running mate, Spiro Agnew, former governor of Maryland, narrowly defeated the Democratic ticket, led by the incumbent vice president, Hubert Humphrey, to win the White House in 1968. It represented a major comeback for Nixon, who had emerged from the wilderness after many had thought they had seen the last of him—at least politically. His had been a turbulent rise. After two terms in the House,

Nixon had gained election in the Senate in 1950, in an ugly red-baiting campaign against the Democratic challenger, Helen Gahagan Douglas, in which Nixon exploited anti-Communist fears. Two years later, at the age of thirty-nine, he became the GOP's vice presidential nominee, providing a youthful balance to the party's sixty-two-year-old standard-bearer, Dwight Eisenhower. Nixon barely held on to his position on the ticket as allegations spread that he had earlier received $18,000 in illegal campaign contributions from wealthy California businessmen. Only a maudlin televised appeal to the American public—the Checkers speech, as it would become known—saved him from being dumped by Ike. Nixon went on to serve for two terms as vice president.

When Nixon won the Republican presidential nomination in his own right in 1960, Eisenhower didn't exactly rally around his number two. Asked by a reporter for a reason why his vice president should be elected president, Eisenhower replied, "Give me a week and I might think of one." It was meant to be a joke, but it stuck. Nixon went on to lose the 1960 election to John F. Kennedy by two-thirds of a percentage point, leaving Washington for private life in his native California. But less than two years later, Nixon was back in the arena, challenging popular Democratic governor Edmund "Pat" Brown for the California statehouse. Brown prevailed easily by three hundred thousand votes, leaving Nixon to call his "last press conference." "Just think of all the fun you'll be missing," he told reporters dejectedly afterward. "You won't have Nixon to kick around anymore." "You reduced him to the nut house," President Kennedy told Brown in a congratulatory phone call afterward. "That last farewell speech of his . . . it shows that he belongs on the couch."[4] Kennedy's doubts about Nixon's psychological shortcomings notwithstanding, Nixon came back after six years in private law practice in New York City to win politics's crown jewel.

While Nixon played out his ambitions in the fifties and sixties—winning and losing—Ford plugged away in the House, where he earned the trust and admiration of his colleagues on both sides of the aisle, rising through the ranks to become minority leader in 1964, the same year President Lyndon Johnson tapped him to be a member of the six-man Warren

Commission investigating Kennedy's assassination. He saw Nixon's potential early, as the two became friends as junior members of the Chowder and Marching Society, an ongoing gathering for conservative congressional Republicans. In 1951, when Ford was charged with producing a speaker for Grand Rapids's biggest annual Republican affair, the Lincoln Day Banquet, he chose Nixon, the new California senator. Not only did Ford respect Nixon for his insight on the issues of the day, a position many Republicans shared, he was one of the few who actually *liked* Nixon and considered him a friend. When others in the party wrote off Nixon after his 1962 gubernatorial loss, Ford continued to support him and believed in his "greatness."[5] He and Nixon talked often about political issues and Republican strategy. After Nixon secured the presidential nomination in 1968, Ford was among those he considered as his running mate, though it was just a courtesy. By the time he approached Ford with the possibility of rounding out the ticket, he had already settled on Agnew—a choice that astounded Ford, who supported New York mayor John Lindsay for the spot. Ford, in any case, was hoping to become House speaker. As it would become known later, Nixon doubted Ford's abilities in the first place.[6]

Nixon took office in 1969 with a pledge to "bring us together." After the divisions of the Vietnam War, which raged through most of the decade, the country needed unity. But it was a promise Nixon was ill suited to deliver on. If the country was divided, so too was he. As he established himself as president, two distinct Nixonian personalities emerged. The first was the one Nixon strove for, the peacemaker, the statesman who sought to find a place in history alongside Woodrow Wilson. It was this Nixon who would draw on his extraordinary knowledge of and interest in foreign affairs to improve America's standing in the world. Consulting closely with his national security adviser and later secretary of state, Henry Kissinger, Nixon worked toward détente with Soviet premier Leonid Brezhnev, carving out an arms agreement to limit the production of nuclear weapons; negotiating a peace treaty between Israel and its neighboring enemies, Egypt and Syria; and, perhaps most spectacularly, providing the opening for establishing diplomatic relations with the People's

Republic of China, which he visited in 1972. But there was another Nixon, the one Kennedy had caught a glimpse of in Nixon's "last press conference": a bitter, angry partisan who believed the world was out to get him. This was Nixon despite himself. It was this Nixon who allowed Watergate to unravel his presidency. America would come to know him in time.

Watergate started off as a simple, bungled robbery of the Democratic National Committee offices in Washington's Watergate Office Building on June 17, 1972. The burglary resulted in the arrests of seven men, including one former FBI agent and two former White House aides who were working for the Committee to Re-elect the President, given the ironic and unfortunate acronym CREEP. Coverage of the story continued throughout the summer and fall, revealing suspicious ties to the White House and implicating others in the administration. Even so, a Gallup poll taken just before Election Day revealed that only half of Americans had heard of Watergate. Nixon went on to win reelection against his challenger, North Dakota senator George McGovern, in a rout, capturing just over 60 percent of the popular vote and every state except Massachusetts. But as would soon be discovered, Watergate was the tip of the iceberg for the web of deceit and trickery that emanated from the Nixon White House.

As the scandal played out in mounting revelations that weighed heavily on Nixon over time—gleaned from investigative reporting and televised congressional hearings on the matter— Spiro Agnew had troubles of his own. In 1973, allegations surfaced that Agnew, while governor of Maryland, accepted kickbacks from state contractors. Nixon was compelled to accept Agnew as his vice president in the first place only because he would appeal to white Southerners put off by the civil rights movement, but he didn't believe Agnew was capable of taking on the presidency. "By any criteria he falls short," Nixon told John Ehrlichman, his chief domestic adviser. "Energy? He doesn't work hard; he likes to play golf. Leadership?" Nixon just laughed. "Consistency? He's all over the place."[7] The American public was even less enthusiastic. Agnew was seen largely as a hatchet man for Nixon. By October 1973, it was a moot point. Agnew resigned before accepting a deal with federal prosecutors that had him pleading no contest to tax evasion and paying $170,000 in fines.

That left Nixon with a vacancy to fill, a particularly important one given the fact that Watergate left his presidency teetering precariously as Congress and the nation continued to question Nixon's involvement in the affair. The provisions of the Twenty-fifth Amendment to the Constitution, passed after Kennedy's assassination, allowed for the appointment of a vice president with the approval of Congress in the event of a "death, resignation or removal," though it had yet to be employed. The amendment was long in coming. Since the Constitution went into effect in 1787, seven presidents had died in office, leaving the incumbent vice president to assume his duties but not allowing for a vice presidential replacement. For about 20 percent of that time, the speaker of the House was the next in line for the presidency. As it stood, with Agnew's departure, Carl Albert, the Democratic House speaker, would be heir to the presidency if it were to be vacated by Nixon.

Nixon's choices for the vice presidential appointment were John Connally, his secretary of the treasury and chosen successor, and Ronald Reagan, governor of California. Nixon liked both men and thought them to be strong leaders. But neither had the support of Congress, and with the dark cloud of Watergate hovering over Nixon, congressional leaders had the upper hand in negotiations. Their choice for the position was Jerry Ford. They knew him and trusted him. And if Nixon were to leave the presidency as Watergate crept closer, they believed Ford would be the right man for the job. "We gave Nixon no choice but Ford," Albert recalled later.[8] Nixon yielded to their wishes by nominating Ford, and Congress promptly approved his choice—92 to 3 in the Senate; 387 to 35 in the House—but he was hardly happy about it. "Can you imagine Jerry Ford in this chair?" he asked incredulously of former New York governor Nelson Rockefeller, pointing to his Oval Office seat.[9] Later, after affixing his signature to Ford's appointment, he forwarded the pen as a souvenir to his lawyer, Fred Buzhardt, with a note that read, "Here's the damn pen I signed Jerry Ford's nomination with."[10]

In 1972, the GOP failed to win a majority in the House, despite Nixon's landslide victory over George McGovern. Ford had made the decision to retire from politics when his term ended in 1975. With no possibility in sight for his promotion to House speaker, he and his wife, Betty, thought it was time to move on. Those plans were now put on hold. On December 6, 1973, with Nixon and Ford's peers from Congress looking on, Ford was sworn in to his new office as the House chamber erupted with applause. Showing his modesty—and self-awareness—the new vice president managed expectations from the start. "I am a Ford, not a Lincoln," he said in a statement just after taking office.

Robert Dole, senator from Kansas, upon seeing a photograph of Jimmy Carter, Ford, and Nixon together after they had all left office, described them respectively in jest as, "speak no evil, see no evil, and evil." As with any good joke there was an element of truth in it. Ford's biggest liability in politics was his naïveté. When he asked Nixon if he had been involved in Watergate, Nixon insisted he hadn't, "I believed what I was told," said Ford later. "So my whole conduct as vice president was predicated on that personal trust."[11] He spent the bulk of his vice presidency doing what he felt was best for the president and the country: touring the United States to proclaim Nixon's innocence in the affair and attempt to restore his credibility. By July of 1974, Ford had logged 130,000 miles on the road across the country in his Nixon goodwill tour, though by the end his trust in the president's word had steadily eroded.[12]

On August 5, Nixon's house of cards fell in. As tapes of Nixon's Oval Office conversations were given over to federal prosecutors, one surfaced providing evidence of Nixon's direct involvement in covering up the affair. The "smoking gun" tape, recorded six days after the Watergate break-in, had Nixon ordering White House chief of staff H. R. "Bob" Haldeman to call off the FBI from looking into the incident. The revelation evaporated Nixon's remaining support on Capitol Hill. Ford's reaction to the news wasn't unlike that of other Americans. He was hurt and, as he wrote later, "the hurt was deep." Even then, though, Ford believed that Nixon, while complicit, had been wronged by his aides John Erlichman and Haldeman, who had led him down the wrong path.[13] In a

White House cabinet meeting on August 6—Nixon's last—Ford informed the president that he too could no longer support him. Henry Kissinger would later write of the situation: *"The presidency was in a state of shambles. The last cabinet meeting of the Nixon Administration had ended in as close to open rebellion as the American system can produce. The balance between the Executive and Legislative branches was shifting to the point where the basic authority of the president was in question. Foreign policy, which depends crucially on Presidential authority and national consensus, had to be conducted against the permanent risk of catastrophe."*[14]

Three days later, 150 million Americans tuned in to watch Nixon from the Oval Office. "I have always tried to do what is best for the nation," he said, looking aged beyond his sixty-one years. "Because of the Watergate matter, I might not have the support of the Congress that I would consider necessary to back the very difficult decisions and carry out the duties of this office in the way the interests of the nation would require. . . . Therefore, I shall resign the Presidency effective at noon tomorrow. Vice President Ford will be sworn in as President at that hour in this office."

Never before in the history of the American republic had a president resigned the office. Never before had the whiff of scandal from the Oval Office been so strong. And never before had an appointee—unelected nationally—advanced to the presidency. But there it was, thrust in the hands of Gerald Ford, appointed by a corrupt president, approved by the members of Congress, and elected only by the voters of Michigan's Fifth Congressional District. The circumstances were, as the historian Roger B. Porter would later assert, "as difficult as those facing Abraham Lincoln and Franklin Roosevelt."[15]

The following day, his family by his side, Nixon gave his farewell to his staff—as beleaguered as he—in the East Room of the White House. At once gracious and self-pitying, the address was as contradictory and paradoxical as the troubled man who gave it. "Always remember," he advised those assembled toward the end, "others may hate you, but those that hate you don't win unless you don't win, unless you hate them. Then you destroy yourself." Afterward, Gerald and Betty Ford somberly es-

corted Richard and Pat Nixon down a red carpet laid carefully across
the rolling South Lawn, leading to Marine One, the presidential helicopter, which would whisk the Nixons off to Andrews Air Force Base and on
to an uncertain private life at their home in San Clemente, California.
Pat Nixon boarded first, followed by her husband, who turned to the
crowd assembled, forced a smile, and, raising his arms over his head,
incongruously flashed his trademark V for victory sign, which turned
into a sweeping, forlorn farewell wave. Then he was gone.

A little over an hour later, at noon, Ford was in the East Room, where
the chairs had been rearranged in another direction, a symbol for the
new administration that would begin as Ford was given the presidential
oath of office by Supreme Court Chief Justice Warren Burger. Shortly
afterward, he gave his first address as president, offering plain, simple
words in his slow Midwestern burr. He acknowledged, "This is an hour
of history that troubles our minds and hurts our hearts," and offered not
an "inaugural speech" but "a little straight talk among friends."

*I am acutely aware that you have not elected me as your President by your
ballots, and so I ask you to confirm me as your President with your prayers.
And I hope that such prayers will also be the first of many.*

*If you have not chosen me by secret ballot, neither have I gained office by
any secret promises. I have not campaigned either for the Presidency or the
Vice Presidency. I have not subscribed to any partisan platform. I am indebted to no man, and only to one woman—my dear wife—as I begin this
very difficult job. . . .*

*I believe that truth is the glue that holds government together, not only our
Government but civilization itself. That bond, though strained, is unbroken at
home and abroad.*

*In all my public and private acts as your President, I expect to follow my
instincts of openness and candor with full confidence that honesty is always
the best policy in the end.*

*My fellow Americans, our long national nightmare is over.*

*Our Constitution works; our great Republic is a government of laws and
not of men. Here the people rule. But there is a higher Power, by whatever*

*name we honor Him, who ordains not only righteousness but love, not only justice but mercy.*

*As we bind up the internal wounds of Watergate, more painful and more poisonous than those of foreign wars, let us restore the golden rule to our political process, and let brotherly love purge our hearts of suspicion and of hate.*

*In the beginning, I asked you to pray for me. Before closing, I ask again your prayers, for Richard Nixon and for his family. May our former President, who brought peace to millions, find it for himself.*

Ford had seen the speech for the first time the day before. It had been written by his aide Robert Hartman as part of the functions of a transition team headed by Ford's former Michigan law partner, Phil Buchen, who had put together the group without Ford's knowledge. Ford asked only that one passage be removed from the address: "Our long national nightmare is over." "If you strike that, I'm quitting," Hartman replied.[16] Ford yielded. The line proved the speech's most resonant and, in conjunction with Ford's steady presence, captured the relief of the nation.

"Openness will be the hallmark of my administration," Ford had promised Senate Majority Leader Hugh Scott the day before taking office.[17] It needed to be. Openness was the remedy to restoring the trust of the American people after the imperious, furtive Nixon years. Nixon, who had promised Americans, "I am not a crook," had left a searing impression of corruption and the worst stereotypes of government abuse.

After the siege of Watergate, Ford was a breath of fresh air. As open and uncomplicated as the plains on which he grew up, he embodied the values of his native Midwest, where he had been born Leslie King Jr. in Omaha, Nebraska, on July 14, 1913, the son of Leslie King and Dorothy Gardner King. Two weeks into her marriage, the newly pregnant Mrs. King moved back to her parents' home of Grand Rapids to escape her abusive husband. After divorcing King, she married Gerald Rudolph Ford, a local paint salesman who never made it in school beyond grade eight. Mr. Ford became the adoptive father to his wife's son, whom they renamed Gerald Rudolph Ford Jr. The couple went on to have three more sons. Growing up in Grand Rapids, young Jerry Ford always had a job and worked hard at everything he did, becoming an Eagle Scout and excelling as an athlete on the gridiron. He went on to attend the University of Michigan, where he starred as the center on the football team. Rejecting offers to play professional football for the Detroit Lions and Green Bay Packers, he went off to Yale Law School, working as a boxing coach to earn extra money. Afterward, he served as a naval officer in the Pacific during World War II, later returning to Grand Rapids, where he soon felt the tug of Republican politics.

As the country got to know the new president, the imperial shadow cast by the Nixon administration receded. The *New York Times* later wrote that Ford "placed no intolerable intellectual or psychological burdens on a weary land."[18] Small things went a long way toward reinforcing the change. Ford ordered that the White House living quarters, referred to as the "mansion" by the Nixon administration, now be called the "residence." When it was appropriate, "Hail to the Chief" was replaced by the University of Michigan "Fight Song."[19] Statements and speeches containing the royal "we" would be changed to "I."[20] He worked closely with Congress and his cabinet, mostly Nixon holdovers in the beginning, which Nixon had all but ignored, and allowed his aides to offer commentary to the press without waiting for official White House clearance.[21]

For eleven days, as the Fords prepared to move into the White House, he commuted from the Alexandria, Virginia, brick ranch-style home he and Betty Ford had built in 1949 for $34,000, looking no different from any other slightly dorky suburban dad going off to the city for work. The only difference was the motorcade of black limousines that transported him door to door. Photographs of Ford going about his daily routine, taken by White House photographer David Hume Kennerly, one of Ford's first hires, bore reassuring evidence of Ford's normality. A simple shot of the president toasting his own breakfast English muffin went a long way toward showing the public that he was "just like us." So did the Ford family. Betty, his wife of twenty-five years, and his children Michael, Jack, Steve, and Susan looked like any other American family. Kennerly called the new first couple, "Ozzie and Harriet in the White House."[22] As Ford settled into the job, it became clear that it wouldn't change him. "I don't

care what he became," said Silas McGee, Ford's former high school football teammate, the team's only African-American member. "He was always the guy I loved. He was always down to earth, like the rest of the
group."[23] Ford's approval ratings in his first few weeks topped 71 percent,
46 percentage points higher than Nixon's when he left office.

But Nixon had not gone away entirely. As Ford set out to resolve the
problems he had inherited from his predecessor—including a foundering
economy beset by double-digit inflation and the slow end to the Vietnam
War—he found that Nixon's legal fate, which hung in the balance, got in
the way of making progress. What *was* the full extent of Nixon's involvement in Watergate? Would he be tried in a court of law? If found guilty,
would he serve jail time as others in his administration were? Those
questions didn't go away as Nixon was in exile behind the gates of his
California estate. "We're all Watergate junkies," Ford was told by his
military aide, Bob Barrett, making an impression. "This will go on and
on unless someone steps in and says that we, as a nation, must go cold
turkey. Otherwise, we'll die of an overdose."[24]

The notion of granting Nixon a presidential pardon had been introduced to Ford when he was vice president. Alexander Haig, Nixon's
chief of staff, made Ford aware of a president's power to grant pardons
on August 1, suggesting that Nixon would be more likely to step down
from office if he knew a pardon would be forthcoming. Unsettled by the
conversation, which could be construed as proposing a deal for the
presidency in exchange for a pardon, Ford, urged by his infuriated
aides, called Haig the following day and read a carefully prepared statement. "I want you to understand," he began, "that I have no intention of
recommending what the president should do about resigning or not resigning, and that nothing we talked about yesterday afternoon should be
given any consideration in whatever decision the President may wish to
make."[25] There would be no further discussions about a pardon while
Nixon was president.

Ford was initially resistant to the idea of pardoning Nixon. "I don't
think the country would stand for it," he said when the subject was raised
during his vice presidential confirmation hearing almost a year earlier.[26]

But after taking office, he began thinking about a pardon as a means of putting Watergate—and the whole Nixon saga—behind. If not, he felt that Nixon's legal fight would continue to dominate news coverage and divide the country. There were other reasons a pardon made sense. He worried about Nixon and his family. Disturbing reports were circulating in the White House that Nixon was behaving erratically. One suggested that he was calling foreign leaders with bizarre ramblings, another that he was suicidal. Nixon's daughter Julie called Ford repeatedly to express concern about her father's depression. Ford also thought that Nixon's resignation was an implicit sign of guilt, and that Nixon had suffered enough. Moreover, he didn't want to see a former president in jail.[27] America needed "recovery, not revenge," he wrote later in his presidential memoir, appropriately titled *A Time to Heal*. He believed then, as he always would, that it was the right thing to do. And he believed the American people would come around to seeing it that way too.[28]

On September 8, a quiet Sunday morning, Ford applied his simple left-handed signature to a "full, free and absolute" pardon of the former president. The day did not remain quiet for long. By afternoon, the news wires were buzzing with the story, which was making its way into households across America.

Ford explained his position in a television address that evening:

> *As President, my primary concern must always be the greatest good of all the people of the United States whose servant I am. As a man, my first consideration is to be true to my own convictions and my own conscience.*
>
> *My conscience tells me clearly and certainly that I cannot continue to prolong the bad dreams that continue to reopen a chapter that is closed. My conscience tells me that only I, as President, have the constitutional power to firmly shut and seal this book. My conscience tells me it is my duty, not merely to proclaim domestic tranquillity but to use every means that I have to insure it.*

He further stated, "I cannot rely upon public opinion polls to tell me what is right."

He was unprepared for the onslaught that ensued. Overnight his lofty approval rating fell from 70 percent to 48 percent, while a Gallup poll showed the public disagreed with the pardon by a two-to-one margin. Protesters, who went away after Nixon's resignation, now resurfaced as fixtures at Ford events, where one picket sign reading FORD, NIXON, SAME OLD SHIT seemed to reflect the sentiments of much of America. The *New York Times* called the pardon "a profoundly unwise, divisive and unjust act" that destroyed Ford's credibility as "a man of judgment, candor and competence."[29] Ford's press secretary, Jerry terHorst, resigned in protest. Most of Ford's former colleagues in Congress, including many conservatives, were appalled that Ford had let Nixon off the hook. Peter Rodino, chairman of the House Judiciary Committee, claimed, contrary to Ford's intentions, "It will reopen a lot of sores."[30] Shortly after issuing the pardon, Ford made the unprecedented move of going to Capitol Hill to testify in front of Rodino and his committee on what led him to the decision—and to ward off notions that it was part of a deal with the Nixon administration—but it didn't do much to mitigate the fallout.

At the same time Fort felt liberated by the pardon. "Finally it was done," he wrote later. "I felt very certain I had made the right decision, and I was confident that I could now proceed without being harassed by Nixon and his problems any more."[31] There would be far-reaching consequences, though, as Tip O'Neill, the Democratic House majority leader, had predicted. When Ford had informed him of the pardon in advance of signing it, O'Neill warned, "I'm telling you right now, this will cost you the [presidential] election [in 1976]." But politics clearly wasn't the issue for Ford. "It feels right in my heart," he told his old friend.[32] Shorter term, it would affect the midterm election of 1974, in which the Democrats picked up forty-nine seats.

Nixon's was not the only controversial pardon Ford issued. In an attempt to heal the divisions the Vietnam War had caused across the country and "draw a real distinction" between the Nixon and Ford administrations, Ford introduced a plan to give limited amnesty to the fifty thousand young Americans who had evaded the Vietnam draft or had deserted their military posts. He looked to Abraham Lincoln for guidance. At the close of the Civil War, Lincoln had offered deserters the chance to be recognized once again as citizens of good standing as long as they withdrew their support of the Confederate cause and pledged allegiance to the union. While Lincoln drew fire for the measure, Ford believed he had "probably [made] the right decision at the time." Ten days after taking office, at a Chicago speech to the Veterans of Foreign Wars, Ford announced his intention. "I foresee their earned reentry—*earned* reentry," he reemphasized, "into a new atmosphere of hope, hard work and mutual trust."[33] The audience greeted the idea with polite applause, but later, when he put the plan into effect on September 16, offering amnesty for two years of public service, it stirred up fury, particularly among conservatives.

But it was nothing close to the pardon of Nixon, which tipped Ford's presidency off balance, never to quite regain its footing. The view of Ford as an ordinary man propelled gracefully into the White House under extraordinary circumstances gave way over time to a cartoonish image of Ford as a clumsy blunderer whose intellect fell well short of presidential standards. The notion had started with Lyndon Johnson while Ford was House minority leader in the sixties and the two clashed on legislative measures. Among other things, Johnson said scathingly that Ford had "played too much football with his helmet off" and "couldn't fart and chew gum at the same time."[34] After the pardon, the image resurfaced. As Ford settled into his tenure as president, it didn't help that he made a series of high-profile gaffes, falls, and errant tee shots in occasional golf rounds, supporting the impression. *Saturday Night Live*, which debuted in 1975, perpetuated the image, helping Chevy Chase to gain national prominence by portraying Ford as the bumbler in chief who fell with alarming regularity. Ford played along with it all, good-naturedly allowing his press secretary Ron Nessen to host the show on April 17, 1976, for which Ford recorded three messages to be included in the broadcast, including its signature line, "Live from New York, it's *Saturday Night!*" Even then, though, he unwittingly became the caricature of himself. After doing the recordings he forgot to remove the microphone from his lapel. As he walked away, stretching the full length of the cord, which was attached to the NBC camera, he was jerked backward, as the camera wobbled, nearly crashing down.[35] (The Fords watched the episode live at Camp David. Though news reports quoted White House aides as saying Ford was "not pleased" with the show, Betty Ford commented that she and the president "laughed and had a good time," but found some of the jokes "a little distasteful."[36]

"I think humor was very important in those days following Nixon's resignation," said Bob Orben, a speechwriter on Ford's White House staff.[37] Ford felt the same way—humor as another healing remedy, even if he was the butt of the joke—though it must have smarted a bit, particularly as it was a largely unfair depiction. After all, he was an accomplished scholar and perhaps the best athlete ever to occupy the Oval Office. Even worse, it hurt him politically.

Embracing pop culture, as Ford had with *Saturday Night Live,* was another manifestation of the openness of the Ford administration. His White House guests included figures who would have made it into the Nixon White House only on an enemies list (and probably did). Among them were Muhammad Ali, who had been stripped of his World Heavyweight Champion title in 1967 after refusing induction into the U.S. armed forces in protest over the Vietnam War, only to earn it back with a title fight against George Foreman two months after Ford took office. Former Beatle George Harrison also visited the White House, looking slightly incongruous with his shoulder-length hair and hippie garb, as did his fellow musician Billy Preston, whose afro was the circumference of a basketball. Ford also made it a point to greet *Saturday Night Live*'s producer Lorne Michaels and cast members Chevy Chase, John Belushi, and Dan Aykroyd at the annual White House Correspondents' Dinner in 1976.

If the resulting photo ops from those meetings helped make Ford a little cooler—he of the loud double-knit seventies suits that Tom Brokaw later said should also have been issued pardons—so did his wife. Betty Ford would become one of the most popular first ladies in history. Born in Chicago in 1918 and raised in middle-class Grand Rapids, Betty Bloomer had studied to be a dancer with her mentor, Martha Graham, in New York for two years, where she supported herself as a model, before returning to Grand Rapids when starring roles didn't come her way. At twenty-four she married a traveling salesman, Bill Warren, whom she divorced four years later. Around the same time, she was introduced to Gerald Ford through a mutual friend at Ford's urging. Over time, the persistent young lawyer turned his friendship with the relationship-wary former model into a romance. They married in 1948, just prior to Ford's election to Congress.

Strong and independent minded, Betty Ford's openness and informality matched that of her husband. Less than two months into her turn as first lady, when she was diagnosed with breast cancer resulting in a mastectomy, Betty Ford disclosed her condition publicly to generate awareness of the disease. Afterward, the number of women requesting breast exams soared. Her support of a proposed Equal Rights Amendment, in opposition to her husband, who believed it was covered in the Constitution, won her admiration for her independence on the issues. In fact, her disarming candor, a refreshing departure from the guarded countenance of first ladies past, could stir up controversy of its own. In an interview on *60 Minutes,* Mrs. Ford was questioned about a number of social issues of the day. Asked her view on the 1973 Supreme Court ruling *Roe v. Wade* legalizing abortion, she proclaimed it "the best thing in the world . . . a great, great decision." She further allowed that she wouldn't be surprised if her eighteen-year-old daughter Susan had had an affair—"she's a big girl"—and that her children had "probably" tried pot, adding that she "probably" would too if she were their age. Those permissive comments and others drew the ire of conservatives.[38]

Ford too gave conservatives plenty to stew about. A self-described "moderate in domestic affairs, a conservative in fiscal affairs, and a dyed-in-the-wool internationalist in foreign affairs," Ford alienated party right-wingers.[39] Already put off by the pardons of Nixon and Vietnam draft dodgers, they were further repelled by Ford's appointment of Nelson Rockefeller as vice president in the fall of 1974. Ford had chosen Rockefeller, the former New York governor, because he believed him to be the most capable of succeeding him. The right wing, which saw Rockefeller as a liberal, hardly agreed. The 1964 fight for the GOP

presidential nomination between the moderate Rockefeller and the conservative favorite, Barry Goldwater—which would go to Goldwater—split
the party, allowing Democrat Lyndon Johnson to carry the election in a
landslide. Conservatives were no more supportive of Rockefeller ten
years on.

Rockefeller wasn't the only new face in the president's inner circle.
Over time, Ford made changes to his cabinet in adherence to Phil Buchen's transition team memo, which advised walking "a delicate line in
compassion and consideration of the former president's staff and the rapid
assertion of your personal control over the executive branch."[40] Infighting
and mistrust between the Nixon and Ford staffers was also becoming a
problem.[41] Chief of staff Alexander Haig, deemed too tied in with "Nixon's image," was replaced by Donald Rumsfeld, who gave the post over to
his protégé, Dick Cheney, in 1975 as Rumsfeld moved on to secretary of
defense.[42] George H. W. Bush was brought in as director of the CIA, over
William Colby. Those changes and others allowed Ford to surround himself with loyalists who had his best interests at heart. A number of them,
including Bush, who remained close to Ford afterward, thought of him as
a "father figure."[43] Ford made an exception for Nixon holdover Henry
Kissinger, whose popularity and ostensible indispensability as secretary of
state rendered him immune to Ford's gentle purge.

Though Ford had his own staff in place and the Nixon administration was all but a bad memory, the atmosphere of crisis in the White
House continued as Ford grappled with the problems that lingered from
his predecessor's tenure. After America's formal role in the Vietnam War
ended in 1973, South Vietnam was eventually overcome by the Communist North Vietnamese. On April 23, 1975, in a speech to students at
Tulane University, Ford announced the war in Vietnam "is finished as
far as America is concerned."[44] A week later came the harrowing fall of
Saigon, South Vietnam's capital, as the few remaining military personnel were evacuated chaotically by helicopter from the roof of the U.S.
embassy before the city was overtaken by the Viet Cong, marking the
true and ignominious end to America's long and futile war.

Moreover, if Watergate had scourged the nation during the tail end of Nixon's presidency, a shaky economy—marked by rapid inflation, due in part to soaring energy costs from the Arab oil embargo, and an unemployment rate that reached 9 percent—hit closer to home for most Americans.[45] Even as Watergate approached its height in June of 1974, 24 percent of Americans believed the biggest problem facing the nation was a lack of trust in government or, more specifically, Watergate, while 48 percent of Americans believed it was the high cost of living.

Ford proposed a cut in government spending along with a 5 percent tax hike for individuals and corporations, though he used his presidential authority to curb inflation on a largely reactive basis, using his veto power to reject more than fifty nonmilitary spending bills.[46] But his tactic of promoting "WIN" buttons, an acronym for "Whip Inflation Now," one of which he sported for a while on his wide, double-knit lapels, did little to ease concerns. In fact, in addition to the persistence of the problem itself, it reinforced the impression of haplessness. Though inflation fell slightly, the problem dogged Ford throughout his tenure. In the spirit of candor, refreshing in today's age of predictable political spin, he opened his 1975 State of the Union address by proclaiming, "I must say that the state of the union is not good. Millions of Americans are out of work. Recession and inflation are eroding the money of millions more. Prices are too high, and sales too slow."

Those issues contributed to the troubles Ford would face in 1975, his first full year in office. In January, his approval rating stood at an anemic 36 percent, half of what it had been the previous August. Despite his best efforts—he believed the harder you worked, the luckier you got—he didn't get much of a break. Prior to the fall of Saigon, Ford journeyed to Helsinki to meet with Soviet premier Leonid Brezhnev and the leaders of Western European nations, resulting in their joint signing of what would become known as the Helsinki Accords. The agreement allowed for American recognition of the Soviet hegemony over Eastern Europe, while the Soviets conceded to its people the recognition of basic human rights as well as allowing for greater information flow and travel within the Soviet Union.[47] Though Ford would later rightfully regard it as a significant step in pushing America's agenda for individual liberties in the midst of the cold war, the accords were roundly criticized at the time as the USSR was continually cited in violation of the human rights of its citizens. Ford had also made strides toward furthering détente with the Soviets by agreeing to terms for a Strategic Arms Limitation Treaty (SALT II), but backed off when conservatives groused that he and Kissinger had conceded too much.

A temporary bump in his approval ratings occurred as he adroitly handled a foreign policy crisis in May. Troops from the Khmer Rouge, which had taken power in Cambodia, seized the *Mayagüez,* an American cargo ship, in international waters. After taking military action, resulting in the deaths of several marines, the members of the ship's crew were released. But the lift in the polls didn't last long. Even two assassination attempts on Ford's life, both made in California in September, did little to rally popular support for the president.[48]

As the election of 1976 neared, Ronald Reagan posed a challenge to Ford's hopes of gaining office on his own steam. A conservative darling like Goldwater had been, Reagan, the former actor and two-term governor of California, considered Ford to be a presidential stand-in not worthy of the position and ran hard for the nomination. "Ultra-liberals in this country hate Ronald Reagan like the devil hates holy water," remarked North Carolina senator Jesse Helms. For the same reasons, the party's right wing lapped up Reagan.[49] Though Ford came out of the gate strong in the primaries, winning the first in New Hampshire, followed by victories in Florida and Illinois, Reagan soon picked up momentum, winning in North Carolina and a string of other states. The contest went all the way to the party's convention in Kansas City, where Ford's camp ensured his nomination on the first ballot. In an uncharacteristically disloyal move—one that would later give Ford pause for a momentary lapse in political nerve—the president decided to bump Vice President Nelson Rockefeller from the ticket well before the convention, ultimately making Robert Dole his running mate as a peace offering to conservatives.[50]

Jimmy Carter posed the next challenge. The former one-term governor of Georgia had gone from being "Jimmy Who?" to the Democratic

Party's presidential nominee after a hard-fought insurgent's campaign against a strong field of well-known members of the party, including Hubert Humphrey and Morris Udall. His rhetoric against the "Nixon-Ford" era, along with his pledge to voters "never to lie" as president and to offer the nation "a government as good as its people," implicitly brought Watergate—and Ford's pardon of Nixon—to the fore as the nation considered who should be its president.

Ford countered by using the Oval Office to his advantage, showing voters he was working hard on their behalf. Throughout the summer, which had him presiding over America's spectacular, brassy bicentennial celebration, he chipped away at a 25 percent deficit in the opinion polls, as the two candidates rode into the fall in a nip-and-tuck chase.[51] The end for Ford may have come in his second presidential debate with Carter in October 1776. When asked a question concerning Eastern Europe by *New York Times* associate editor Max Frankel, Ford replied, "There is no Soviet domination of Eastern Europe, and there never will be under a Ford Administration." It was a misstatement; Ford meant to say that his administration would not accept a Soviet domination of the region, nor would Eastern Europe's people. An incredulous Frankel gave Ford the chance to retract or amend his answer, but Ford continued to stumble. "I was stepping through a minefield," Ford later wrote, "but I failed to recognize that at the time."[52]

*Time* magazine, in a piece titled "The Blooper Heard Round the World," wrote, "For a President, especially one who is running partly on a campaign theme of experience in foreign policy, the mistake reawakened many voters' suspicions that Ford is a bumbler."[53] Afterward, Carter gained traction in the polls, holding on through Election Day, when he narrowly took 51 percent of the popular vote to Ford's 48. While Ford's comment in the debates hurt, the pardon of Nixon was a deciding factor: 7 percent of voters claimed they pulled the lever for Carter as a result of the pardon.[54]

Jack Ford, Ford's oldest son, captured the sentiments of his father after the election. "You know," he said, "when you come so close, it's really hard to lose. But at the same time, if you can't lose as graciously as you had planned to win, then you shouldn't have been in the thing in the first place."[55] Though he had never before lost a political office and believed he had earned the White House "based on the merits," Ford, as always, was gracious in defeat.[56] Vindictiveness and bitterness were not in his nature.

The public, for the most part, appreciated that, knowing that without Ford's decency, things might have been far different for the country after Watergate. As he passed the presidency to Carter on January 20, 1977, he had earned an approval rating of 53 percent. Despite his mistakes, Ford, in doing his best, had earned the goodwill of most of his country. Carter spoke for them as he began his inaugural address. "For myself and our nation," he said in his soft Southern drawl, "I want to thank my predecessor for all he has done to heal our land."

A few weeks before the ninety-three-year-old Ford's health gave out, as his fragile condition continued to slide, I wrote the following op-ed piece. It ran in the *Boston Globe, Cleveland Plain Dealer,* and *San Francisco Chronicle* two days after the thirty-eighth president's death on December 26, 2006, bearing testimony to his legacy, not of greatness but of goodness.

> *When I interviewed Gerald Ford in 2004 for my book,* Second Acts: Presidential Lives and Legacies After the White House, *I asked him how he wished to be remembered. "That's easy, Mark," was his quick reply. "I was a healer and a builder. And if I am remembered that way, I would be most grateful."*
>
> *The healing Ford offered in the form of the presidential pardon of Richard Nixon and limited pardon of Vietnam War draft dodgers was acutely unpopular at the time—the former almost certainly cost him the 1976 election to Jimmy Carter. But he never doubted then or later that it was the right thing to do. Ford thought that those pardons were the price the divided country—and ultimately he—needed to pay in order to put the past behind us and move forward.*
>
> *Over the years, historians and the public began to appreciate the wisdom of those decisions, and the political selflessness it took to make them. Only a*

*third of Americans approved of the pardon of Nixon when it was granted in September 1974, a number that grew to 54 percent just ten years later. Indeed, the honor Ford was most proud of in his post-presidency was the Profiles in Courage Award given to him under the auspices of the John F. Kennedy Library in 2001, by a committee composed of historians and Kennedy family members, including Ted Kennedy and Caroline Kennedy Schlossberg. "You can't beat that," he told me with some pride in the same interview.*

*But while he lived long enough to see his most controversial decisions vindicated, he also grew increasingly dismayed by the "poisonous" political atmosphere in Washington. He recalled fondly the times when he would battle Democratic opponents such as Tip O'Neill in the House of Representatives on a typical day, then go hoist beers together after hours.*

*When the House threatened the impeachment of Bill Clinton in 1998, he counseled Republicans out for blood to censure Clinton instead, sending a strong message to the president but stopping short of a draconian measure driven largely by bitter partisanship. They ignored his advice, to their detriment. In more recent years, he became concerned about zealous Democrats and their anti-Bush tactics, even as he worried that President George W. Bush had made the wrong decision to invade Iraq under the guise of ridding the world of a dictator and eliminating weapons of mass destruction.*

*As we move forward after his death, I believe Ford, defined as a president and as a man by his inherent decency, would want politicians in Washington and across America to make decisions based on right or wrong, and not by partisan boundaries; he would want rabid Republicans on the right and passionate Bush-haters on the left to moderate their tones, and be more respectful toward one another; he would want Americans to stop seeing our country as a divided patchwork of blue and red states and start defining it by the values we share at its core. And I believe if we were to honor his memory in that way, Gerald Ford would be most grateful.*[57]

# EPILOGUE

"Even as we celebrate tonight," said Barack Obama upon winning the White House on November 4, 2008, "we know the challenges that tomorrow will bring are the greatest of our lifetime—two wars, a planet in peril, the worst financial crisis in a century." What can President Obama do or say in his first days in office to rally the nation and boost our self-assurance? What steps can he take to dispel our fears of economic calamity and to restore our standing in the world—and our own faith in our role within it? And what lessons can he draw from those who went before him as he faces his own unprecedented crises?

"The only thing new in the world," Harry Truman once said, "is the history you don't know."[1] As George W. Bush recedes into private life, he leaves the burdens of his presidency—many of his own doing—in fresh hands. Barack Obama may be mindful of all or some of these examples as he takes office, like the men who provide them, in a time of unprecedented crisis. And then, he may not. Within the stories our new president can find timeless guidance in leadership to be upheld, as well as pitfalls to be avoided, particularly as he embarks on the formative stages of his presidency. Some lessons are obvious and risk reading like platitudes; others are less cliché.

One lesson is clear: Words matter. The words spoken by a president at the outset of his term can set the tone of his administration as much as any action he takes. Particularly in a time of crisis, they can quell fear and anxiety, and instill confidence and buoyancy. As former British prime minister Clement Attlee once said, referring to his predecessor and successor Winston Churchill's gift for oratory, "Words at great moments of history are deeds."[2] A new administration offers America a fresh start and an opportunity to set direction—and raise hopes—anew, at home and aboard. The president's inaugural address is the overture.

> *We are all Republicans. We are all Federalists.*
> *The only thing we have to fear is fear itself.*
> *Ask not what your country can do for you—ask what you can do for your country.*
> *Our long national nightmare is over.*

These words are as enduring as nearly any part of the presidential legacy of the men who spoke them. At the time they were offered, they were simply sound bites, memorable rhetoric that struck a chord during a difficult time. They resonated at the moment by extending a promise of sorts, providing a glimpse of the character of the new man in charge. They echoed in history when the promise was fulfilled. (Indeed, it is difficult to conjure up passages of inaugural speeches from presidents—no matter how historically significant—who were sworn in during a more placid period. Do any memorable phrases from inaugural addresses of Wilson, Eisenhower, or Reagan come to mind?) The new president on the day of his inaugural has the chance to assuage our moral uncertainty by defining who we are at the dawn of the twenty-first century, and, by extension, what our role in the world should be. The presidency "is preeminently a place for moral leadership," said Franklin Roosevelt. "All our great presidents were leaders of thought at times when certain historic ideas in the life of the nation had to be clarified."[3]

But a president's words don't have to be immortal, or spoken in an inaugural address, to be important. Some just have to be spoken often and with authority, particularly during an anxious time. Anyone who has been stuck on an airport runway in an idle plane well after takeoff time knows that any words from the cockpit are better than none. If nothing else, they give the helpless passengers a sign that someone in a position to do something is aware of the situation, even if it doesn't mean an immediate resolution of the problem.

Roosevelt's regular Fireside Chats—part cheerleading, part progress reports—gave Americans an ongoing sense that the president was firmly in control and that things were being done to address the nation's plight, even though the Depression would not abate until the outset of World War II. His frequent press briefings had the same effect. Active communication reflected the activism and openness of Roosevelt's administration, which was seen as part of the solution, and stood in marked contrast to the administration of his unpopular predecessor, Herbert Hoover, who wasn't big on either frequent communication with the American public on the nation's state of affairs or government intervention in mitigating them. Similarly, Kennedy's ongoing press conferences demonstrated his confidence, visible in his wit and cool manner, despite the weight he carried from the cold war, civil rights, and Southeast Asia and other trouble spots.

While words are important, only deeds can fulfill the pledge of unity. George W. Bush came to office as a self-proclaimed "uniter, not a divider." But his words rang hollow, undone by his policies—though division was not his intention. The war in Iraq's central failure was in the White House's decision to politically alienate the Sunnis, the dominant force in Saddam Hussein's Baathist regime, giving them no stake in the new Iraq, a move that resulted in the unleashing of ancient tribal hatred and ultimately in fueling the insurgency. But the last straw for Bush's presidency, at least as far as popular support went, came at home, where the administration's slow, inadequate response to Hurricane Katrina reinforced the impression that the president was more interested in the country's "haves" than the "have-nots." Even before the onset of the global financial crisis in August

2008, Bush's presidential disapproval rating was the highest in history, at 71 percent, nudging past Truman, the previous record holder, whose disapproval rating stood at 68 percent in January 1952. The new president must take the necessary steps to bring the American people together.

Washington, through his towering example as president, personified unity, just as he had in leading the Continental army through the six desolate years of the revolution. But as the historian Thomas Bailey put it, "Perhaps [Washington's] only flaw, at least administratively, was his failure to mix fire and water, that is, to persuade Hamilton and Jefferson to work together harmoniously in his Cabinet."[4] Lincoln, putting aside all thoughts of retribution, enacted policies that extended a hand to the vanquished South and urged the nation to carry on "with malice toward none" after the Civil War had torn it apart. Truman did the same on a global scale after the Second World War, rebuilding Central and Western Europe through the Marshall Plan, while integrating the armed forces at home. Likewise, Ford's pardon of Richard Nixon and his limited pardon to Vietnam draft dodgers were meant to heal the nation's wounds in the wake of Watergate and the Vietnam War.

The most immediate means by which the president can foster a sense of unity is by reaching out to Congress. If our government can work together effectively, putting aside differences for the betterment of the nation, Americans are more likely to come together themselves. While Bush alone is not culpable for the partisan rancor in Washington, which escalated when Newt Gingrich engineered a GOP majority in Congress in 1994 and put Bill Clinton and his party in its crosshairs, resulting in counterattacks, he did little to lessen its ferocity.

Though he came to office after what was perhaps the most divisive election in American history, Jefferson worked skillfully with the committees of Congress to enact his Republican agenda. He was reelected four years later in a decisive victory as the deep political divisions in the body politic just a few years earlier had given way to a path of progress. Roosevelt's first hundred days saw a flurry of legislation that necessitated Congress's ready cooperation and consent (though Roosevelt didn't have to exert much influence to see it through, given his rousing mandate).

Through strong leadership and consensus building, FDR ensured that the engine of government was humming even if the economy wasn't.

Presidential image is, of course, paramount, as important today as it was in the days when Washington was transported through the streets in a souped-up canary yellow chariot as a message to European onlookers that the American government was as magisterial as theirs. Bush's cowboy image, which has been characterized by "wanted, dead or alive" rhetoric and go-it-alone decisions, as well as the folksy Texan persona he has cultivated, was largely rebuffed by the American public just as it played into the worst of American stereotypes abroad. It will be important for the new president to set a defining new tone. Symbolism and appearance have substance of their own. Kennedy's graceful image, perhaps his best political asset (and one that has given him a lift in history), boosted American pride and played well on the world stage, where the young president matched wits with formidable figures like Khrushchev and de Gaulle. The coolness of his image was reinforced in the darkest hour of his presidency as he skillfully handled the missile crisis off the shores of Cuba. Roosevelt, with his jaunty, ebullient manner, uplifting voice, and cigarette holder propped upward by teeth clenched in a defiant smile, was the very picture of resilience despite his crippling disability—and the country's desperate economic predicament.

In addition, the Bush administration was tarnished by its insularity and almost obsessive furtiveness, a throwback to the Nixon regime, when paranoia led to Watergate. Ford made good on his promise to former congressional colleagues that "openness" would be the "hallmark" of his administration, providing a much-needed contrast to the closed-door Nixon White House. A simple photograph of the newly sworn in Ford in the kitchen making his own breakfast bore refreshing testimony to his normality and provided an antidote to the imperious Nixon. But though intellectually able, Ford was not helped by his *Saturday Night Live* caricature as a hapless, albeit good-natured, clod, a perception he unwittingly perpetuated by making a number of high-profile gaffes and stumbles.

Truman's image also set him back. By coming off as a thin-skinned, carping partisan, he only reinforced perceptions of himself as a little man out of his depth in the Oval Office, despite a more than capable performance that indicated otherwise. Though he won reelection in 1948 through a remarkable campaign attesting to his grit and tenacity, he spent the better part of his second term battling anemic approval ratings that hurt his efforts with Congress and standing overall.

Jefferson and Kennedy offer reminders that boldness of vision can galvanize the nation, capturing its imagination and shaping its destiny. In 1961, Kennedy's challenge to send a manned spacecraft to the moon within the decade roused America's shoddy space efforts, inspiring NASA to surge ahead of the Soviets and to achieve its goal by the summer of 1969. While much of the space race was cold war bravado, holding the promise of celestial bragging rights, the achievement captured the best of the American—indeed, the human—spirit. When Jefferson dispatched Lewis and Clark to explore the West, it resulted not only in the epic tales and exotic fruits of a brave new world but also planted the seeds of manifest destiny, a sign to the nation and to the world that America's future lay beyond the Mississippi.

The importance of the West, and of another key leadership trait— flexibility—was nowhere more obvious than in the Louisiana Purchase. In authorizing the buy in 1803, Jefferson violated the core of his own intrinsic views on the national government's role in American life, including accruing a massive federal debt and temporarily abandoning his own constructionist view of the Constitution. Justifying his questionable use of federal authority in authorizing the purchase, he later wrote, perhaps as a mandate to his successors, "It is incumbent on those who accept great charges to risk themselves on great occasions."[5] The electorate seemed to agree, forgiving him his inconsistencies with his resounding reelection in 1804.

Tyler achieved his best results when he subordinated his own reflexive stubbornness. Convinced that his vice presidential inauguration was enough to make him president upon William Henry Harrison's death, despite the ambiguities in the Constitution at the time, he yielded to the advice of his advisers, who suggested that he take the presidential oath as a symbolic rite to validate his assumption of the role of president. Had he stuck to his guns, doubts about the transfer of power might have continued to linger and intensify. And, like Jefferson in the Louisiana Purchase, Tyler kept his constructionist views in check over the matter of Texas annexation, allowing for a joint resolution of Congress to determine the matter rather than the Constitution's requirement of a two-thirds vote in the Senate, which likely would have resulted in its defeat. But ultimately, Tyler was compromised by his inflexibility. Determined to be his own man as president, he made few concessions to the Whig Party that rode him into office. Exasperated, the party eventually froze him out and did what it could to undermine him. As a result, Tyler was a largely reactive leader, exercising his authority primarily in the form of veto power.

In the previous administration, we saw Bush hampered by his stringent hold on ideological principles, as reflected in his intransigence on Iraq. Despite mounting proof that the war was failing as executed, he consistently stayed the course when a more pragmatic approach—one that might contradict earlier plans—might have better served Iraq and the United States. Given that, the next commander in chief would do well to remember that courage in decision, though subject to drawing political fire in its time, is often rewarded in history. This is especially important as he inherits the war—itself a daring decision initially, which will require tough new strategies and reimagining—and an economy severely weakened by deregulation. Jay's Treaty was a political disaster for Washington, further alienating the already wary Jeffersonian Republicans, who saw it as a sellout to the British, and speeding up the inevitability of the two-party system Washington himself had hoped to forestall. However, it was the best hope in keeping the United States out of war at a time when fighting one would have threatened the country's viability. While acutely unpopular in its day, it was ultimately vindicated as the right thing to do. So was Ford's pardon of Nixon. When it was issued, the pardon was seen in the most cynical terms by a skeptical public, frowned on by two-thirds of Americans who sent Ford's approval ratings plunging overnight—and voted him out of office just over two years later. But Ford would live to see the day when the majority of Americans appreciated not only the pardon as he intended it—as the price the nation needed to pay to move beyond Watergate—but also his political courage and inherent decency in granting it.

Truman, too, was underappreciated in his time, leaving office with a 31 percent approval rating. He almost surely would have been defeated had he chosen to run again in 1952. But now Truman is considered a great, or at least a near-great, president, shored up by his most controversial decisions, including the drop of atomic bombs on Hiroshima and Nagasaki to prevent further bloodshed in the war with Japan, and his unpopular fight for civil rights, as well as for his bold stand in containing the Communist threat from the Soviet Union. Perhaps the best example of a bold decree, unpopular in its day, is Lincoln's Emancipation Proclamation, which not only stands out in history but dramatically changed it.

The forty-fourth president may be mindful of all or some of these examples as he takes office, like the men who provided them, in a time of unprecedented crisis. And then, he may not.

Rather, he may find that the sagest wisdom comes from just one of them, Lincoln, who, in a written message to Congress sent a month before signing the Emancipation Proclamation, held:

*The dogmas of the quiet past are inadequate to the stormy present. The occasion is piled high with difficulty and we must rise with the occasion. As our case is new, so we must think anew and act anew. We must disenthrall ourselves, and then we shall save our country.*

# NOTES

## INTRODUCTION

1. Walter Isaacson, *Benjamin Franklin: An American Life* (New York: Simon & Schuster, 2003), 458–59.

2. Arthur M. Schlesinger Jr. *The Cycles of American History* (Boston: Houghton Mifflin, 1986), 8.

3. Hugh Sidey, "Time and the Presidency" (traveling exhibit created by *Time* magazine, which appeared at select presidential museums, 1999–2002).

4. University of Virginia, "Thomas Jefferson on Politics and Government," http://etext.virginia.edu/jefferson/quotations/jeff1290.htm.

5. Edward P. Crapol Jr., *John Tyler: The Accidental President* (Chapel Hill: University of North Carolina Press, 2006).

6. *National Geographic Eyewitness to the 20th Century* (Washington, D.C.: National Geographic Society, 1998), 126.

7. David McCullough, *Truman* (New York: Simon & Schuster, 1992), 353.

8. PBS, *The American Experience,* "The Presidents: Truman," www.pbs.org/wgbh/amex/presidents/video/truman_18.html#v175.

9. "Paying the Price," *Time,* April 2, 1990.

10. *Newsweek,* May 12, 2008.

11. CNN, CNN/Opinion Research poll data, July 2, 2008, http://political-ticker.blogs.cnn.com/2008/07/04/poll-founding-fathers-would-be-disappointed-in-america/.

## I. George Washington: The First

1. Catherine Drinker Bowen, *Miracle at Philadelphia: The Story of the Constitutional Convention, May to September, 1789* (Boston: Little, Brown, 1966), 54–62.

2. Bowen, *Miracle at Philadelphia*, 60–61.

3. Bowen, *Miracle at Philadelphia*, 61.

4. Joseph J. Ellis, *Founding Brothers: The Revolutionary Generation* (New York: Knopf, 2000), 120.

5. Richard Norton Smith, *Patriarch: Washington and the New American Nation* (Boston: Houghton Mifflin, 1993), xix.

6. Smith, *Patriarch*, xix; Ellis, *Founding Brothers*, 124.

7. Frank Freidel, *The Presidents of the United States of America* (Washington, D.C.: White House Historical Association, 1964), 2.

8. Smith, *Patriarch*, 8.

9. R. W. B. Lewis and Nancy Lewis, *American Characters: Selections from the National Portrait Gallery* (New Haven: Yale University Press, 1999), 26.

10. Michael Beschloss, ed., *American Heritage Illustrated History of the Presidents* (New York: Crown, 2000), 18.

11. Thomas A. Bailey, *Presidential Greatness: The Image and the Man from George Washington to the Present* (New York: Appleton-Century, 1966), 68.

12. Ellis, *Founding Brothers*, 120.

13. Smith, *Patriarch*, 68.

14. Michael Beschloss, "Washington Slept Here," *Newsweek*, September 3, 2007; John Lloyd and John Mitchinson, *The Book of General Ignorance* (New York: Harmony, 2006), 13.

15. Smith, *Patriarch*, xix.

16. PBS, *Rediscovering George Washington*, "Appearance and Reality," www.pbs.org.georgewashington/father/appearance.html.

17. *We the People: The Commission of the Bicentennial of the United States Constitution, 1985–1992* (Washington, D.C.: The Commission, 1992), 125.

18. *We the People*, 125.

19. David McCullough, *John Adams* (New York: Simon & Schuster, 2001), 404.

20. Thomas L. Connelly and Michael D. Senecal, eds., *Almanac of American Presidents from 1789 to the Present* (New York: Facts on File, 1991), 27.

21.  Kenneth C. Davis, *Don't Know Much About History: Everything You Need to Know About American History but Never Learned* (New York: Crown, 1990), 51.

22.  David McCullough, *1776* (New York: Simon & Schuster, 2005), 49.

23.  Connelly and Senecal, *Almanac*, 106.

24.  Ellis, *Founding Brothers*, 130.

25.  Lewis and Lewis, *American Characters*, 26.

26.  Ellis, *Founding Brothers*, 130.

27.  Smith, *Patriarch*, 28.

28.  Beschloss, *Illustrated History*, 27.

29.  John Whitcomb and Claire Whitcomb, *Real Life at the White House: 200 Years of Daily Life at America's Most Famous Residence* (New York: Routledge, 2000), 2.

30.  Whitcomb and Whitcomb, *Real Life*, 2.

31.  Whitcomb and Whitcomb, *Real Life*, 2.

32.  Smith, *Patriarch*, 25.

33.  Beschloss, *Illustrated History*, 28.

34.  McCullough, *1776*, 43.

35.  Gaillard Hunt, ed., *The Writings of James Madison*, Vol. V (New York: Putnam, 1904), 356.

36.  Beschloss, *Illustrated History*, 24–25.

37.  University of Chicago, "The Founders' Constitution," "Epilogue: Securing the Republic," http://press-pubs.uchicago.edu/founders/documents/v1ch18s21.html.

38.  McCullough, *John Adams*, 436.

39.  Richard Brookhiser, *Founding Father: Rediscovering George Washington* (New York: Free Press, 1996), 78–83.

40.  Davis, *Don't Know Much*, 95.

41.  Ellis, *Founding Brothers*, 50.

42.  Ellis, *Founding Brothers*, 80.

43.  Miller Center, University of Virginia, "Essays on George Washington and His Administration," http://millercenter.org/academic/american-president/washington.

44.  Brookhiser, *Founding Father*, 83.

45.  Smith, *Patriarch*, 19.

46.  Smith, *Patriarch*, 226.

47.  Whitcomb and Whitcomb, *Real Life*, 4–5.

48.  Whitcomb and Whitcomb, *Real Life*, 7; McCullough, *John Adams*, 543.

49.  Whitcomb and Whitcomb, *Real Life,* 7.

50.  Whitcomb and Whitcomb, *Real Life,* 3.

51.  Newt Gingrich, *Rediscovering God in America: Reflections on the Role of Faith in Our Nation's History and Future* (Nashville: Integrity House, 2006), 110.

52.  Whitcomb and Whitcomb, *Real Life,* 4–5.

53.  Kathryn Moore, *The American President: A Complete History* (New York: Fall River Press, 2007), 13–14.

54.  Margaret Brown Klapthor, *The First Ladies* (Washington, D.C.: White House Historical Association, 1975), 8.

55.  Connelly and Senecal, *Almanac,* 360.

56.  Ellis, *Founding Brothers,* 140.

57.  Davis, *Don't Know Much,* 96.

58.  Ellis, *Founding Brothers,* 143.

59.  Ellis, *Founding Brothers,* 135.

60.  Ellis, *Founding Brothers,* 131.

61.  James Thomas Flexner, *George Washington: Anguish and Farewell (1793–1799)* (Boston: Little, Brown, 1969), 144.

62.  AmericanRevolution.com, "John Jay's Treaty," www.Americanrevolution.com/JaysTreaty.htm.

63.  Ellis, *Founding Brothers,* 136.

64.  Brookhiser, *Founding Father,* 96.

65.  Smith, *Patriarch,* 231.

66.  AmericanRevolution.com, "John Jay's Treaty."

67.  Frank E. Grizzard Jr., *George Washington: A Biographical Companion* (Santa Barbara, Calif.: ABC-CLIO, 2002), 178.

68.  Smith, *Patriarch,* 236.

69.  Brookhiser, *Founding Father,* 96.

70.  Ellis, *Founding Brothers,* 137.

71.  Bailey, *Presidential Greatness* (New York: Appleton-Century, 1966), 251.

72.  Bailey, *Presidential Greatness,* 251.

73.  U.S. Senate, "Art & History: Uproar Over Senate's Approval of Jay's Treaty," www.senate.gov/artandhistory/history/minute/Uproar_Over_Senate_Treaty_Approval.htm.

74.  AmericanRevolution.com, "John Jay's Treaty."

75.  Smith, *Patriarch,* 237.

76.  Donald L. Miller and John Sargent, eds., *From George . . . to George: Two*

*Hundred Years of Presidential Quotations* (Alexandria, Va.: Braddock Communications, 1989), 258.

77.  Ellis, *Founding Brothers*, 135.

78.  McCullough, *John Adams*, 467.

79.  McCullough, *John Adams*, 467.

## II. Thomas Jefferson: "We are all Republicans, we are all Federalists"

1.   John Whitcomb and Claire Whitcomb, *Real Life at the White House: 200 Years of Daily Life at America's Most Famous Residence* (New York: Routledge, 2000), 14.

2.   Thomas A. Bailey, *Presidential Greatness: The Image and the Man from George Washington to the Present* (New York: Appleton-Century, 1966), 270.

3.   Paul J. Boller Jr., *Presidential Inaugurations* (New York: Harcourt, 2001), 220.

4.   Joseph J. Ellis, *Founding Brothers: The Revolutionary Generation* (New York: Knopf, 2000), 181.

5.   R. B. Bernstein, *Thomas Jefferson* (New York: Oxford University Press, 2003), 133.

6.   Paul J. Boller Jr., *Presidential Anecdotes* (New York: Penguin Books, 1982), 36.

7.   Natalie Bober, PBS, Interview for *Thomas Jefferson* by Ken Burns, www.pbs.org/jefferson/archives/interviews/frame.htm.

8.   Michael Beschloss, ed., *American Heritage Illustrated History of the Presidents* (New York: Crown, 2000), 52.

9.   Joseph J. Ellis, *American Sphinx* (New York: Knopf, 1997), 44.

10.  Ellis, *Founding Brothers*, 213.

11.  Donald L. Miller and David Sargent, eds., *From George . . . to George: Two Hundred Years of Presidential Quotes* (Alexandria, Va.: Braddock Communications, 1989), 32.

12.  Walter Kirn, "Life, Liberty and the Pursuit of Thomas Jefferson," *Time*, June 30, 2004.

13.  Ellis, *American Sphinx*, 198.

14.  Ellis, *American Sphinx*, 310.

15.  Beschloss, *Illustrated History*, 56.

16.  Boller, *Presidential Anecdotes*, 32.

17.  David McCullough, *John Adams* (New York: Simon & Schuster, 2001), 544.

18.  Miller Center, University of Virginia, "Essays on Thomas Jefferson and His Administration," http://millercenter.org/academic/americanpresident/jefferson.

19.   McCullough, *John Adams*, 543.

20.   Beschloss, *Illustrated History*, 56.

21.   McCullough, *John Adams*, 543–44.

22.   Ellis, *American Sphinx*, 211.

23.   Ellis, *American Sphinx*, 206.

24.   Whitcomb and Whitcomb, *Real Life*, 16.

25.   Ellis, *American Sphinx*, 201.

26.   Bernstein, *Thomas Jefferson*, 136.

27.   Whitcomb and Whitcomb, *Real Life*, 16.

28.   Paul M. Zall, ed., *Jefferson on Jefferson* (Lexington: University Press of Kentucky, 2002), 106.

29.   Bernstein, *Thomas Jefferson*, 137; Whitcomb and Whitcomb, *Real Life*, 15.

30.   Kirn, "Life, Liberty and the Pursuit of Thomas Jefferson."

31.   Whitcomb and Whitcomb, *Real Life*, 20–21.

32.   Zall, *Jefferson on Jefferson*, 109.

33.   *Jefferson on Jefferson*, 109; Bernstein, *Thomas Jefferson*, 140–41.

34.   Kathryn Moore, *The American President: A Complete History* (New York: Fall River Press, 2007), 41.

35.   Whitcomb and Whitcomb, *Real Life*, 20.

36.   Ellis, *American Sphinx*, 224–25.

37.   Bernstein, *Thomas Jefferson*, 140.

38.   Ellis, *American Sphinx*, 228; Whitcomb and Whitcomb, *Real Life*, 20.

39.   Bernstein, *Thomas Jefferson*, 138.

40.   U.S. Department of State, *Outline of U.S. Government*, "The Judicial Branch: Interpreting the Constitution," http://usinfo.state.gov/products/pubs/outusgov/ch5.htm.

41.   Geoffrey C. Ward and Ken Burns, *Baseball: An Illustrated History* (New York: Knopf, 1994), 155–56.

42.   National Park Service, "The Lewis and Clark Journey of Discovery," www.nps.gov/archive/jeff/LewisClark2/Circa1804/Heritage/Louisiana Purchase/LouisianaPurchase.htm.

43.   Stanislaus Murray Hamilton, ed., *The Writings of James Monroe*, Vol. 7 (New York: Putnam, 1903), 299–300.

44.   Monticello.org, "The Louisiana Purchase: Jefferson's Big Deal," www.monticello.org/jefferson/lewisandclark/louisiana.html; Beschloss, *Illustrated History*, 58–59.

45.   Beschloss, *Illustrated History*, 58–59.

46. National Park Service, "Louis and Clark Journey of Discovery."

47. Monticello.org., "Lewis and Clark," www.monticello.org/jefferson/lewis andclark/louisiana.html.

48. Ellis, *American Sphinx*, 249.

49. Monticello.org., "Lewis and Clark."

50. Zall, *Jefferson on Jefferson*, 110.

51. Ellis, *American Sphinx*, 253.

52. Ellis, *American Sphinx*, 247–48; Kenneth C. Davis, *Don't Know Much About History: Everything You Need to Know About American History but Never Learned* (New York: Crown, 1990), 103.

53. Walter Kirn, "Lewis and Clark," *Time*, July 8, 2002.

54. Whitcomb and Whitcomb, *Real Life*, 22.

55. Davis, *Don't Know Much*, 103–04.

56. Walter Kirn, "Lewis and Clark, *Time*, July 8, 2002.

57. Beschloss, *Illustrated History*, 61.

58. Miller Center, "Essays on Thomas Jefferson."

59. Bailey, *Presidential Greatness*, 272,

60. Monticello.org, "Sanctum Sanctorum," www.monticello.org/jefferson/ dayinlife/sanctum/home/html.

61. Encyclopedia Britannica, "Thomas Jefferson," www.britannica.com/ presidents/article-61882.

62. Daniel Boorstin, PBS, Interview for *Thomas Jefferson* by Ken Burns, www .pbs.org/jefferson/archives/interviews/Boorstin.htm.

63. Ellis, *American Sphinx*.

## III. JOHN TYLER: THE ACCIDENTAL PRESIDENT

1. Michael Beschloss, ed., *American Heritage Illustrated History of the Presidents* (New York: Crown, 2000), 131.

2. U.S. Senate, "Art & History: John Tyler, Tenth Vice President," www.senate .gov/artandhistory/history/common/generic/VP_John_Tyler.htm; John Whitcomb and Claire Whitcomb, *Real Life at the White House: 200 Years of Daily Life at America's Most Famous Residence* (New York: Routledge, 2000), 85.

3. Whitcomb and Whitcomb, *Real Life*, 85.

4. Frank Freidel, *The Presidents of the United States of America* (Washington, D.C.: White House Historical Association, 1964), 24.

5. Miller Center, University of Virginia, "Essays on John Tyler and His Administration," http://millercenter.org/academic/americanpresident/tyler.

6.   Miller Center, "Essays on John Tyler."

7.   Miller Center, "Essays on John Tyler."

8.   Miller Center, "Essays on John Tyler."

9.   Beschloss, *Illustrated History,* 133.

10.  U.S. Senate, "Art & History: John Tyler"; Beschloss, *Illustrated History,* 133.

11.  Edward P. Crapol, *John Tyler: The Accidental President* (Chapel Hill: University of North Carolina Press, 2006), 10–11.

12.  Charles Francis Adams, ed., *Memoirs of John Quincy Adams,* 12 vols. (Philadelphia: Lippincott, 1876).

13.  Whitcomb and Whitcomb, *Real Life,* 85.

14.  Robert Seager II, *And Tyler Too: A Biography of John & Julia Gardiner Tyler* (New York: McGraw-Hill, 1963), 50.

15.  Thomas L. Connelly and Michael D. Senecal, eds., *Almanac of American Presidents from 1789 to the Present* (New York: Facts on File, 2006), 86.

16.  Miller Center, "Essays on John Tyler."

17.  White House Historical Association, "First Ladies of the United States: Letitia Christian Tyler," www.whitehouse.gov/history/firstladies/lt10.html.

18.  Beschloss, *Illustrated History,* 133.

19.  Whitcomb and Whitcomb, *Real Life,* 85.

20.  U.S. Senate, "Art & History: John Tyler."

21.  U.S. Senate, "Art & History: John Tyler."

22.  Beschloss, *Illustrated History,* 138.

23.  U.S. Senate, "Art & History: John Tyler."

24.  Whitcomb and Whitcomb, *Real Life,* 87.

25.  White House Museum, "East Sitting Hall," www.whitehousemuseum.org/floor2/east-sitting-hall.htm.

26.  Whitcomb and Whitcomb, *Real Life,* 87.

27.  U.S. Senate, "Art & History: John Tyler"; Connelly and Senecal, *Almanac,* 13–14.

28.  Beschloss, *Illustrated History,* 137.

29.  White House Historical Association, "First Ladies of the United States: Letitia Christian Tyler."

30.  Connelly and Senecal, *Almanac,* 71.

31.  White House Historical Association, "First Ladies of the United States: Letitia Christian Tyler."

32.  Whitcomb and Whitcomb, *Real Life*, 88.

33.  John F. Kennedy, *Profiles in Courage* (New York: Harper, 1956), 56.

34.  U.S. Department of State, "Webster-Ashburton Treaty, 1842," www.state
     .gov/r/pa/ho/time/dwe/14323.htm.

35.  Beschloss, *Illustrated History*, 137.

36.  Miller Center, "Essays on John Tyler."

37.  Beschloss, *Illustrated History*, 138.

38.  Beschloss, *Illustrated History*, 138–39.

39.  Beschloss, *Illustrated History*, 139.

40.  Whitcomb and Whitcomb, *Real Life*, 92.

41.  Whitcomb and Whitcomb, *Real Life*, 92.

42.  Carl Sandburg, *Abraham Lincoln: The Prairie Years and the War Years* (New
     York: Harcourt, 1954), 182.

43.  Max J. Skidmore, *After the White House: Former Presidents as Private Citizens*
     (New York: Palgrave Macmillan, 2004), 56–57.

44.  Harrison Tyler, interview with the author, Richmond, Virginia, October
     2007.

## IV. Abraham Lincoln: "The Union is unbroken"

1.  Newt Gingrich, *Rediscovering God in America: Reflections on the Role of Faith in
    Our Nation's History and Future* (Nashville: Integrity House, 2006), 75–77.

2.  Joshua Wolf Shenk, *Lincoln's Melancholy: How Depression Challenged a Presi-
    dent and Fueled His Greatness* (Boston: Houghton Mifflin, 2005), 173; Carl
    Sandburg, *Abraham Lincoln: The Prairie Years and the War Years* (New York:
    Harcourt, 1954), 185.

3.  Michael Beschloss, ed., *American Heritage Illustrated History of the Presidents*
    (New York: Crown, 2000), 245.

4.  Beschloss, *Illustrated History*, 426.

5.  David Herbert Donald, *Lincoln* (New York: Simon & Schuster, 1995),
    279.

6.  PBS, *Thomas Jefferson* by Ken Burns, www.pbs.org/jefferson/archives/
    interviews/Franklin.htm.

7.  Howard Zinn, *A People's History of the Unites Stated* (New York: Harper,
    1980), 167.

8.  Zinn, *A People's History*, 184.

9.  PBS, "Africans in America: Dred Scott, the Supreme Court Decision,"
    www.pbs.org/wgbh/aia/part4/4h2933.html.

10.   Kenneth C. Davis, *Don't Know Much About History: Everything You Need to Know About American History but Never Learned* (New York: Crown, 1990), 158.

11.   Beschloss, *Illustrated History*, 189.

12.   Frank Freidel, *The Presidents of the United States of America* (Washington, D.C.: White House Historical Association, 1964), 38.

13.   William Lee Miller, *Lincoln's Virtues: An Ethical Biography* (New York: Knopf, 2002), 12.

14.   Miller, *Lincoln's Virtues*, 37.

15.   Miller, *Lincoln's Virtues*, 38.

16.   Thomas L. Connelly and Michael D. Senecal, eds., *Almanac of American Presidents from 1789 to the Present* (New York: Facts on File, 1991), 40–41.

17.   Benjamin P. Thomas, *Abraham Lincoln: A Biography* (New York: Knopf, 1952), 45.

18.   Connelly and Senecal, *Almanac*, 93.

19.   Donald, *Lincoln*, 149.

20.   Donald, *Lincoln*, 149.

21.   Davis, *Don't Know Much*, 159.

22.   Paul J. Boller Jr., *Presidential Anecdotes* (New York: Penguin Books, 1982), 122–23.

23.   William H. Herndon and Jesse William Weik, *Herndon's Lincoln: The True Story of a Great Life* (Springfield, Ill.: Herndon's Lincoln Publishing Company, 1888), 587.

24.   Shenk, *Lincoln's Melancholy*, 4.

25.   Shenk, *Lincoln's Melancholy*, 19.

26.   Miller, *Lincoln's Virtues*, 68.

27.   Donald, *Lincoln*, 108.

28.   Miller Center, University of Virginia, "Essays on Abraham Lincoln and His Administration," http://millercenter.org/academic/americanpresident/lincoln.

29.   Donald, *Lincoln*, 221.

30.   Beschloss, *Illustrated History*, 191.

31.   Donald, *Lincoln*, 221–22.

32.   Beschloss, *Illustrated History*, 194.

33.   Donald, *Lincoln*, 222.

34.   Donald, *Lincoln*, 222.

35.   Thomas, *Abraham Lincoln*, 192; Donald, *Lincoln*, 228.

36.   Donald, *Lincoln*, 228.

37. Thomas, *Abraham Lincoln*, 206.

38. Miller Center, "Essays on Abraham Lincoln."

39. Thomas, *Abraham Lincoln*, 219.

40. Thomas, *Abraham Lincoln*, 225.

41. Sandburg, *Abraham Lincoln*, 161.

42. Sandburg, *Abraham Lincoln*, 161.

43. Donald, *Lincoln*, 283.

44. Donald, *Lincoln*, 286.

45. Thomas, *Abraham Lincoln*, 234.

46. Thomas, *Abraham Lincoln*, 235.

47. Sandburg, *Abraham Lincoln*, 189.

48. Donald, *Lincoln*, 282.

49. Thomas, *Abraham Lincoln*, 253–54.

50. Beschloss, *Illustrated History*, 197.

51. Thomas, *Abraham Lincoln*, 254.

52. Donald, *Lincoln*, 295.

53. Sandburg, *Abraham Lincoln*, 202.

54. Davis, *Don't Know Much*, 165–67.

55. Sandburg, *Abraham Lincoln*, 222–23.

56. Donald, *Lincoln*, 221, 285, 311.

57. Kathryn Moore, *The American President: A Complete History* (New York: Fall River Press, 2007), 187.

58. Donald, *Lincoln*, 82.

59. White House Historical Association, "Mary Todd Lincoln," www.white house.gov/history/firstladies/ml16.html.

60. Sandburg, *Abraham Lincoln*, 71.

61. Donald, *Lincoln*, 312.

62. Donald, *Lincoln*, 313.

63. Geoffrey C. Ward, Ken Burns, and Ric Burns, *The Civil War: An Illustrated History* (New York: Knopf, 1990), 76.

64. Sandburg, *Abraham Lincoln*, 222.

65. Moore, *American President*, 187.

66. Sandburg, *Abraham Lincoln*, 248.

67. Donald, *Lincoln*, 336.

68. Moore, *American President*, 187.

69. Thomas, *Abraham Lincoln*, 200.

70. Miller Center, "Essays on Abraham Lincoln."

71. Donald, *Lincoln,* 489.

72. Miller Center, "Essays on Abraham Lincoln."

73. Donald, *Lincoln,* 490.

74. Malcolm Jones, "Death of a Nation," *Newsweek,* January 21, 2008.

75. Gene Smith, *Lee and Grant: A Dual Biography* (New York: McGraw-Hill, 1984), 122; Jones, "Death of a Nation."

76. Smith, *Grant and Lee,* 228.

77. Donald, *Lincoln,* 489.

78. Donald, *Lincoln,* 489.

79. Miller Center, "Essays on Abraham Lincoln."

80. Miller, *Lincoln's Virtues,* 406–07.

81. Shenk, *Lincoln's Melancholy,* 214.

82. Miller, *Lincoln's Virtues,* 69; Shenk, *Lincoln's Melancholy,* 8.

83. Ushistory.org, "Thomas Kunders House Site," www.ushistory.org/german town/lower/kunders.htm.

84. Thomas, *Abraham Lincoln,* 311; Miller Center, "Essays on Abraham Lincoln."

85. Donald, *Lincoln,* 364.

86. Moore, *American President,* 188.

87. Miller Center, "Essays on Abraham Lincoln."

88. Beschloss, *Illustrated History,* 202.

89. Davis, *Don't Know Much,* 171.

90. Davis, *Don't Know Much,* 89.

91. Beschloss, *Illustrated History,* 203.

92. William Safire, ed., *Lend Me Your Ears: Great Speeches in History* (New York: Norton, 1992).

93. Moore, *American President,* 190.

94. Ward, Burns, and Burns, *Civil War,* 400.

95. Donald, *Lincoln,* 526.

96. Thomas, *Abraham Lincoln,* 492.

97. Donald, *Lincoln,* 529.

98. Beschloss, *Illustrated History,* 204.

99. Donald, *Lincoln,* 531.

100. Donald, *Lincoln,* 506.

101. Ward, Burns, and Burns, *Civil War,* 364.

102. Sandburg, *Abraham Lincoln,* 56; Donald, *Lincoln,* 576.

103. Sandburg, *Abraham Lincoln*, 564.

104. Bruce Catton, *The American Heritage Picture History of the Civil War* (New York: American Heritage, 1960), 592–93.

105. Ward, Burns, and Burns, *Civil War*, 364.

106. Thomas, *Abraham Lincoln*, 513.

107. Beschloss, *Illustrated History*, 225.

108. Sandburg, *Abraham Lincoln*, 565.

109. Beschloss, *Illustrated History*, 225; Thomas, *Abraham Lincoln*, 514.

110. Sandburg, *Abraham Lincoln*, 566.

111. EyeWitnessToHistory.com, "The Civil War Ends: A Small Town's Reaction, 1865," www.eyewitnesstohistory.com/civilwarends.htm.

112. Ward, Burns, and Burns, *Civil War*, 382.

113. Thomas, *Abraham Lincoln*, 515.

114. Thomas, *Abraham Lincoln*, 517.

115. Sandburg, *Abraham Lincoln*, 578.

116. Thomas, *Abraham Lincoln*, 518; Donald, *Lincoln*, 593.

117. Sandburg, *Abraham Lincoln*, 578.

118. Thomas, *Abraham Lincoln*, 522.

119. Donald, *Lincoln*, 399.

120. Sandburg, *Abraham Lincoln*, 599.

121. Sonofthesouth.net, "The Assassination of Abraham Lincoln: Civil War *Harper's Weekly*, April 29, 1865," www.sonofthesouth.net/leefoundation/civil-war/1865/assassination-abraham-lincoln.htm.

122. Joshua Wolf Shenk, "The True Lincoln," *Time*, June 26, 2005.

## V. FRANKLIN D. ROOSEVELT: NOTHING TO FEAR

1. Ted Morgan, *FDR* (New York: Simon & Schuster, 1985), 377.

2. Fred I. Greenstein, ed., *Leadership in the Modern Presidency* (Cambridge, Mass.: Harvard University Press, 1988), 12.

3. Jon Meacham, *Franklin and Winston: An Intimate Portrait of an Epic Friendship* (New York: Random House, 2003), 40.

4. Miller Center, University of Virginia, "Essays on the Franklin Roosevelt Administration," http://millercenter.org/academic/americanpresident/fdroosevelt.

5. "Franklin Delano Roosevelt," *Time*, August 14, 2007.

6. Conrad Black, *Franklin Delano Roosevelt: Champion of Freedom* (Cambridge, Mass.: PublicAffairs, 2003), 242.

7.    Jon Meacham, "Arthur Schlesinger, 1917–2007," *Newsweek*, March 12, 2007.

8.    Black, *Franklin Delano Roosevelt*, 268.

9.    Morgan, *FDR*, 375.

10.   Julia Baird, "The Woman the President Loved," *Newsweek*, May 5, 2008.

11.   Kathryn Moore, *The American President: A Complete History* (New York: Fall River Press, 2007), 381.

12.   Morgan, *FDR*, 375.

13.   Doris Kearns Goodwin, *No Ordinary Time: Franklin and Eleanor Roosevelt: The Home Front in World War II* (New York: Simon & Schuster, 1994), 57.

14.   Ronald Reagan, *An American Life* (New York: Simon & Schuster, 1990), 19.

15.   Thomas A. Bailey, *Presidential Greatness: The Image and the Man from George Washington to the Present* (New York: Appleton-Century, 1966), 255.

16.   Lewis L. Gould, *The Modern American Presidency* (Lawrence: University Press of Kansas, 2003), 21.

17.   Gould, *Modern American Presidency*, 85.

18.   Bailey, *Presidential Greatness*, 255.

19.   Gould, *Modern American Presidency*, 85.

20.   Tennessee Valley Authority, "From the New Deal to a New Century," www.tva.gov/abouttva/history.htm.

21.   U-S-History.com, "National Industrial Recovery Act," www.u-s-history.com/pages/h1663.html.

22.   Miller Center, "Essays on the Roosevelt Administration."

23.   Morgan, *FDR*, 377.

24.   Moore, *American President*, 374.

25.   Michael Beschloss, ed., *American Heritage Illustrated History of the Presidents* (New York: Crown, 2000), 31.

26.   Time/CBS News, *People of the Century: One Hundred Men and Women Who Shaped the Last One Hundred Years* (New York: Simon & Schuster, 1999), 113.

27.   Time/CBS News, *People of the Century*, 113.

28.   Meacham, *Franklin and Winston*, 34.

29.   Morgan, *FDR*, 247.

30.   Beschloss, *Illustrated History*, 378.

31.   Morgan, *FDR*, 259.

32.   Morgan, *FDR*, 261.

33.    Beschloss, *Illustrated History*, 378.

34.    Kenneth C. Davis, *Don't Know Much About History: Everything You Need to Know About American History but Never Learned* (New York: Crown, 1990), 276.

35.    Peter Collier and David Horowitz, *The Roosevelts: An American Saga* (New York: Simon & Schuster, 1994), 355.

36.    Erwin C. Hargrove, *The Power of the Modern Presidency* (Philadelphia: Temple University Press, 1974), 53.

37.    Gould, *Modern American Presidency*, 86.

38.    Norman Augustine and Kenneth Adelman, *Shakespeare in Charge: The Bard's Guide to Leading and Succeeding on the Business Stage* (New York: Hyperion, 1999), 168, 185.

39.    Richard Brookhiser, "Acting Like a President," *Time*, April 5, 2007.

40.    Black, *Franklin Delano Roosevelt*, 382.

41.    Greenstein, *Leadership in the Modern Presidency*, 19.

42.    Goodwin, *No Ordinary Time*, 586–87.

43.    Black, *Franklin Delano Roosevelt*, 347.

44.    Greenstein, *Leadership in the Modern Presidency*, 8.

45.    Arthur M. Schlesinger Jr., "Franklin Delano Roosevelt," *Time*, April 13, 1998.

46.    Beschloss, *Illustrated History*, 381.

47.    Greenstein, *Leadership in the Modern Presidency*, 33.

48.    Hugh Sidey, "Time and the Presidency" (a traveling exhibit created by *Time* magazine, which appeared at select presidential museums, 1999–2002).

49.    Goodwin, *No Ordinary Time*, 57.

50.    Epluribus Media, "FDR's Brain Trust," www.epluribusmedia.org/features/2006/200609_FDR_pt3.html.

51.    Greenstein, *Leadership in the Modern Presidency*, 29.

52.    Beschloss, *Illustrated History*, 383.

53.    Black, *Franklin Delano Roosevelt*, 347.

54.    Black, *Franklin Delano Roosevelt*, 347.

55.    Frederick S. Voss, *Portraits of the Presidents: The National Portrait Gallery* (New York: Rizzoli, 2000), 112.

56.    Goodwin, *No Ordinary Time*, 64.

57.    Goodwin, *No Ordinary Time*, 19–20.

58.    Joseph E. Persico, *Franklin and Lucy* (New York: Random House, 2008).

59.  Julia Baird, "The Women the President Loved," *Newsweek*, May 5, 2008.

60.  Miller Center, "Essays on the Roosevelt Administration."

61.  Morgan, *FDR*, 430.

62.  Miller Center, "Essays on the Roosevelt Administration."

63.  *National Geographic Eyewitness to the 20th Century* (Washington, D.C.: National Geographic Society, 1998), 147.

64.  Miller Center, "Essays on the Roosevelt Administration."

65.  Time/CBS News, *People of the Century*, 88.

66.  Miller Center, "Essays on the Roosevelt Administration."

67.  American Studies at the University of Virginia, "Court Packing: Judicial Re-organization and the End of the New Deal," http://xroads.virginia.edu/~MA02/volpe/newdeal/court.html.

68.  Black, *Franklin Delano Roosevelt*, 409.

69.  Black, *Franklin Delano Roosevelt*, 408.

70.  K. Daniel Glover, enterstageright.com/archive/articles/0799fdrcourt.htm.

71.  Miller Center, "Essays on the Roosevelt Administration."

72.  *National Geographic Eyewitness*, 151.

73.  Morgan, *FDR*, 541–42.

74.  Miller Center, "Essays on the Roosevelt Administration."

75.  Time/CBS News, *People of the Century*, 84.

76.  Moore, *The American President*, 384.

77.  Time/CBS News, *People of the Century*, 86.

78.  Eleanor Roosevelt, *This Is My Story* (New York: Harper, 1937), 84.

79.  "Franklin Roosevelt," *New York Times*, April 13, 1945.

## VI. Harry S. Truman: "If you pray, pray for me now"

1.  U.S. Senate, "Art & History: Harry S. Truman," www.senate.gov/artandhistory/history/common/generic/VP_Harry_Truman.htm.

2.  Kathryn Moore, *The American President: A Complete History* (New York: Fall River Press, 2007), 403.

3.  Merle Miller, *Plain Speaking: An Oral Biography of Harry S. Truman* (New York: Berkley, 1974), 196.

4.  Moore, *American President*, 403.

5.  David McCullough, *Truman* (New York: Simon & Schuster, 1992), 341.

6.  Miller, *Plain Speaking*, 197.

7.  McCullough, *Truman*, 325.

8.  McCullough, *Truman*, 346.

9.  Arthur Gelb, A. M. Rosenthal, and Marvin Siegel, eds., *New York Times Great Lives of the Twentieth Century* (New York: Times Books, 1988), 615.

10. McCullough, *Truman*, 353.

11. McCullough, *Truman*, 355.

12. McCullough, *Truman*, 353.

13. Louis L. Gould, *The Modern American Presidency* (Lawrence: University Press of Kansas, 2003), 75.

14. Gelb, Rosenthal, and Siegel, *New York Times Great Lives*, 621; Gould, *Modern American Presidency*, 45.

15. White House, Biography of Bess Truman, www.whitehouse.gov/history/firstladies/et33/html.

16. Gelb, Rosenthal, and Siegel, *New York Times Great Lives*, 621.

17. Michael Beschloss, ed., *American Heritage Illustrated History of the Presidents* (New York: Crown, 2000), 392.

18. U.S. Senate, "Art & History: Henry A. Wallace," www.senate.gov/artand history/history/common/generic/VP_Henry_Wallace.htm.

19. McCullough, *Truman*, 314.

20. McCullough, *Truman*, 411.

21. Robert H. Ferrell, ed., *Dear Bess: The Letters from Harry to Bess Truman, 1910–1959* (New York: Norton, 1983), 526.

22. McCullough, *Truman*.

23. Gelb, Rosenthal, and Siegel, *New York Times Great Lives*, 618.

24. Miller, *Plain Speaking*, 199.

25. Gould, *Modern American Presidency*, 101; Gelb, Rosenthal, and Siegel, *New York Times Great Lives*, 618.

26. James T. Patterson, *Grand Expectations: The United States, 1945–1974* (New York: Oxford University Press, 1997), 106–07.

27. Patterson, *Grand Expectations*, 106.

28. Patterson, *Grand Expectations*, 106–07.

29. Miller, *Plain Speaking*, 199.

30. Miller, *Plain Speaking*, 200.

31. Patterson, *Grand Expectations*, 108.

32. Ferrell, *Dear Bess*, 522.

33. Gelb, Rosenthal, and Siegel, *New York Times Great Lives*, 619.

34. McCullough, *Truman*, 438.

35. McCullough, *Truman*, 437.

36. Miller Center, University of Virginia, "Essays on the Harry Truman Administration," http://millercenter.org/academic/americanpresident/Truman.

37. McCullough, *Truman*, 439.

38. Harry S. Truman Library, Independence, Missouri, "Pages from President Truman's diary, July 17, 18, and 25, 1945," www.trumanlibrary.org/whistlestop/study_collections/bomb/large/documents/fulltext.php?fulltextid=15.

39. McCullough, *Truman*, 454.

40. PBS, *The American Experience*, "The Presidents: Harry Truman," www.pbs.org/wgbh/amex/presidents/33_truman/psources/ps_hiroshima.html.

41. Gelb, Rosenthal, and Siegel, *New York Times Great Lives*, 624.

42. Harry S. Truman, *Truman Speaks* (New York: Columbia University Press, 1960), 45.

43. Gelb, Rosenthal, and Siegel, *New York Times Great Lives*, 619.

44. Beschloss, *Illustrated History*, 394.

45. PBS, *The American Experience*, "Harry Truman," www.pbs.org/wgbh/amex/presidents/33_truman/truman_foreign.html.

46. William Safire, ed., *Lend Me Your Ears: Great Speeches in History* (New York: Norton, 1992), 864.

47. Gould, *Modern American Presidency*, 108–09.

48. National Park Service, "Henry Wallace," www.nps.gov/archive/elro/glossary/wallace-henry.htm.

49. McCullough, *Truman*, 517.

50. Patterson, *Grand Expectations*, 105.

51. Beschloss, *Illustrated History*, 396.

52. McCullough, *Truman*, 564.

53. Beschloss, *Illustrated History*, 397.

54. McCullough, *Truman*, 565.

55. Miller, *Plain Speaking*, 246.

56. Gelb, Rosenthal, and Siegel, *New York Times Great Lives*, 621.

57. Miller, *Plain Speaking*, 233.

58. Harry S. Truman, *Where the Buck Stops: The Personal and Private Writings of Harry S. Truman* (New York: Warner Books, 1989), 81.

59. Safire, *Lend Me Your Ears*, 82.

60. Gould, *Modern American Presidency*, 56.

61. Harry S. Truman Library, "Truman Trivia," www.trumanlibrary.org/trivia/letter.htm.

62. Thomas A. Bailey, *Presidential Greatness: The Image and the Man from George Washington to the Present* (New York: Appleton-Century, 1966), 323.

63. Fred I. Greenstein, ed., *Leadership in the Modern Presidency* (Cambridge, Mass.: Harvard University Press, 1988), 44.

64. Ferrell, *Dear Bess*, 526.

65. Miller Center, "Essays on Truman Administration."

66. Gelb, Rosenthal, and Siegel, *New York Times Great Lives*, 620.

67. Ferrell, *Dear Bess*, 536.

68. Miller Center, "Essays on Truman Administration."

69. Beschloss, *Illustrated History*, 397.

70. McCullough, *Truman*, 630.

71. *National Geographic Eyewitness to the 20th Century* (Washington, D.C.: National Geographic Society, 1998), 192–93.

72. McCullough, *Truman*, 631.

73. Michael R. Gardner, *Harry Truman and Civil Rights: Moral Courage and Political Risks* (Carbondale: Southern Illinois University Press, 2002).

74. Harry S. Truman Library, Letter to Ernie Roberts.

75. Gould, *Modern American Presidency*, 106.

76. U.S. Congress, House, *Congressional Record*, April 8, 1948, 4270–72.

77. Ferrell, *Dear Bess*, 431.

78. Time/CBS News, *People of the Century: One Hundred Men and Women Who Shaped the Last One Hundred Years* (New York: Simon & Schuster, 1999), 84.

79. Miller Center, "Bess Truman," http://millercenter.org/academic/americanpresident/truman/essays/firstlady.

80. John Whitcomb and Claire Whitcomb, *Real Life at the White House: 200 Years of Daily Life at America's Most Famous Residence* (New York: Routledge, 2000), 326.

81. Miller Center, "Bess Truman."

82. Miller, *Plain Speaking*, 105.

83. Miller, *Plain Speaking*, 104.

84. Miller, *Plain Speaking*, 105.

85. Whitcomb and Whitcomb, *Real Life*, 326; Miller, *Plain Speaking*, 106.

86. McCullough, *Truman*, 694–95.

87. Gelb, Rosenthal, and Siegel, *New York Times Great Lives*, 626.

88.   *National Geographic Eyewitness*, 212.

89.   Cabell Phillips, "A Man Who 'Done His Damndest,'" *New York Times*, December 31, 1972.

90.   Phillips, "A Man Who 'Done His Damndest.'"

## VII. John F. Kennedy: "The torch has been passed"

1.   Hugh Sidey, *John F. Kennedy, President* (New York: Atheneum, 1964), 31–32.

2.   John Eisenhower, *Strictly Personal* (Garden City, N.Y.: Doubleday, 1974), 285.

3.   Richard Reeves, *President Kennedy: Profile in Power* (New York: Simon & Schuster, 1993), photo sections.

4.   Reeves, *President Kennedy*, 4.

5.   *National Geographic Eyewitness to the 20th Century* (Washington, D.C.: National Geographic Society, 1998), 203.

6.   Kenneth C. Davis, *Don't Know Much About History: Everything You Need to Know About American History but Never Learned* (New York: Crown, 1990), 344.

7.   *National Geographic Eyewitness*, 250.

8.   Jonathan Alter, "Love That Grover!" *Newsweek*, March 17, 2003.

9.   Sidey, *John F. Kennedy*, 8.

10.  Arthur M. Schlesinger Jr., *A Thousand Days* (New York: Black Dog & Leventhal, 2005), 160.

11.  Reeves, *President Kennedy*, 23.

12.  Reeves, *President Kennedy*, 24.

13.  Sidey, *John F. Kennedy*, 34.

14.  Fred I. Greenstein, ed., *Leadership in the Modern Presidency* (Cambridge, Mass.: Harvard University Press, 1988), 120.

15.  Greenstein, *Leadership*, 120.

16.  Reeves, *President Kennedy*, 36.

17.  William Taubman, *Khrushchev: The Man and His Era* (New York: Norton, 2003), 485; Kathryn Moore, *The American President: A Complete History* (New York: Fall River Press, 2007), 452.

18.  Robert Dallek, *An Unfinished Life: John F. Kennedy, 1917–1963* (Boston: Little Brown, 2003), 28.

19.  Moore, *American President*, 444.

20.  David Greenberg, "Was Nixon Robbed?" October 16, 2000, www.slate.com/id/91350.

21.  Kurt Andersen, "Working Hard for the Last Laugh," *Time*, August 15, 1983.

22.  Theodore H. White, "In Search of History," *Time*, July 3, 1978.

23.  Peter Collier and David Horowitz, *The Kennedys: An American Drama* (New York: Summit Books, 1984), 256.

24.  Clyde Haberman, "NYC; Fleeting Wisp of Glory, and Eloquence," *New York Times*, November 21, 2003.

25.  Greenstein, *Leadership*, 114.

26.  Greenstein, *Leadership*, 115.

27.  Sidey, *John F. Kennedy*, 56.

28.  Reeves, *President Kennedy*, 73.

29.  Reeves, *President Kennedy*, 73.

30.  Greenstein, *Leadership*, 131.

31.  Sidey, *John F. Kennedy*, 36.

32.  Taubman, *Khrushchev*, 493.

33.  Taubman, *Khrushchev*, 493.

34.  Theodore Sorensen, interview with the author, New York, January 31, 2008.

35.  David Talbot, "Warrior for Peace," *Time*, July 2, 2007.

36.  Moore, *American President*, 450.

37.  Miller Center, University of Virginia, "Essays on John F. Kennedy and His Administration," http://millercenter.org/academic/americanpresident/kennedy.

38.  Reeves, *President Kennedy*, 106.

39.  Reeves, *President Kennedy*, 106.

40.  Peter Beinart, "The War Over Patriotism," *Time*, July 7, 2008.

41.  Taubman, *Khrushchev*, 494.

42.  Reeves, *President Kennedy*, 153.

43.  Taubman, *Khrushchev*, 485.

44.  Hugh Sidey, *The Presidency* (New York: Thornwillow Press, 1991), 40.

45.  *National Geographic Eyewitness*, 253.

46.  Moore, *American President*, 452.

47.  Collier and Horowitz, *Kennedys*, 277.

48.  Hugh Sidey, "Locking Eyes at the Top," *Time*, November 22, 1982.

49.  Sidey, *The Presidency*, 42.

50.  Sorensen, interview with the author.

51.  Sidey, *The Presidency*, 38.

52.  Taubman, *Khrushchev*, 500.

53. Miller Center, "Jacqueline Kennedy," http://millercenter.org/academic/americanpresident/kennedy/essays/firstlady.

54. Arthur and Barbara Gelb, "Culture Makes a Hit at the White House," *New York Times,* January 28, 1962.

55. David Friend, "A Claim to Camelot," *Vanity Fair,* April 2008.

56. PBS, *The American Experience,* "Eyes on the Prize, America's Civil Rights Movement, 1954–1985," www.pbs.org/wgbh/amex/eyesontheprize.

57. PBS, "Eyes on the Prize."

58. Robert Dallek, "His Cautious Path to Civil Rights," *Time,* July 2, 2007.

59. PBS, "Eyes on the Prize."

60. PBS, "Eyes on the Prize."

61. Collier and Horowitz, *Kennedys,* 296.

62. Schlesinger, *A Thousand Days,* 798.

63. Schlesinger, *A Thousand Days,* 798.

64. Moore, *American President,* 454.

65. Hugh Sidey, "Time and the Presidency" (a traveling exhibit created by *Time* magazine, which appeared at select presidential museums, 1999–2002).

66. Talbot, "Warrior for Peace."

67. Schlesinger, *A Thousand Days,* 798.

68. Sorensen, interview with the author.

69. Schlesinger, *A Thousand Days,* 426.

70. Talbot, "Warrior for Peace."

71. Schlesinger, *A Thousand Days,* 829–30.

72. Hugh Sidey, conversation with the author, 1999.

73. Nikita Khrushchev, *Khrushchev Remembers* (Boston: Little, Brown, 1970), 496.

74. Sorensen, interview with the author.

75. Khrushchev, *Khrushchev Remembers,* 499–500.

76. Schlesinger, *A Thousand Days,* 826.

77. Sheldon M. Stern, "The Cuban Missile Crisis Myth You Probably Believe," The History News Network, George Mason University, http://hnn.us/articles/7982.html.

78. Theodore Sorensen, *Counselor: A Life at the Edge of History* (New York: Harper, 2008).

79. Khrushchev, *Khrushchev Remembers,* 500.

80. Schlesinger, *A Thousand Days,* 830.

81.   Salon.com, "Letter from a Birmingham Jail," August 19, 2003, http://archive.salon.com/opinion/freedom/2003/08/19/king/index.html.

82.   Miller Center, "Essays on John F. Kennedy."

83.   Dallek, "Cautious Path to Civil Rights."

84.   Miller Center, "Essays on John F. Kennedy."

85.   PBS, "Eyes on the Prize."

86.   William Styron, "Politics as Glamour," *Esquire*, September 1963.

87.   Reeves, *President Kennedy*, 661.

88.   William Styron, "The Short Classy Voyage of JFK," *Esquire*, December 1983.

89.   Styron, "The Short, Classy Voyage of JFK."

## VIII. GERALD R. FORD: "OUR LONG NATIONAL NIGHTMARE IS OVER"

1.    Miller Center, University of Virginia, "Essays on Gerald Rudolph Ford and His Administration," http://millercenter.org/academic/american-president/ford.

2.    Hugh Sidey, "Time and the Presidency" (a traveling exhibit created by *Time* magazine, which appeared at select presidential museums, 1999–2002).

3.    Miller Center, "Essays on Gerald Rudolph Ford"; Hugh Sidey, "Gerald Ford," *Time*, February 28, 2000.

4.    Christopher Matthews, "Former Governor Called Nixon 'Psycho,'" *San Francisco Chronicle*, December 6, 1998.

5.    Richard Reeves, *A Ford, Not a Lincoln* (New York: Harcourt, 1975), 115.

6.    U.S. Senate, "Art & History: Gerald R. Ford," www.senate.gov/artandhistory/history/common/generic/VP_Gerald_Ford.htm.

7.    U.S. Senate, "Art & History: Spiro Agnew," www.senate.gov/artandhistory/history/common/generic/VP_Spiro_Agnew.htm.

8.    "Gerald R. Ford," editorial, *New York Times*, December 28, 2006.

9.    "Gerald R. Ford," *New York Times*.

10.   Robert Sam Anson, *Exile: The Quiet Oblivion of Richard Nixon* (New York: Simon & Schuster, 1984), 11.

11.   James M. Naughton and Adam Clymer, "President Gerald R. Ford . . . Dies at 93," *New York Times*, December 28, 2006.

12.   Naughton and Clymer, "President Gerald R. Ford."

13.   Gerald R. Ford, interview with the author, Rancho Mirage, California, October 30, 2004.

14.   Henry Kissinger, introduction to Gerald R. Ford, *A Time to Heal: The Auto-biography of Gerald R. Ford* (New York: Harper, 1979), 2.

15.   Lewis L. Gould, *The Modern American Presidency* (Lawrence: University Press of Kansas, 2003), 2.

16.   Miller Center, "Essays on Gerald Rudolph Ford."

17.   Gould, *Modern American Presidency*, 206.

18.   Naughton and Clymer, "President Gerald R. Ford."

19.   Gould, *Modern American Presidency*, 21.

20.   Hugh Sidey, *The Presidency* (New York: Thornwillow Press, 1991), 77.

21.   *Washington Post*, December 28, 2006.

22.   David Hume Kennerly, conversation with the author, 2007.

23.   Hugh Sidey (text) and Fred Ward (photographs), *Portrait of a President* (New York: Harper, 1975), 40.

24.   Ford, *A Time to Heal*, 160.

25.   Ford, *A Time to Heal*, 6.

26.   Scott Shuger, "Indo-amnesia," *Slate*, September 9, 1999.

27.   Barry Werth, *31 Days: The Crisis That Gave Us the Government We Have Today* (New York: Doubleday, 2006), 317.

28.   Ford, interview with the author.

29.   "Gerald R. Ford," editorial, *New York Times*.

30.   Sidey, *Portrait of a President*, 70.

31.   Werth, *31 Days*, 327.

32.   Werth, *31 Days*, 317.

33.   Ford, *A Time to Heal*, 141.

34.   Reeves, *A Ford*.

35.   Doug Hill and Jeff Weingrad, *Saturday Night: The Backstage History of* Saturday Night Live (New York: Morrow, 1986), 182–83.

36.   Hill and Weingrad, *Saturday Night*, 187.

37.   Hill and Weingrad, *Saturday Night*, 178.

38.   Ford, *A Time to Heal*, 307.

39.   Frank Freidel, *The Presidents of the United States of America* (Washington, D.C.: White House Historical Association, 1964), 80.

40.   Gould, *Modern American Presidency*, 201.

41.   Michael Beschloss, ed., *American Heritage Illustrated History of the Presidents* (New York: Crown, 2000), 485.

42.   Gould, *Modern American Presidency*, 202.

43. George H. W. Bush, interview with the author, Houston, March 22, 2006.

44. Quang X. Pham, "Ford's Finest Legacy," *Washington Post*, December 30, 2006.

45. J. Y. Smith and Lou Cannon, "Gerald R. Ford, 93, Dies," obituary, *Washington Post*, December 27, 2006.

46. Smith and Cannon, "Gerald R. Ford."

47. Smith and Cannon, "Gerald R. Ford."

48. Smith and Cannon, "Gerald R. Ford."

49. Beschloss, *Illustrated History*, 461.

50. Richard Norton Smith, conversation with the author, Alexandria, Virginia, March 2007.

51. Naughton and Clymer, "President Gerald R. Ford."

52. Ford, *A Time to Heal*, 422.

53. *Time*, October 18, 1976.

54. Douglas Brinkley, *The Unfinished Presidency: Jimmy Carter's Journey to the Nobel Peace Prize* (New York: Viking, 1998), 14.

55. Ford, *A Time to Heal*, 436.

56. Beschloss, *Illustrated History*, 463.

57. Mark K. Updegrove, op-ed, *The Boston Globe*, December 28, 2006.

## EPILOGUE

1. Merle Miller, *Plain Speaking: An Oral Biography of Harry S. Truman* (New York: Berkley, 1974).

2. "Chief Trumpet," *New York Times*, August 12, 1990.

3. Hugh Sidey, *John F. Kennedy, President* (New York: Atheneum, 1964), 256.

4. Thomas A. Bailey, *Presidential Greatness: The Image and the Man from George Washington to the Present* (New York: Appleton-Century, 1966), 268.

5. University of Virginia, "Thomas Jefferson on Government & Politics," http://etext.virginia.edu/jefferson/quotations/jeff1275.htm.

# BIBLIOGRAPHY

Adams, Charles Francis, ed. *Memoirs of John Quincy Adams*. 12 vols. Philadelphia: Lippincott, 1870.

Anson, Robert Sam. *Exile: The Unquiet Oblivion of Richard Nixon*. New York: Simon & Schuster, 1984.

Augustine, Norman, and Kenneth Adelman. *Shakespeare in Charge: The Bard's Guide to Leading and Succeeding on the Business Stage*. New York: Hyperion, 1999.

Bailey, Thomas A. *Presidential Greatness: The Image and the Man from George Washington to the Present*. New York: Appleton-Century, 1966.

Bernstein, R. B. *Thomas Jefferson*. New York: Oxford University Press, 2003.

Beschloss, Michael, ed. *American Heritage Illustrated History of the Presidents*. New York: Crown, 2000.

Black, Conrad. *Franklin Delano Roosevelt: Champion of Freedom*. Cambridge, Mass.: PublicAffairs, 2003.

Boller, Paul J., Jr. *Presidential Anecdotes*. New York: Penguin Books, 1982.

———. *Presidential Inaugurations*. New York: Harcourt, 2001.

Bowen, Catherine Drinker. *Miracle at Philadelphia: The Story of the Constitutional Convention, May to September, 1789*. Boston: Little, Brown, 1966.

Brinkley, Douglas. *The Unfinished Presidency: Jimmy Carter's Journey to the Nobel Peace Prize*. New York: Viking, 1998.

Brookhiser, Richard. *Founding Father: Rediscovering George Washington.* New York: Free Press, 1996.

Burns, James MacGregor. *John Kennedy: A Political Profile.* New York: Harcourt, 1960.

Cannon, James. *Time and Chance: Gerald Ford's Appointment with History.* Ann Arbor: University of Michigan Press, 1998.

Catton, Bruce. *The American Heritage Picture History of the Civil War.* New York: American Heritage, 1960.

Collier, Peter, and David Horowitz. *The Kennedys: An American Drama.* New York: Summit Books, 1984.

———. *The Roosevelts: An American Saga.* New York: Simon & Schuster, 1994.

Connelly, Thomas L., and Michael D. Senecal, eds. *Almanac of American Presidents from 1789 to the Present.* New York: Facts on File, 1991.

Crapol, Edward P. *John Tyler: The Accidental President.* Chapel Hill: University of North Carolina Press, 2006.

Davis, Kenneth C. *Don't Know Much About History: Everything You Need to Know About American History but Never Learned.* New York: Crown, 1990.

Donald, David Herbert. *Lincoln.* New York: Simon & Schuster, 1995.

Editors of Time. *Hugh Sidey's Portraits of the Presidents: Power and Personality in the Oval Office.* New York: Time Inc., 2000.

———. *75th Anniversary Gala.* New York: Time Inc., 1998.

Eisenhower, John. *Strictly Personal.* Garden City: Doubleday, 1974.

Ellis, Joseph J. *American Sphinx: The Character of Thomas Jefferson.* New York: Knopf, 1997.

———. *Founding Brothers: The Revolutionary Generation.* New York: Knopf, 2000.

Ferrell, Robert H., ed. *Dear Bess: The Letters from Harry to Bess Truman, 1910–1959.* New York: Norton, 1983.

———. *Harry Truman and the Modern Presidency.* Boston: Little, Brown, 1983.

Flexner, James Thomas. *George Washington: Anguish and Farewell (1793–1799).* Boston: Little, Brown, 1969.

Freeman, Douglas Southall. *Washington: A Biography.* An Abridgment in one volume by Richard Harwell of the seven-volume *George Washington.* New York: Scribner, 1968.

Ford, Gerald R. *A Time to Heal: The Autobiography of Gerald R. Ford.* New York: Harper, 1979.

Fredericks, Vic. *The Wit and Wisdom of the Presidents.* New York: Frederick Fell, 1966.

Freidel, Frank. *The Presidents of the United States of America.* Washington, D.C.: White House Historical Association, 1964.

Fuller, J. F. C. *Grant & Lee: A Study in Personality and Generalship.* Bloomington: Indiana University Press, 1957.

Gardner, Michael R. *Harry Truman and Civil Rights: Moral Courage and Political Risks.* Carbondale: Southern Illinois University Press, 2002.

Gelb, Arthur, A. M. Rosenthal, and Marvin Siegel, eds. *New York Times Great Lives of the Twentieth Century.* New York: Times Books, 1988.

Gingrich, Newt. *Rediscovering God in America: Reflections on the Role of Faith in Our Nation's History and Future.* Nashville: Integrity House, 2006.

Goodwin, Doris Kearns. *No Ordinary Time: Franklin and Eleanor Roosevelt: The Home Front in World War II.* New York: Simon & Schuster, 1994.

Gould, Lewis L. *The Modern American Presidency.* Lawrence: University Press of Kansas, 2003.

Greenstein, Fred I., ed. *Leadership in the Modern Presidency.* Cambridge, Mass.: Harvard University Press, 1988.

Grizzard, Frank E., Jr. *George Washington: A Biographical Companion.* Santa Barbara: ABC-CLIO, 2002.

Halliday, E. M. *Understanding Thomas Jefferson.* New York: Harper, 2001.

Hamby, Alonzo L. *Man of the People: A Life of Harry S. Truman.* New York: Oxford University Press, 1995.

Hargrove, Erwin C. *The Power of the Modern Presidency.* Philadelphia: Temple University Press, 1974.

Herndon, William H., and Jesse William Weik. *Herndon's Lincoln: The True Story of a Great Life.* Springfield, Ill.: Herndon's Lincoln Publishing Company, 1888.

Hill, Doug, and Jeff Weingrad. *Saturday Night: The Backstage History of Saturday Night Live.* New York: Morrow, 1986.

Hunt, Gaillard, ed. *The Writings of James Madison.* Vol. V. New York: Putnam, 1904.

Hunt, John Gabriel, ed. *The Inaugural Addresses of the Presidents: From George Washington to George W. Bush.* New York: Gramercy Books, 1997.

Kennedy, John F. *Profiles in Courage.* New York: Harper, 1956.

Kennerly, David Hume. *Photo Op.* Austin: University of Texas Press, 1995.

Khrushchev, Nikita. *Khrushchev Remembers.* Boston: Little, Brown, 1970.

Kissinger, Henry. *Years of Renewal.* New York: Simon & Schuster, 1999.

———. *Years of Upheaval.* Boston: Little, Brown, 1982.

Klapthor, Margaret Brown: *The First Ladies.* Washington, D.C.: White House Historical Association, 1975.

Lewis, R. W. B., and Nancy Lewis. *American Characters: Selections from the National Portrait Gallery*. New Haven: Yale University Press, 1999.

Lloyd, John, and John Mitchinson. *The Book of General Ignorance*. New York: Harmony, 2006.

McCullough, David. *John Adams*. New York: Simon & Schuster, 2001.

———. *1776*. New York: Simon & Schuster, 2005.

———. *Truman*. New York: Simon & Schuster, 1992.

Meacham, Jon. *Franklin and Winston: An Intimate Portrait of an Epic Friendship*. New York: Random House, 2003.

Miller, Donald L., and John Sargent, eds. *From George . . . to George: Two Hundred Years of Presidential Quotations*. Alexandria, Va.: Braddock Communications, 1989.

Miller, Merle. *Plain Speaking: An Oral Biography of Harry S. Truman*. New York: Berkley, 1974.

Miller, William Lee. *Lincoln's Virtues: An Ethical Biography*. New York: Knopf, 2002.

Moffitt, Phillip. *Esquire, Fiftieth Anniversary Collector's Issue*. New York: Hearst Publications, 1983.

Moore, Kathryn. *The American President: A Complete History*. New York: Fall River Press, 2007.

Morgan, Ted. *FDR: A Biography*. New York: Simon & Schuster, 1985.

*National Geographic Eyewitness to the 20th Century*. Washington, D.C.: National Geographic Society, 1998.

Nixon, Richard. *RN: The Memoirs of Richard Nixon*. New York: Grosset & Dunlap, 1978.

Patterson, James T. *Grand Expectations: The United States, 1945–1974*. New York: Oxford University Press, 1997.

Reagan, Ronald. *An American Life*. New York: Simon & Schuster, 1990.

Reeves, Richard. *A Ford, Not a Lincoln*. New York: Harcourt, 1975.

———. *President Kennedy: Profile in Power*. New York: Simon & Schuster, 1993.

Roosevelt, Eleanor. *This I Remember*. New York: Harper, 1949.

———. *This Is My Story*. New York: Harper, 1937.

Safire, William, ed. *Lend Me Your Ears: Great Speeches in History*. New York: Norton, 1992.

Sandburg, Carl. *Abraham Lincoln: The Prairie Years and the War Years*. New York: Harcourt, 1954.

Schlesinger, Arthur M., Jr. *The Cycles of American History*. Boston: Houghton Mifflin, 1986.

————. *A Life in the 20th Century*. Boston: Houghton Mifflin, 2000.

————. *A Thousand Days*. New York: Black Dog & Leventhal, 2005.

Seager, Robert, II. *And Tyler Too: A Biography of John & Julia Gardiner Tyler*. New York: McGraw-Hill, 1963.

Shenk, Joshua Wolf. *Lincoln's Melancholy: How Depression Challenged a President and Fueled His Greatness*. Boston: Houghton Mifflin, 2005.

Sidey, Hugh. *John F. Kennedy, President*. New York: Atheneum, 1964.

————. *The Presidency*. New York: Thornwillow Press, 1991.

Sidey, Hugh (text), and Fred Ward (photographs). *Portrait of a President*. New York: Harper, 1975.

Skidmore, Max J. *After the White House: Former Presidents as Private Citizens*. New York: Palgrave Macmillan, 2004.

Smith, Gene. *Lee and Grant: A Dual Biography*. New York: McGraw-Hill, 1984.

Smith, Richard Norton. *Patriarch: George Washington and the New American Nation*. Boston: Houghton Mifflin, 1993.

Sorensen, Theodore C. *Counselor: A Life at the Edge of History*. New York: Harper, 2008.

————. *Kennedy*. New York: Harper, 1965.

Stiles, T. J., ed. *The Citizen's Handbook: Essential Documents and Speeches from American History*. New York: Berkley, 1993.

Taubman, William. *Khrushchev: The Man and His Era*. New York: Norton, 2003.

Thomas, Benjamin P. *Abraham Lincoln: A Biography*. New York: Knopf, 1952.

Thomas, Evan. *Robert Kennedy: His Life*. New York: Simon & Schuster, 2000.

Time/CBS News, *People of the Century: One Hundred Men and Women Who Shaped the Last One Hundred Years*. New York: Simon & Schuster, 1999.

Truman, Harry S. *Truman Speaks*. New York: Columbia University Press, 1960.

————. *Where the Buck Stops: The Personal and Private Writings of Harry S. Truman*. New York: Warner Books, 1989.

————. *Years of Decisions*. Vol. 1 of *Memoirs*. Garden City, N.Y.: Doubleday, 1955.

Updegrove, Mark K. *Second Acts: Presidential Lives and Legacies After the White House*. Guilford, Conn.: Lyons Press, 2006.

Vidal, Gore. *Lincoln: A Novel*. New York: Random House, 1984.

Voss, Frederick S. *Portraits of the Presidents: The National Portrait Gallery*. New York: Rizzoli, 2000.

Ward, Geoffrey C., and Ken Burns. *Baseball: An Illustrated History*. New York: Knopf, 1994.

Ward, Geoffrey C., Ken Burns, and Ric Burns. *The Civil War: An Illustrated History*. New York: Knopf, 1990.

Washington, George. *George Washington's Rules of Civility and Decent Behaviour in Company and Conversation*. Bedford, Mass.: Applewood Books, 1989.

*We the People: The Commission of the Bicentennial of the United States Constitution, 1985–1992*. Washington, D.C.: The Commission, 1992.

Werth, Barry. *31 Days: The Crisis That Gave Us the Government We Have Today*. New York: Doubleday, 2006.

Whitcomb, John, and Claire Whitcomb. *Real Life at the White House: 200 Years of Daily Life at America's Most Famous Residence*. New York: Routledge, 2000.

White, Theodore. *Breach of Faith: The Fall of Richard Nixon*. New York: Atheneum, 1975.

Woodward, Bob, and Carl Bernstein. *The Final Days*. New York: Simon & Schuster, 1976.

Zall, Paul M., ed. *Jefferson on Jefferson*. Lexington: University Press of Kentucky, 2002.

Zinn, Howard. *A People's History of the United States*. New York: Harper, 1980.

# INDEX